modernizing the little red schoolhouse

the economics of improved education

modernizing the little red schoolhouse

the economics of improved education

Edward J. Willett, Austin D. Swanson, Eugene A. Nelson

EDUCATIONAL TECHNOLOGY PUBLICATIONS
ENGLEWOOD CLIFFS, NEW JERSEY 07632

Library of Congress Cataloging in Publication Data

Willett, Edward J
    Modernizing the little red schoolhouse.

    Bibliography: p.
    Includes index.
    1. Education—Economic aspects—United States.
2. Educational technology—United States. I. Swanson,
Austin D., joint author. II. Nelson, Eugene A., joint
author. III. Title.
LC66.W48   371.3'078   78-26604
ISBN 0-87778-133-8

Printed in the United States of America.

Library of Congress Catalog Card Number:
78-26604.

International Standard Book Number:
0-87778-133-8.

First Printing: April, 1979.

PREFACE

This book is the product of the concerns of the three authors over society's present lack of ability to afford the quality and quantity of educational services now possible and necessary for the citizens of a post-industrial era.

Despite warnings to the contrary, even five years ago it was difficult for most people to recognize the real limits of the American economy to provide bountifully for the needs of all its citizens whether through the private or public sectors. At that time, as a nation, we were still basking in the euphoria of one of Mankind's greatest technological accomplishments—placing humans on the moon. The public had not yet been fully impressed with the severity of the energy crisis, unfavorable balances of trade, abnormal inflation, and the decline of the dollar as a world currency. While taxpayers had periodically rejected school budgets and bond issues, they had not revolted in the manner of California's "Proposition 13." A sense of optimism still governed our social, political, economic, and biological dealings: that Man's creative genius, and the resulting technology, could provide the means of overcoming any and all obstacles to unlimited growth and development. Although such aggregate optimism now seems out of place, a more limited, but practical optimism characterizes the orientation of the authors as they consider the future with respect to education.

Technology is helpful only if it is used wisely. In the private sector, the market provides powerful incentives for most firms to maintain high productivity through advanced technology. The alternatives are bankruptcy, or receipt of government relief through subsidies, loans, tariffs, etc. On the other hand, the public sector, now constituting about 34 percent of the economy, rarely faces the prospect of bankruptcy, and only occasionally and sporadically faces the discipline of outraged taxpayers. As a result, public sector activities tend to be less technologically progressive, and are lower in productivity; they tend to be governed by tradition. Reform, if it takes place at all, frequently must depend upon an internal recognition of the problems and a willingness to deal with them. The willingness is often lacking, or is frustrated by inertia.

The authors have viewed with alarm what they perceive as a deterioration in the quality and relevance of the educational services being offered to the traditional school age population of the nation. At the same time, there appear to be millions of persons equally in need of educational services who are not receiving them because of not being among that "traditional population." This is despite the fact that the proportion of the Gross National Product allocated to education has increased from less than two percent to nearly eight percent in the past three decades.

Education has become expensive because it has responded to cultural and financial crises in its traditional labor-intensive mode. This is particularly serious in education because of the high level of training required of teachers and the correspondingly high level of wages they deserve. But when children are unable to master basic skills, rather than modifying the method of teaching, the children are placed by the present educational system into "special programs" which are taught by "special teachers" who use the *same* method of instruction which originally failed. Program is added to program. With little coordination, new programs frequently conflict with other programs. Pupils become confused and/or bored; attention drops; discipline and control become problems; achievement fails to improve, while total educational costs escalate.

A similar labor-intensive bias permeates the use of the specific technological devices which *have* found their way into the schools. There is an attitude that information, if it is to be understood, must proceed from the lips of the teacher. "Audio-visual aids," being used primarily in an add-on fashion for "enrichment," gather dust in closets much of the time. Thus, technology, rather than reducing costs by making labor more productive, as is generally the case in the private sector, has little impact on productivity, while adding to total cost.

The purpose of this book is to sketch out feasible schooling designs which elevate teachers to truly professional status and enhance the productivity of those professionals through the integration of technology, paraprofessionals, and student assistants into a "man-machine *system.*" Existing research points to significantly lower costs, with no drop in pupil cognitive achievement, and the possibility of real gains, particularly in the affective and psychomotor domains.

Events which led to the writing of this book started with Professor Edward J. Willett, an economist at Houghton College, and a former businessman, who was disturbed over the labor-intensiveness of both public and private schools and their failure to take full advantage of the cost-saving potential of educational technology. In seeking an educationist who at the least could understand the basis of his concern, he established contact with the second author, Professor Austin D. Swanson, a specialist in school administration and finance at the State University of New York at Buffalo. They in turn sought a specialist in curriculum and learning theory who had a vision of the full benefits which an integrated man-machine system could generate. This they found in the person of Mr. Eugene A. Nelson, a private educational consultant, dedicated to the cause of making an individualized curriculum a reality for every child.

The ideas presented in this book have been examined and strongly endorsed by a variety of educators. Early among those intrigued by the potential of the models set forth herein were the superintendents heading the intermediate school districts serving the Buffalo (New York) metropolitan area: Dr. Clifford Crooks and Mr. William Crocoll. They were instrumental in bringing the models to the attention of superintendents of the regular school districts in that metropolitan area, several of whom were also intrigued by the potential. Even in the face of declining enrollments, these educators saw no problem in financing, at the local level, pilot-model, capital-intensive schools. However, neither the intermediate nor local districts could provide developmental and start-up costs, but together with the authors, sought such support from the New York State Education Department.

At the State Education Department, there were those who were receptive, and those who were not. Among those particularly receptive were Dr. John J. Polley, then Acting Deputy Commissioner for Elementary and Secondary Education, Dr. Robert E. Lamitie, Administrator of Educational Finance Research Services, and Dr. Carl E. Wedekind, Director, Division of Research. It was at the State Education Department level that the authors came face to face with the politics of change discussed at some length in Chapter X. About this time also, the State of New York was experiencing one of those rare instances of a government on the brink of bankruptcy.

With these severe political and economic constraints, the best that supporters in the State Education Department could do was to endorse a proposal to the National Science Foundation for funding of the development and start-up costs of a pilot model of a capital-intensive school. The reviews of the proposal ran the gauntlet from "the . . . principal investigators lacked background in dealing with young children" to "if the project were successful, it would make a major change in instructional practice and the impact would be felt widely." With such mixed reviews, funding of the proposal was not recommended.

Somewhat battered, but undaunted, the authors have now embarked upon a strategy of presenting their arguments in book form intended for a national audience. The hope is that, by weaving the threads of knowledge about educational technology and its use into a complete fabric, more people will recognize its potential, and the possibility for gaining the necessary support for financing developmental and start-up costs of pilot models will be enhanced. In the opinion of the authors, the eventual widespread implementation of such models will be an *economic necessity* within 20 years, or less.

It is interesting to note that several large firms specializing in various aspects of educational technology (both hardware and software) are presently increasing their efforts in the educational fields relating to business, health organizations, higher education, and the military. None of these firms, however, though possessing the overall capability, are willing to tackle the educational establishment controlling public elementary and secondary education in the United States. (Two nationally-known firms are fully aware of the research herein discussed.)

The authors are in the debt of the above mentioned persons for their assistance in shaping the ideas, and in giving encouragement when there was little to be encouraged about. They are also grateful to Mrs. Nancy Hunt Myers, who was meticulous in typing the manuscript through its various phases of development; and to Mrs. Ruth Shea Willett, who set up the Appendices. To them we express our deepest appreciation.

A final "thank you" goes to Mr. Lawrence Lipsitz, our editor, who sensed from his first acquaintance with the potential manuscript the relevance of its theme, and who has patiently guided us in producing the final version.

Edward J. Willett	Austin D. Swanson	Eugene A. Nelson
Houghton, New York	Buffalo, New York	Snyder, New York

February 2, 1979

TABLE OF CONTENTS

PREFACE v

I TECHNOLOGY AND SCHOOLING: Modernizing
   the Little Red Schoolhouse 3

II EDUCATION PRODUCTION FUNCTIONS: Analogy
    or Pedagogy 23

III THE LUDDITE MENTALITY: Anti-technology and
     Education 37

IV MAN-MACHINE SYSTEMS IN EDUCATION: Indi-
    vidualization 51

V AN ALTERNATIVE—CAPITAL-INTENSIVE IN-
   STRUCTION: Samples of Possible Designs—The Fu-
   ture Today 67

VI A MANAGEMENT SYSTEM FOR INDIVIDUAL-
    IZED INSTRUCTION: Coping with Complexity 89

VII CONCEPTUAL MODELS OF A MAN-MACHINE
SYSTEM: Reallocating Scarce Educational Resources ... 119

VIII THE FIVE-DAY CAPITAL-INTENSIVE MODEL:
Description and Costs 131

IX THE THREE-DAY CAPITAL-INTENSIVE MODEL:
Description and Costs 165

X CAN CHANGE OCCUR? Implications for Policy and
Further Research and Development 181

BIBLIOGRAPHY 205
APPENDIX 225
GLOSSARY 267
AUTHOR INDEX 273
SUBJECT INDEX 277

Appendices

A Cost Estimates for Media Equipment Units for an
800-1200 Student Learning Center 227

B Cost Estimates for Media *Preparation* Equipment for
an 800-1200 Student Learning Center 230

C Cost Estimates for Instructional Television Production and Systems Utilization for an 800-1200 Student
Learning Center 232

D Cost Estimates for Purchase of Media *Materials* for an
800-1200 Student Learning Center 233

E-1 Cost Estimates of Capital Outlay for Art, Music,

Physical Education, and Science Equipment for an
800-1200 Student Learning Center 235

E-2 Cost Estimates of Annual Outlay for Supplies and
Replacement of Equipment for Print-Medium, Art,
Music, Physical Education, and Social Science 236

F   Cost Estimates for *Annual Replacement* of Media
Equipment and Materials for an 800-1200 Student
Learning Center 237

G   Cost Estimates of Annual Outlay for Media Design
and Preparation *Supplies* for an 800-1200 Student
Learning Center 238

H   Cost of Estimated *Annual Outlay* for Miscellaneous
Audio-visual Media Service Items for an 800-1200
Student Learning Center 239

I   Summary of Estimated Costs for Nonhuman Media
and Media Services (Excluding District Services) for
an 800-1200 Student Learning Center—Stated in
1977 Dollars—Five-Day Design (Transitional) 240

J   Cost Estimates of Annual Outlay for Audio-visual
Media Specialist Staff at District Level (To serve
Districts of 12,000 to 24,000 students) 242

K   Cost Estimates of *Annual Outlay for Equipment and
Supplies* for the Design and Preparation of Audio-
visual Media by District Staff—Five-Day Design (Transitional) 243

L-1 Cost Estimates of Salaries of Professional Staff for an
800-Student Learning Center (Not Including Fringe
Benefits)—Five-Day Design (Transitional) 244

L-2 Cost Estimates of Salaries of Professional Staff for a 1000-Student Learning Center (Not Including Fringe Benefits)—Five-Day Design (Transitional) 245

L-3 Cost Estimates of Salaries of Professional Staff for a 1200-Student Learning Center (Not Including Fringe Benefits)—Five-Day Design (Transitional) 246

M-1 Cost Estimates of Salaries of Paraprofessional Staff for an 800-Student Learning Center (Not Including Fringe Benefits)—Five-Day Design (Transitional) 247

M-2 Cost Estimates of Salaries of Paraprofessional Staff for a 1000-Student Learning Center (Not Including Fringe Benefits)—Five-Day Design (Transitional) 248

M-3 Cost Estimates of Salaries of Paraprofessional Staff for a 1200-Student Learning Center (Not Including Fringe Benefits)—Five-Day Design (Transitional) 249

N Cost Estimates of Wages for Student Assistants—Five-Day Design (Transitional) 250

O Cost Estimates of Fringe Benefits for Professional and Paraprofessional Staff (Except District Staff)—Five-Day Design (Transitional) 251

P Calculation of Per Student Per Year Cost for *Non-human Media* (except CAI): Based on 10 Percent Blocks of Instructional Time 252

Q Calculation of Per Student Per Year Cost of *Computer-Assisted Instruction*: Based on 10 Percent Blocks of Instructional Time 253

R   1974-75 Per Student Per Year Costs for Instructional Services—Traditional (Plus Audio-visual)—In Western New York 254

S-1   Cost Estimates of Salaries of Professional Staff for an 800-Student Learning Center Accommodating 1600 Students During a Five-Day Week (Not Including Fringe Benefits)—Three-Day Design (Future) 255

S-2   Cost Estimates of Salaries of Professional Staff for a 1000-Student Learning Center Accommodating 2000 Students During a Five-Day Week (Not Including Fringe Benefits)—Three-Day Design (Future) 256

S-3   Cost Estimates of Salaries of Professional Staff for a 1200-Student Learning Center Accommodating 2400 Students During a Five-Day Week (Not Including Fringe Benefits)—Three-Day Design (Future) 257

T-1   Cost Estimates of Salaries of Paraprofessional Staff for an 800-Student Learning Center Accommodating 1600 Students During a Five-Day Week (Not Including Fringe Benefits)—Three-Day Design (Future) 258

T-2   Cost Estimates of Salaries of Paraprofessional Staff for a 1000-Student Learning Center Accommodating 2000 Students During a Five-Day Week (Not Including Fringe Benefits)—Three-Day Design (Future) 259

T-3   Cost Estimates of Salaries of Paraprofessional Staff for a 1200-Student Learning Center Accommodating 2400 Students During a Five-Day Week (Not Including Fringe Benefits)—Three-Day Design (Future) 260

U   Cost Estimates of Wages for Student Assistant— 1974-75 Dollars—Three-Day Design (Future) 261

V-1 Cost Estimates of Fringe Benefits for Professional Instructional Staff (Except District Staff)—Three-Day Design (Future) 262

V-2 Cost Estimates of Fringe Benefits for Paraprofessional Instructional Staff (Except District Staff)—Three-Day Design (Future) 263

W   Estimates of Costs for Nonhuman Media and Media Services (Excluding District Services) for 800-1200 Student Learning Center Designed to Accommodate 1600 to 2400 Students in Two Alternating Shifts (Plus All-School Activity Day) During Five-Day Week—Three-Day Design (Future) 264

X   Cost Estimates of *Annual* Outlay for Equipment and Supplies for the Design and Preparation of Audiovisual Media by District Staff—Three-Day Design (Future) 265

Y   Estimated Percentage Savings in Per Student Per Year Costs Over Western New York State Traditional Education Format (Figures are from the Five-Day and Three-Day Designs) 266

Tables

7.1 Five-Day (Transitional) and Three-Day (Future) Designs: Summary of Descriptive Features 121

8.1 Five-Day Design (Transitional): Description of Educational District 133

8.2 Five-Day Design (Transitional): Calculation of Number of Professional Staff Needed per Learning Center 135

8.3   Five-Day Design (Transitional): Calculation of Number of Paraprofessional Staff per Learning Center; Ratio of Professional to Paraprofessional: 2 to 3 137

8.4   Five-Day Design (Transitional): Summary of Instructional Hardware and Software: Equipment, Maintenance, Repair, Replacement, and Supply Costs (Based on Erickson) 145

8.5   Five-Day Design (Transitional): Summary of Instructional Hardware and Software: Equipment, Maintenance, Repair, Replacement, and Supply Costs (Based on Kiesling) 148

8.6   (Erickson Study) Five-Day Design—800 Students: Summary of Estimated per Student per Year Instructional Costs for a Capital-Intensive Man-Machine System of Individualized Education Below College Level 152

8.7   (Erickson Study) Five-Day Design—1000 Students: Summary of Estimated per Student per Year Instructional Costs for a Capital-Intensive Man-Machine System of Individualized Education Below College Level 153

8.8   (Erickson Study) Five-Day Design—1200 Students: Summary of Estimated per Student per Year Instructional Costs for a Capital-Intensive Man-Machine System of Individualized Education Below College Level 154

8.9   (Kiesling Study) Five-Day Design—800 Students: Summary of Estimated per Student per Year Instructional Costs for a Capital-Intensive Man-Machine

System of Individualized Education Below College
Level 156

8.10 (Kiesling Study) Five-Day Design—1000 Students:
Summary of Estimated per Student per Year Instruc-
tional Costs for a Capital-Intensive Man-Machine
System of Individualized Education Below College
Level 157

8.11 (Kiesling Study) Five-Day Design—1200 Students:
Summary of Estimated per Student per Year Instruc-
tional Costs for a Capital-Intensive Man-Machine
System of Individualized Education Below College
Level 158

9.1 Three-Day Design (Future): Calculation of Number
of *Professional* Staff Needed per Learning Center;
Ratio of Professional to Paraprofessional—2/3 to 1 166

9.2 Three-Day Design (Future): Calculation of Number
of *Paraprofessional* Staff per Learning Center; Ratio
of Professional to Paraprofessional—2/3 to 1 ....

9.3 (Erickson Study) Three-Day Design—1600 Students:
Summary of Estimated per Student per Year Instruc-
tional Costs for a Capital-Intensive Man-Machine
System of Individualized Education Below College
Level 170

9.4 (Erickson Study) Three-Day Design—2000 Students:
Summary of Estimated per Student per Year Instruc-
tional Costs for a Capital-Intensive Man-Machine
System of Individualized Education Below College
Level 171

9.5 (Erickson Study) Three-Day Design—2400 Students: Summary of Estimated per Student per Year Instructional Costs for a Capital-Intensive Man-Machine System of Individualized Education Below College Level 172

9.6 (Kiesling Study) Three-Day Design—1600 Students: Summary of Estimated per Student per Year Instructional Costs for a Capital-Intensive Man-Machine System of Individualized Education Below College Level 174

9.7 (Kiesling Study) Three-Day Design—2000 Students: Summary of Estimated per Student per Year Instructional Costs for a Capital-Intensive Man-Machine System of Individualized Education Below College Level 175

9.8 (Kiesling Study) Three-Day Design—2400 Students: Summary of Estimated per Student per Year Instructional Costs for a Capital-Intensive Man-Machine System of Individualized Education Below College Level 176

Figures

4.1 McMullen's computer framework for programs 59

6.1 Major components of an individualized man-machine instructional system 93

6.2 An information matrix for needs assessment 105

6.3 A management system for individualized instruction 109

8.1 Five-day design—Average total cost curves: Instruction only 161

9.1 Three-day design—Average total cost curves: Instruction only 178

10.1 Relationships between productivity, unit costs, wages, and taxes 185

modernizing the little red schoolhouse
the economics of improved education

Chapter I

TECHNOLOGY AND SCHOOLING:

Modernizing the Little Red Schoolhouse

... the task of preventing the new generation from changing in any deep or significant way is precisely what most societies require of their educators (Leonard, 1968:7).

Critics of 20th century education in the United States—from the advocates of "de-schooling" to the proponents of a free market voucher approach—agree on one essential: *the individual needs of individual students are being poorly met* by what Morrison (1940) called "the discontinuous school system." Underlying the problems of rising costs, racism, teacher strikes, student unrest, and taxpayer obstinacy is an uneasiness which is difficult to define but which manifests itself in unguarded moments in the conversation of the man-in-the-street and the man-in-the-ivy-covered-tower.

There is growing national concern over declining average scores on standardized tests. With the revelation that many high school graduates are functionally illiterate, state after state is adopting minimum competency standards for high school diplomas, and

3

there is strong support in Congress for federal educational standards. Teenage unemployment is rampant and crime rates among juveniles are rising. There appears to be a lower level of interest among pupils in school activities as discipline becomes a serious problem and vandalism and absenteeism mount.

At the same time, no matter how they are measured, education costs are going up at an alarming rate. As the Great Depression was beginning, the United States was devoting 3.1 percent of its Gross National Product (GNP) to education. Shrinking national production boosted the percentage to 4.1 percent in 1934 even though the absolute expenditure declined. Rising production during World War II caused the percentage to drop to 1.8 percent in 1944. Since that time, the increases in educational expenditures have outstripped increases in production, causing the percentage to steadily rise to 7.8 percent during 1974-75. Expenditures at the elementary and secondary level for public and private institutions combined for 1974-75 was $68 billion (Grant and Lind, 1976:2-3). While the importance of education to the political and economic health of the country is generally acknowledged, evidence is accumulating that the nation has passed the point of diminishing returns in its expenditures for education, given the present educational arrangements.

There are three major causes of this phenomenal increase. First, the number of persons enrolled in schools has nearly doubled since the 1930's. The second influence is simply inflation. But interestingly, during the 1950's and 1960's, in spite of increasing enrollments, inflation, a teacher shortage, and a relatively inelastic tax base (property), education became more and more labor-intensive—a counter-trend to the general economy. The declining enrollments of the 1970's have accelerated the process of labor-intensiveness as a third factor in rising education costs. Data pertaining to New York State vividly illustrate what has happened in this respect. In 1936 there were 36.8 professional employees for every 1,000 students. By 1973 this had increased to 61.2. While for American industry as a whole, approximately 66 percent of total product cost is for labor, a random sample of school districts in western New York State showed that labor costs in education ranged between 79 and 89 percent of the total costs (Swanson and Willett, 1974).

If it could be shown that educators working more intensively with children produced more learning, the greater costs might be justified. But such is not the case. In a study submitted to the President's Commission on School Finance in 1971, the Rand Corporation concluded that, "Increasing expenditures on traditional educational practices is not likely to improve educational outcomes substantially." The report goes on to say:

> Researchers have examined many variants of the existing educational system. As we have indicated, none of these variants has been shown to improve educational outcomes consistently. A fact often overlooked is that few have been shown to lead to significantly worse outcomes either. Consequently, educational research has provided a long list of equally effective variants of the existing system. And if these variants are not all equally expensive, then choosing the least expensive provides opportunities to redirect (or even reduce) costs without also reducing effectiveness (i.e., effectiveness as now measured) (Averch *et al.*, 1971:155).

A review of research on alternative instructional media by Dean Jamison, Patrick Suppes, and Stuart Wells points to the frustration of those experimenting with educational technology and to the need for carefully designed and carefully evaluated demonstrations:

> On the one hand, it seems almost inevitable that productivity improvements in the schools, if they are to occur, will require the use of technology. On the other hand, in spite of very considerable expenditures on educational technology for many years, we are pressed to find an example of its use to improve productivity. What is required is a carefully designed, carefully evaluated demonstration that main-line instructional costs can be reduced without sacrificing quality—indeed it is important to

attempt to improve quality—by use of a technology or mix of technologies (1974:58).

The Benefits versus the Costs

Defenders of the status quo in education are hard to find, not because there are so few of them—some would say the defenders are a large majority—but because they are not articulate or vocal. Perhaps they were educated in and for a world which no longer exists, but for which they envision no suitable substitute.

It has often been suggested that the major disagreement between the critics and defenders of modern education is the role which innovation should play in the educational process. Critics say, what can be done should be done; defenders reply, this is not necessarily so. The result is that other valid areas of discussion—for example, social benefits versus vested interests, centralization versus decentralization, economic efficiency versus non-economic values—are relegated to the periphery where little can be gained from research into their possible interrelationships. The more one listens to each side of this debate, the more one is tempted to ask: what if they are *both* correct?

There is a concept—and a technique—which, if applied, makes it possible to view this continuing argument from the vantage of reasonable objectivity and minimum bias. The concept is known in academic jargon as *opportunity cost*; the technique involves the simulation of alternatives.

All disciplines recognize this concept. Theology comments on man's mortality. The humanities romantically point out that we pass this way but once. Physical scientists state that time is irretrievable. The social sciences recognize the possibility of but one course of action at a time. Educators intone: a path once chosen may be irreversible.

Once the concept of opportunity cost is understood, the logic of the technique of investigating alternatives becomes obvious. If there is but one goal, the possible ways of reaching that goal may not be numerous, but they will be plural. If many goals are involved, the range of alternatives can become complex, but (a) solution(s) can be found.

The realization that alternative solutions are possible suggests that a systematic procedure for identifying, ranking, and choosing among alternatives is required. It should also suggest that some arrangement is needed for monitoring any ongoing process in order to redefine both problems and alternative solutions as changes occur, i.e., an arrangement for feedback.

Opportunity cost as a concept, and choosing among alternatives as a technique, have become part of the world of economic decision-making, and to a more limited degree, of the world of political activity. While education has taught the concept, only in the last few years have both the concept and the technique been seriously considered as applicable to the problems of education. As Vaizey remarks:

> ... a great deal of the tenor of educational administration is non-quantitative, and to a considerable extent it tends to choose the costliest solution rather than the least costly solution because the people who run education (... people who have been teachers, and in many countries ... people who have little or no experience in administration) have not been trained to think in terms of opportunity cost ... (1967:233).

When the opportunity (or alternative) cost approach is applied to educational decisions, the role of innovation in education is given its correct perspective: a means to an end, rather than an end in itself. Archer (1970) appropriately points out that under these conditions, the conventional wisdom is properly reworded: what should be done can be done.

Ignorance of, or resistance to, the opportunity cost analysis of educational processes has carefully kept covered the most obvious economic problem of education in the United States today. Given the technology now available, there are too many people employed in elementary and secondary education, and they are improperly deployed.

This volume focuses on one aspect of the problem: the economic efficiency of the present educational process, which commits, nationally, about 83 percent of the *instructional* budgets of public elementary and secondary education to salaries of instructional staff.[1] The concept of "efficiency" encompasses the *quality* of performance as well as the quantity of inputs, as developed further in Chapter III.

Productivity in Service Industries

If productivity[2] improvements in education can probably occur only by the use of improved technology, why does society not move forcibly in this direction, thus reducing the amount of scarce resources devoted to schooling? Baumol (1967:415) argues that "inherent in the technological structure" of such economic service industries as education "are forces working almost unavoidably for progressive and cumulative increases in the real costs incurred in supplying them."

In non-service industries (e.g., manufacturing), it is generally understood that the "technological structure" is not inalterably fixed, especially under market conditions of competition. Instead, the emphasis is on alternative methods of producing the desired product, each alternative production possibility being judged by its opportunity cost versus every other alternative. Education, however, appears to be locked into one mode of production. On this point Baumol comments:

> On the other hand, there are a number of services in which the labor is an end in itself, in which quality is judged directly in terms of amount of labor. Teaching is a clear-cut example, where class size (number of teaching hours expended per student) is often taken as a critical index of quality. Here, despite the invention of teaching machines and the use of closed circuit television and a variety of other innovations, there still seem to be fairly firm limits to class size. We are deeply concerned when elementary school classes grow to 50 pupils and are disquieted by the idea of college lectures attended by 2000 underclassmen. *Without a complete revolution in our approach to teaching,* there

is no prospect that we can ever go beyond these levels (or even up to them) with any degree of equanimity (1967:416) [italics added].

The idea of "a complete revolution in our approach to teaching" may have been improbable, if not impossible, prior to 1970 in the United States, largely due to institutional arrangements for mass education which had been formalized over the preceding 50-75 years by American society. These arrangements, however, were, in *their* infancy, a complete revolution from the unique American concept of the Common School where the teacher was primarily a "manager of learning" rather than a transmitter of information. During the 1970's the public and professional focus has returned to "individualized" instruction. Indeed, the United States Congress has legislated individualized curricula for children with handicapping conditions; it is only a matter of time until such mandates are extended to all children.

It is the considered conclusion of the authors that new arrangements are possible for the improvement of productivity in education, arrangements which can demonstrate that the technological structure of education is not inherently predisposed to increase the real costs of providing schooling in today's world. Further, we argue that education does not need to be viewed as a service (i.e., parasitic) sector of the society, but preferably can be understood as a non-service industry producing a *good,* under input conditions that are variable and therefore responsive to technological change.

In order to clarify the basis for these arguments, it is necessary to introduce some specific analyses pertaining to the similarities between the "production" of education and the production of other output in a technologically advanced society.

Education as an Industry

The view of education as an industry which produces a product would have been considered professional sacrilege prior to World

War II. Schooling, defined as time spent in an institution called a school, was considered an inviolable extension of the training of the home, and parallel to the emphasis of religion in the preparation of the citizenry for their adult responsibilities.

The specific forces that resulted in a more pragmatic appraisal of education are difficult to isolate. The arms race, global wars, demographic changes, and space exploration could all qualify as contributors to the growing realization of just how limited were the resources of the economy, given the proliferation of programs competing for resource use. As a user of economic resources, public education in affluent societies has reached the point where some ultimate limitation of the resource capacity to support education must be recognized. Because levels of technology can, and do, rise (especially in developed economies), largely as a function of education, this ultimate limitation may be obscure. It becomes clear only when the competing demands for economic resources aggregate more than the economy can produce at current prices and levels of technology without a reduction in the standard of living, or an abnormal rate of inflation, which is the same thing, and which has characterized the 1970's.

Resource allocation, then, becomes the name of the game in modern economies, just as it has been historically. The industrial revolution with its resulting use of real capital (i.e., productive goods) only postponed the time when allocation of economic resources on a national, or global, scale would reassert its importance[3] and emphasize the economic axiom that resources are limited but wants tend toward infinity.

The sizeable amount of additional resources committed to education since 1944 has brought education into the category of a major competitor for a share of the economy's productive capacity because of (1) the role education plays in developing new technology, which is the prime defense against a reduction in affluence, and (2) the rising educational aspirations of an increasingly literate population. Education's part in new technology illustrates the need for supporting education as a social investment, whereas the desire of people to obtain more education reflects a personal view which sees education as a long run investment, as a short run intermediate good which is re-saleable, and as a market (or consumption) good yielding individual satisfaction.

Education as a social investment implies not only the further-ance of economic growth, but also the development of the most important of all economic resources—human beings. This latter concept has resulted in a growing body of research in the area of Human Capital.

The realization that "labor is people" has come about slowly even in societies that are now only a few generations removed from permitting actual physical slavery. Human resources are indeed the labor component of the creation of any product. The more democratic societies, however, are committed to the principle that the individual can develop as a *person* as well as a worker. Today, support for this principle can be objectively asserted as a result of the discovery that in any good random sample of any large population, the intellectual abilities of people cluster around the mean, i.e., form a "normal," or bell-shaped, curve. This knowledge, along with the rising awareness of the unconstitutional discriminatory practices toward various segments of American society, has propelled research into the development-al aspects of the individual.

Ginsburg (1972:12-13) proposes neither a hereditary (nativist) nor an environmental (empiricist) view of human personality. He uses the term "poor children" as a "simple and direct" synonym for those in a "lower socioeconomic status." From the standpoint of *present* psychological research, Ginsburg asserts:

> The real issue is not why poor children are deficient, but why they develop as well as they do . . . This is the question which the developmental view seeks to answer. The fact seems to be that poor children develop an adequate intellectual life . . . Like everyone else, they organize their own learning, they are curious about the world, they practice what needs to be learned, they

work out a reasonable adjustment to the environment. Poor children take an active role in devising solutions to the reality which confronts them (1972:15-16).

In light of these insights, Ginsburg suggests that:

> ... Traditional education approaches are based on several faulty assumptions. One is that the child's knowledge is a simple quantitative trait, like height . . . second . . . that knowledge is most effectively acquired through systematic instruction . . . Genuine intellectual work in many areas—writing, mathematics, science—often proceeds best on a relatively self-directed and intrinsically motivated basis (1972:17).

Thus, the potential which is present in modern society for the development of people forms the foundation for research into the methods by which a society can make an increasing investment in its people as a *capital* resource as well as a labor resource.

While investment in human capital is increasingly expensive, such investment properly should be related to the substantial growth in real income in the United States "after the growth in physical capital and labor has been accounted for (Becker, 1964:xv)." What might be an even more shocking comparison, but difficult to estimate, is the loss of economic growth as well as the loss in human resources which have resulted from the under-investment and misplaced investments in people as human capital.

Much of the current interest in and research on investment in human capital was stimulated by T.W. Schultz (1961, 1963, 1970) who early recognized that many of the concepts of economic analysis should be applied to education:

> Schools may be viewed as firms that specialize in producing[4] schooling.[5] The educational establishment, which includes all schools, may be viewed as an industry (Schultz, 1963:4).

Schultz also viewed the concept of opportunity cost as "a key to a number of puzzles about education (1963:5)." Becker (1964) isolates what is often referred to as the "spillover" effect of education: "Completely general training increases the marginal [i.e., extra] productivity of trainees by exactly the same amount in the firms providing the training as in other firms . . . (1964:18)," and adds, "A School can be defined as an institution specializing in the production of training, as distinct from a firm that offers training in conjunction with the production of goods (1964:29)."

Becker also points out that:

> . . . conventional measures of ability—intelligence tests or aptitude scores, school grades, and personality tests . . . do not reliably measure the talents required to succeed in the economic sphere. The latter consists of particular kinds of personality, persistence, and intelligence. Accordingly, some writers have gone to the opposite extreme and argued that the only relevant way to measure economic talent is by results, or by earnings themselves. This approach goes too far . . . The main reason for relating ability to earnings is to distinguish its effects from difference in education, training, health, and other such factors, and a definition equating ability and earnings *ipso facto* precludes such a distinction (1964:61-62).

The concept of human capital and the role of education in its development is now receiving respectful attention in texts dealing with the theory and process of economic growth. Kindleberger (1965:107), who published his first text on economic development in 1958, incorporates a special section in the second edition on investment in human capital. Denison (1962:67-79) discusses the role of education in improving the quality of the labor force, and in increasing the total amount of useful knowledge available to society. He feels that extending years of schooling (i.e., a quantitative approach) would yield a much smaller return than improving education (i.e., a qualitative approach). Kuznets concludes his very complete study of economic growth:

> Whatever the source, the increase in the stock of useful knowledge and the extension of its application are of the essence

in modern economic growth . . . No matter where these technological and social innovations emerge . . . the economic growth of
any given nation depends upon their adoption . . . One easily
observable corollary of such dependence is the spread in
developed nations of modern education (1966:286-287).

B.F. Skinner puts it even more succinctly:

Everything which is now taught must have been learned at least
once by someone who was not being taught, but thanks to
education we no longer need to wait for these rare events
(1968:5).

The concept of human capital, and the concept of education as
an industry, are both part of a rising area of research termed the
Economics of Education which, since 1966,[6] has begun to live a
life very much its own. Although grounded in basic economic
ideas (e.g., resource allocation, opportunity cost, return on
society's investment, etc.), it uses these as tools to explore in
minute detail the relationship of the costs of education to learning
theory, to educational processes, to environmental factors, and to
both private and social benefits in a society. It is probable that
most economists today would concur that Vaizey (1962:13),
among the first economists to study the economic effect of
education, was overly optimistic in writing, "It is the theme of this
book that education can help to make us rich and, being rich (as
Keynes pointed out), we can be free to be uneconomic," since the
events of the succeeding decade have given *scarcity* at least as
much publicity as *affluence*. But educators should be the first to
point out that richness of life is not primarily due to the
abundance of material possessions—that an educated individual is
one who has learned to use wisely for personal achievement, and
for the social group, whatever resources are available, striving
constantly to increase total benefits both personally and on behalf
of society. Personal satisfaction from education is related to, but
not parallel with, the gain to be obtained by society as a result of
investment in the education of its citizens.[7]

A Caveat About the Use of the Word "Capital"
In referring to discussions among economists, Professor Lionel Robbins has written:

> We all talk about the same thing, but we have not yet agreed what it is we are talking about . . . As Mill pointed out a hundred years ago, the definition of a science has almost invariably, not preceded, but followed the creation of the science itself (1946:1-2).

If economic scholars, both those who read and those who write, tend to assume that economic terms are understood, even when such terms are imprecise, it follows that non-economists will be confused to an even greater extent. The term "capital" is a case in point.

General agreement[8] on the concept of capital in economic analysis goes back to the Austrian economist of the late 19th century, Bohm-Bawerk,[9] though embryonic portions of the idea can be traced at least to the early 17th century. Capital is real, physical *means of production*—factories, machines, tools—which is itself the product of the combination of the two other basic inputs in any production process, human and natural resources. To this "production capital" is added the major structural investments of the society—airports, dams, highways, railroads, etc.—and the combined total is known to economists as the *capital stock* of an economic system. Such a precise rendering is absolutely necessary to clearly distinguish each basic input: human resources (*labor*), and natural resources (*land*), from produced resources (*capital*). Some analysts also argue that management (enterprise) should be included as a fourth input (or factor of production).

Real capital has both a quantitative and a qualitative character. Increasing the amount of equipment at the same technological level (e.g., providing a calculator for each student), or raising the technological level of the capital (e.g., time-sharing a computer), may each result in increases in the productive use of student and teacher time. *Or*, both quantitative and qualitative changes in capital may be made together. It is the *application*, not cost.

Capital *as a tangible productive resource* is the way in which the term is used throughout this book. When it is combined, as in the adjective "capital-intensive," the reference is to a relatively larger percent of the "production mix" being found in the form of capital rather than in the form of human resources ("labor-intensive"), or in the form of natural resources ("land-intensive").

Where does this leave *real* capital in relation to the much more recent, and still imprecise, term "human capital"? This latter concept might better be rendered "investment in people," since it is an elaboration on the concept of "labor"—not "capital"—giving to it, as with real capital, a qualitative as well as a quantitative character.

Three aspects are involved in investment in people. In modern history, the first aspect was clearly isolated by Robert Owen (1771-1858), an English factory owner, who provided all of his workers with proper food, clean, well-lighted, and well-ventilated factories, plus other attentions to physical welfare, with resulting increases in output, i.e., a rise in the productivity of his work force. The importance of the second and third aspects of investment in people was recognized through analytical work (in the 1950-1970 period) which (1) related increases in the *knowledge base* (through research and development activities) to the productivity of the production process, and (2) analyzed the contribution to productivity increases resulting from raising the levels of education and training of people beyond those of mere literacy and minimum skills. As Freeman,[10] in Shapiro and White (1977:117-118), points out:

> In the absence of changes in knowledge the potential for growth by investing in physical capital, discovering new sources of natural resources, and investing in education eventually appears to run out . . . This point is that the difference in *what* is learned . . . is the key factor differentiating modern from fourteenth century economies. More positively, one of the most remarkable aspects of the contribution of the stock of knowledge to growth is that even the most abstract scientific work . . . has historically turned

out to have significant consequences that are unlikely to be
captured in the simple marginal productivity growth accounting.

Thus, the term *human capital*[11] must not be confused with the
term *real capital.* Investment in people (human capital) has the
potential effect of improving human resources (labor) as an input
in the production process, but its actual use in the production of
any good or service is a function of the individual's decision to be
(or not to be) available as a productive factor. Investment in
equipment (real capital), however, can be an immediate addition
to the production process. Its amount, disposition, and employment is (or should be) determined by the change in productivity
which will result from its use.

The inclusion of more, and better, real capital in the productive
capacity of the United States has accounted for 21.6 percent of
the economic growth in the period 1948-69 (Denison, 1972). But
advances in knowledge and increased education per worker
accounted for 34.1 percent[12] and 11.9 percent, respectively, in
the same time period, for a total economic growth increase
attributable to these two categories of 46 percent. Investment in
people can thus be seen to be extremely important to a
post-industrial society such as the United States, because it is both
a complement to, and a determinant of, the sophistication of real
capital which, when applied to the production process, gives
increasing leverage to the allocation of all resources at the disposal
of the society: human, natural, and capital.

Investment in people is also what this book is about. The
process of education as it is now carried on is extremely wasteful of
human resources, both of those who attempt to educate, and of
those who attempt to learn, in relation to energy and time.
Systematic, planned incorporation of the technologically advanced
real capital, now available, into the production of education is not
being done. Until this is done, the gains from an increased
knowledge base, and from increased education per worker, cannot
contribute to greater improvement in the effectiveness of the
nation's education delivery system.

The Perspective of a New, Yet Old, Approach

Early in its history, the United States had made educational arrangements to provide the politically literate citizenry needed by a fledgling democracy. The economic gains from the industrial revolution brought additional pressure to form (or reform) institutional arrangements (e.g., mass public education) to keep a supply of trained manpower abreast of the rate of entrepreneurial innovation in the industrial processes. The initial result was a universally available, but non-mandatory, educational system with a curriculum devoted almost entirely to mastery of the basic skills of reading, writing, and arithmetic. The family still retained the primary role of teaching moral values and occupational skills. As the industrial revolution progressed, the position of the family as a basic economic and social unit continued to weaken. Work was taken out of the home and with it for eight to twelve hours a day so was the father and, to an increasing extent, the mother. Correspondingly, schooling became compulsory and its curriculum became comprehensive. The conformity of public education was partially tempered, however, by the *decentralization* of control which allowed local communities some opportunity to shape the system in terms of local expressions of norms and values (Tyack, 1974).

As the 20th century moved toward its midpoint, an increasing trend toward greater centralization of education decision-making became apparent. One influence contributing to this trend had to be the larger and larger share of the costs of education being assumed at the state level. Another factor was the improvement in efficiencies of operation and enrichment of curriculum which consolidation of very small units made possible. Behind both of these forces pushing against decentralization was the changing technology of the period, especially in transportation, where the use of school buses, and subsequent improvement of roads, created a whole new concept of mass education for rural and suburban America. One by one, in the name of progress, the "little red schoolhouses" which had epitomized the individualized yet homogeneous learning experience of the American Common School disappeared. The pendulum now swung more and more in the direction of the social utility of education and farther and farther away from personal benefit of education. In the words of Morrison (1940), *continuous* education was fast becoming *discontinuous* education.

The economies which mass education on an ever larger scale made possible coincided with the drive for similar economies of mass production as the industrialization of the United States proceeded (Kliebard, 1971). Lock-step learning became institutionalized in bricks and mortar, methods of instruction, homogeneous grouping by age and ability, and bureaucratic administration. World War I, the "business-of-America-is-business" climate of the 1920's, the Great Depression, and World War II all tended to camouflage the forces of change which, by 1960, would make mass education more and more costly, and less and less up-to-date in its technology and in its application of modern learning theory.

There is a literal plethora of analyses of "what is wrong"; fortunately, there are also many serious-minded investigators who have produced a wide variety of research into what *could* be done if our society can be persuaded to marshal the human and technological resources now at its disposal to deal with the change which should no longer be postponed. In a period of skyrocketing educational costs, the immediate response to such an "idealistic" bit of rhetoric is to ask: "What resources are we not already making available in greater quantity and quality than ever before?" While this is a fair question, it only accentuates the mode of thinking which has pervaded present-day American education to a point of near paralysis. A counter question is: *"What should be done, and are we able to do it?"*

Revisiting the Little Red Schoolhouse

What should be done? In an increasingly literate and sophisticated society we must find ways to meet the unique needs of individual students. At the same time we must stabilize, and if possible reduce, the share of real resources allocated to formal education. Today, these two goals are *not* mutually exclusive. They are attainable if, (1) educators are permitted to restructure the proportionate arrangement of human and other inputs in the schooling process, and (2) the society is as committed to taking advantage of the technology of information transmission now possible as it was committed in the 1960's to putting men on the moon.

This approach to "up-dating the little red schoolhouse" can be stated in the form of a question:

> *If education production functions for elementary and secondary education in the United States were to become more capital-intensive, and less labor-intensive, would the change be positive in terms of both economic efficiency, and of meeting the needs of individual students?*

Are we able to do it? The format for determining this part of the problem can be outlined in a series of sub-questions, which are discussed, and answered, in subsequent chapters.

1. What does existing evidence reveal concerning individualized, programmed, and supervised learning procedures as compared with traditional, teacher-intensive learning procedures?

2. How might costs of capital-intensive schooling compare with costs of traditional, labor-intensive schooling?

3. If capital-intensive schooling appears to offer any significant per pupil cost reductions for at-least-equal student cognitive achievement, what might be the possible effect(s) upon change(s) in the roles of professional, paraprofessional, and non-professional personnel in education?

4. If capital-intensive schooling appears to offer significant per pupil cost reductions for at-least-equal student cognitive achievement, then what revisions might occur in such educational components as: buildings (whether owned or leased); administration; transportation; maintenance; and miscellaneous support functions?

Existing research already provides the data necessary to make valid cost-comparisons between: (1) the procedures of traditional instruction (teacher, plus audio-visual add-ons), and (2) completely integrated man-machine systems (incorporating the appropriate "mix" of human and nonhuman media in a framework of individualized instruction).

Now that the industrial revolution has given way to the technological revolution, a post-industrial society must conduct a re-evaluation of its use of economic resources in the education of future generations. Whether or not the fantastic changes in the mechanics of information handling and transmission are in today's world, what printing was to the world of yesterday, is not the most important point for consideration. Of much greater import is the fact that it now appears possible for both personal benefit and societal benefit to expand independently, yet in complement. The *key* is herein alleged to be educational technology,[13] which makes education no longer only a dependent, but also an independent, variable in society.[14]

To investigate this key, we next look at *education production functions.*

Notes

1. As a percent of all public elementary and secondary expenditure in 1973-74, this is reduced to 57.2 percent. The 83 percent figure above is calculated in the following manner. Total "instructional staff" in public elementary and secondary schools in 1973-74 was 2,425,445. Estimated average annual salary of instructional staff (supervisors, principals, classroom teachers, and others) was $11,185 in 1973-74 dollars, for a total of $27.129 billion. Total expenditure for "instruction" in public elementary and secondary schools in 1973-74 was $32.609 billion, of which amount instructional staff salaries were 83 percent. (Grant and Lind, 1976:51, 55 and 69.)

2. In economic terms, productivity is a ratio: the output divided by the input(s). Productivity increase occurs when (1) more output is obtained with the same inputs, or (2) the same output is obtained with less inputs.

3. This does not imply a purely Malthusian view. Technological develop-ment as a function of research which is a function of education has in the advanced economies pushed back the specter of want to a reasonable degree for the majority but has not been successful for total populations.

4. Instructional inputs are: teachers, teacher aides, teaching devices, and teaching materials.

5. It may be significant in the light of present discussion that Schultz defined the product of schools as schooling. Paradoxically, Schultz felt "that schooling is the largest investment in human capital" (1963:x).

6. Burkhead *et al.,* in 1967, developed the first serious, *published* attempt to grapple with education as an industrial "production function." Discussion of this pioneering contribution is to be found in Chapter II.

7. Personal satisfaction (i.e., "utility" in the economic sense) from education may be greater, equal to, or less than, the utility of education to society.

8. The reader is referred to any standard textbook in Principles of Economics (Samuelson, McConnell, etc.) under "capital."

9. Eugene von Bohm-Bawerk. *The Positive Theory of Capital.* Published in German in 1889. Trans. W. Smart. London and New York: Macmillan and Company, 1891.

10. R.B. Freeman. "Investing in Human Capital and Knowledge."

11. For the most recent summary of human capital theory, see: Mark Blaug, "The Empirical Status of Human Capital Theory: A Slightly Jaundiced Survey," *Journal of Economic Literature, 14*(3), September 1976, 827-855.

12. Less some small percent for changes which could not be classified under any of the five determinants: advances in knowledge; more work done; more capital; increased education per worker; and improved resource allocation.

13. "Educational technology has been defined as the application of scientific knowledge, including learning theory, to the solution of problems in education" (Hempel, 1971: 34).

14. Prior to World War II, education primarily focused on preparing people for existing niches in society. Thus, it was a *dependent* variable. Since World War II, education, through research, has also laid and is laying the groundwork for new vocations which did not then, or do not now, exist. This makes education an *independent* variable, as well.

Chapter II

EDUCATION PRODUCTION FUNCTIONS:

Analogy or Pedagogy

> In practice, the efficiency aspects of education are complicated by the presence of public sector financing or provision of schooling (O'Donoghue, 1971:149).

If the idea of education as an industry can be accepted, then some of the jargon of the economic analysis of industrial activity must be introduced.

The term "production function" might be likened in some respects to the word "recipe." It connotes a "mix" of ingredients. The ingredients of a production function are economic resources, usually thought of as: human resources (labor); natural resources (land); and synthetic[1] resources (capital). Some analysts like to include, as a fourth resource, management. Any product (or output) of a production process is a function of some combination of these resources, often symbolized as

$$Output = f\ (Inputs)$$

In a market-oriented society, management decisions are based upon the monetary amount which must be paid for the use of economic resources. This sum is referred to as cost. Profit is always included in cost; thus, when a production function is stated in monetary terms, it is properly written

$$\text{PRICE of Product} = \text{COST of Output}$$

since the price cannot be more than the sum of all the claims to product (including profit) which comprise the cost of production (including profit).[2]

Public elementary and secondary education in the United States is a *de facto* monopoly.[3] As a result, any change (usually an increase) in the *cost* of public schooling is automatically reflected as an increase in the *price* of public schooling to such an extent that the word "price" is rarely used in reference to the output of education. The emphasis is exclusively on "cost."

Economic analysis of production functions also demonstrates that there is an inverse relationship between the productivity represented in a production function and the unit cost of the output. This follows from the definition of productivity, which is: the ratio of the output to the input(s). As productivity rises, unit cost declines, and vice versa.

In relation to public education, changes in productivity, either positive or negative, are difficult to isolate because of continuing changes in other variables, such as the nature and size of enrollment, qualifications for teachers, societal composition, and the transmission media (human and mechanical) used to disseminate knowledge. The translucence—almost opaqueness—of the problem has caused many researchers to despair of a solution.

In applying the concept of production functions to public education, the identifiable inputs are natural resources (students),[4] human resources (staff), and capital resources (equipment). The product is variously viewed as being the educational services rendered or the resulting behavioral changes in students.

The concept of human capital holds implications for both inputs and product. On the production or input side of the equation, public education is a primary means through which society "invests" in human capital thereby improving the human capital stock. Public education is also a consumer of a portion of that stock of human capital in that professional and supporting personnel are important inputs to the schooling process.

Since the number of students to be educated is a function of the population,[5] this number must be taken as a given. Staff and equipment, however, are both variable (i.e., show different "production possibilities") in two ways: (1) their absolute quantity can be changed relative to each other; and (2) their level of performance, i.e., qualitative deployment, can have variegated arrangements. Once the range of alternative production-possibilities in any existing school budget has been delineated, an optimal, or most efficient, alternative can be selected. Should this prove politically unacceptable under existing conditions, other, less optimal, but more palatable arrangements can be offered. It is a very rare situation indeed where some improvement in resource allocation cannot occur, with a resulting positive effect on both unit cost and productivity.

Prior research on education production functions has dealt almost entirely with analyses of the inputs of students, staff, and equipment as presently arranged, or structured, against outputs of cognitive achievement by students. An early unpublished[6] attempt to grapple with education production function analyses was made in 1962. Later, a published study by Burkhead *et al.* (1967:3-4, 12) pointed out that to achieve more "effective"[7] elementary and secondary education there must be "attention to the economic evaluation of educational practices" and development of "leadership for educational innovation."

The Burkhead study also suggested three *caveats:*

> First, school outputs are multiple . . . test scores . . . drop-out rates . . . post high school education . . . lifetime earnings . . . Sec-

ond, school output is a function of joint inputs whose marginal products are difficult to measure.[8] Third, there are community and home influences that affect school outcomes.

Burkhead concludes:

> The most important finding of this study is that variations in educational outcomes in large-city high schools, measured in terms of test scores, are almost wholly conditioned by the socioeconomic environment of the neighborhood (1967:88).

In dealing with the allocation of societal resources to education, Burkhead assumes a production "mix" which is traditional. Thus, the possible policy alternatives of the Burkhead study (1967:90-92) are: (1) "accentuation" (of the present unequal distribution of educational resources); (2) "perpetuation" (defined as "approximately equal resources to the education of all students in the system" which has essentially a neutral effect because of the socioeconomic predestination of educational outcomes); and (3) "amelioration," where:

> equal educational opportunity would be defined as equal opportunity, in accordance with ability, to be accepted for and pursue a college education or equal opportunity from the kindergarten on to score in the upper quartile on school achievement tests.

The "amelioration" policy was estimated by Burkhead to perhaps "require a doubling or tripling of educational resources per pupil for some low-income areas," with "no way of knowing in advance whether . . . it would 'work' . . ."

From the enhanced perspective of the present, it is easy to look back on Burkhead's pioneering use of production function analysis in education and ask why the assumption was made that only the traditional production-possibility curve could exist. In actuality, Burkhead anticipates the reasonableness of some rearrangement of inputs:

> ... we will not be able to assess the outcomes of ... innovations unless systematic attention is directed to resource costs, to *resource combinations* [italics added] and to educational outputs (1967:94).

Although not using a production function conceptualization, the analysis of James Coleman *et al.* (1966) in *Equality of Educational Opportunity* is similar in many respects to that of Burkhead—as are its conclusions. Coleman and restudies by Mayeske *et al.* (1972) and Moynihan (1972) have offered what is (to many) convincing evidence that the independent effect of schooling inputs upon pupil's cognitive achievement is—at best—minimal. Jencks *et al.* (1972) came to a similar conclusion with reference to the effect of schooling input on lifetime earnings of individuals.

Not unexpectedly, such conclusions have generated widespread controversy. Bowles and Levin (1968) were among the multitude attacking the statistical bias of the Coleman study. In reply, Coleman (1968) accused educators and educational researchers of having "an initial bias in favor of the effects of school factors." Were it not for the demonstrated effect of such research on public policy decisions, this debate could be dismissed as academic. However, the implications for the expenditure of public funds for schooling is of considerable economic magnitude.

Both the ineffectiveness and inefficiency of present education production functions are well summarized by Katzman (1971). Building upon his earlier study (1968), he relates present learning theory research to current use of economic resources in education, and raises such questions as:

> ... Why are schools unable to solve persistent educational problems? To what extent are the failures of schools traceable to lack of technology, to instructional failure, or to political conflict? To what extent are educational problems amenable to purely technical solutions (1971:3)?

He feels there is little understanding of "social technology," that is, "the controllable factors that contribute to the existence of a social problem, and thereby to its potential solution (1971:4)." He adds:

> The delivery of social services . . . is largely in the hands of monopolies or oligopolies administered by those who perceive themselves as professionals . . . professionals are rarely concerned with technical efficiency in the strict sense (1971:5).

Further compounding the problem, in Katzman's view, is the fact that the quality of an economic resource used in education is measured in monetary terms: expenditure per student;[9] but, unfortunately, "expenditure measures do not distinguish between high costs owing to inefficiency and those needed to maintain quality (1971:21)." Consequently, when socioeconomic background and number of years of schooling are held constant, "there seems to be no relationship between school expenditures per pupil and long-term student achievement (1971:22)."[10] Katzman's conclusion as to the value of additional analysis of education production functions under present institutional arrangements indicates diminishing returns. He summarizes:

> Because of the high intercorrelations among school resources and social class of students, no studies reviewed here were able to identify more than two or three effective resources. To that extent these studies remain inconclusive (1971:42-44).

Similarly, after a very careful review of the extensive research on educational effectiveness (including, but not limited to, production function studies), the Rand Corporation report to the President's Commission on School Finance (cited in Chapter I), stated: "Research has not identified a variant of the existing system that is consistently related to students' educational outcomes (Averch *et al.*, 1971:154)." They go on to elaborate:

> We must emphasize that we are not suggesting that nothing makes

a difference, or that nothing 'works.' Rather we are saying that research has found nothing that consistently and unambiguously makes a difference in students' outcomes.

While many studies of education production functions have focused on inputs and outputs, they have made few, if any, assumptions about the interaction of the known variables. Their failure to identify significant school effects is beginning to suggest to the research community that if such effects do exist, they must be sought in the interactive relationships *within* schools. In his review of Jenck's (1972) study of *Inequality,* Levine (1972:163) writes:

> If effective educational practice is a matter of interactions, then attention must center on those ultimately responsible for structuring and controlling the interactions; that is, teacher and students. The use that these agents make of the school resources usually measured in input-output analysis may be more signifi- cant than the absolute levels and kinds of resources.

The matter of "interactive relationships" is treated at length in Chapter VI.

* * *

The recent beginnings made in education production function analysis, cited above, should not be confused with a comple- mentary approach which derives its heritage from the adaptation of the concepts of industrial and agricultural economics to public policy decisions for the expenditure of public funds. This is called benefit-cost analysis, and has proven extremely useful in applying the theory of marginalism[11] to obtain optimal public resource allocation where three or more alternatives exist. Marginal analysis states that the most efficient use of scarce resources will result at that point where the extra (or marginal) benefit(s) to be obtained from a given alternative most nearly approximate but are never less than the extra (or marginal) cost(s) of that course of action. If both benefit(s) and cost(s) can be quantified, and measured in monetary units, then this approach is a highly refined tool for decision-makers in the public sector, just as the marginal revenue-marginal cost rule is a guide to businessmen in the private sector. As Eckstein puts it:

> The ideal principle for budget decisions is clear enough. *Push expenditures for each public purpose to that point where the benefit of the last dollar spent is greater than or at least equal to the dollar of cost* (1967:24).

When this technique is directed to the educational sector, however, a basic weakness becomes obvious: the extra output (i.e., benefits) cannot be quantified and therefore "priced" in monetary units in any way which will be comparable to the extra cost of production.[12] The way out of this cul-de-sac is a hybrid technique known as cost-effectiveness analysis. As defined by Swanson:

> Cost-effectiveness analysis is the use of systematic and quantitative techniques to compare the effects of alternate techniques of applying resources (input) in order to accomplish desired objectives (outputs) (1971:288).

Goldman suggests that

> Cost-effectiveness analysis is specifically directed to problems in which the output cannot be evaluated in market prices, but where the inputs can, and where the inputs are substitutable at exchange relationships developed in the market (1967:18).

Two approaches similar to those used in benefit-cost analysis become available to cost-effectiveness approaches: (1) minimizing cost(s) and (2) maximizing efficiency. The first approach assumes that the desired educational objective(s) is (are) attainable by more than two alternative courses of action. The goal then becomes selection of the specific alternative which will attain the objective for the least cost. The second approach recognizes that, given some level of technology, educational objectives and educational costs may both vary. To secure the optimal (or more efficient) solution will involve "tradeoffs," i.e., having less of this in order to have more of that, and vice versa. Hinrichs and Taylor (1969:10) consider proper statement of the problem to be the crucial factor, "for if one knows the problem, one already has the solution (given free computer time)."

The literature about the methodology of cost-effectiveness analysis is, in the words of Levin (1968:2), "a profuse outpouring," some of which he proceeds to list. However, he lists only those he considers "the most extensive." Some education production function studies that use cost-effectiveness methodology to a greater or lesser degree include: Kiesling (1968 and 1971); Katzman (1968); Levin (1968 and 1970); Hanushek (1970 and 1971); Gintis (1971); and Swanson *et al.* (1971 and 1976).

Insufficient time has elapsed for an adequate critique of cost-effectiveness analysis to emerge, but one illustrative comment may indicate the trend of constructive criticism: in the discussion which followed the presentation of Hanushek's 1971 paper to the American Economic Association (December 29, 1970), Garner (1971:300) pointed out that "it is the *services* [italics added] of productive units, not the units themselves, which are factors of production." Thus, it is the "behaviors" of teachers, and students, which are the real inputs in schooling. This reasoning was also extended by Garner to include the "relevant technology," since it is necessary to know "not only how much of each resource was used, but how it was used."

A seemingly prophetic pessimist about the future returns from such activities as dissecting education production functions was Baumol (1967), who suggested that the economy is divided into a (technologically) progressive sector and a (technologically) non-progressive sector.[13] In the former, any increases in productivity tend to offset increases in real wages, a situation which is "sporadically" true in the latter. While Baumol considers education to be in the non-progressive sector, he leaves for his reader an interesting loophole in his assessment of education as having only "sporadic increases in productivity." As cited in Chapter I, Baumol believes no improvement is possible:

> *"without a complete revolution in our approach to teaching"*
> (1967:416) [italics added].

Whether Baumol thinks that education has always been in the non-progressive sector of the economy is not clear; but he does not rule out the possibility that a drastic change could bring improvement. In other words, education has been a *dependent* societal variable, but it now is also an *independent* variable, and as such can improve the external productivity (i.e., efficiency) of society, while also doing something about its own internal efficiency (cf. Edding, 1969:22).[14]

To consider education as an independent variable, it is necessary to investigate alternative structures of education production functions. Two reasons are paramount: (1) an apparent consensus that existing education production functions are inefficient; and (2) the alleged failure of present education production functions to cope with the individual differences of the students who are being "processed." What Silberman (1970), Kozol (1967), Mayer (1961), and others said existentially has been reiterated empirically, including: Koerner (1963); Coleman (1966); Jencks (1966); Stodolsky and Lesser (1967); and Conant (1959).

Edding sums up appropriately:

> All the simple approaches recommended not so long ago under the labels "manpower approach," "returns approach," or "correlations approach" have been discovered to be dubious as theory and often almost useless practically for the decision-maker. More and more factors (e.g., the ability to learn as solely an inherited trait) formerly considered to be explanatory variables in the analysis of past developments and as parameters in planning education are now seen as policy variables in a wide field of interdependencies (1969:25-26).

More concisely stated, the present arrangement(s) of inputs into the education process bear(s) little, sometimes no, relationship to the desired output(s).

We should then ask the unasked question: would rearrangement of the inputs—students, staff, and facilities—(1) improve economic efficiency both internally and externally and (2) permit the professed ideal of modern education—individualized learning—to take place?

In a world where "R & D" [Research and Development] is almost a dictionary term, it is logical to view the production of education as requiring both rearrangement of the inputs and upgrading of technology. Thus, the research problem advanced herein hypothesizes *less* labor-intensive and *more* capital-intensive education production functions by incorporating into the sample designs the highest quality and greatest quantity of educational technology now available.

The present level of analysis of education production functions appears to be more pedagogy[15] than analogy:[16] that is, something from which to learn, rather than a reasoned process which has the likely probability of accomplishing a specific objective, such as greater economic efficiency in education. Pessimism concerning what further (if anything) could be learned from education production function analysis is primarily due to what Goldman would call an "attention bias" which can be "caused by cherished belief or an unconscious adherence to a 'party line' (1967:8)."

In the case of mid-20th century education, the "party line" has been: increase the monetary inputs; but underlying this imperative has been an assumption which has never been seriously challenged: lower and lower student-teacher ratios imply better education. Grant and Lind state:

> Over-all, the trend in recent years has been for the number of public school teachers to grow at a faster rate than the number of pupils. The result is a continuing improvement in the pupil-teach-

er ratio. This fall (1975) there are about 20.7 pupils per teacher as compared with 24.7 pupils for each teacher 10 years ago (1976:2).

Given this comparative statistic, the question remains: why is the tax-paying public more and more disenchanted with the "cognitive output" of American elementary and secondary education?

There is a growing body of research which suggests that a shift in direction is overdue. It talks of man-machine systems of education, and proposes that capital-intensive education production functions are a large share of the answer to what schooling should be, and can become, in terms of both accomplishment and cost. In essence, it points out that the future increase in productivity which can result from modifications of traditional approaches[17] to education is severely limited because it is a linear extrapolation of present educational methods. Only with a higher level of technology and a complete rearrangement of inputs can we break out of the prevailing parameters on productivity improvement. Only capital-intensive education production functions qualify as the higher level of technology, which must be combined with *less* labor-intensive input of human resources.

It is the purpose of this book to give serious consideration to technologically up-dated education production functions. Rather than restricting the machine to assisting the teacher, such a production function is designed as a "man-machine *system*" which

> is a set of planned procedures in which man and machine capabilities are used in an integrated manner to achieve results man could not achieve without the machine (Loughary *et al.*, 1966:5).

Conceived as "machine-dependent," such a system places planned reliance upon the machine—that is, the various types of audio-visual, electronic, and programmed hardware now available—for the complete range of abilities, but subject to man's direction, planning, and control. People are still absolutely essential; but their roles are changed.

Before proceeding to a detailed discussion of man-machine systems in education, one difficulty must be addressed. That difficulty is the perennial bias found in a segment of any society toward *change*—especially technological change. We next consider this "anti-technology bias."

Notes

1. A term the writers use to designate that capital refers to *produced* means-of-production.
2. Algebraically, this would be expressed:
$$P = P_1 N_1 + P_2 N_2 \ldots + P_j N_j$$
where P equals Price of unit 1, N_1 equals the number of units of the first input purchased, N_2 equals the number of units purchased of the second input, and N_j equals the number purchased of the jth input.
3. It is not a *de jure* monopoly, since private education is permitted; however, in practice this is offset by the fact that *all* citizens contribute either directly or indirectly to the support of public education. Burkhead (1967:2), in discussing the spillover effect of education, likened local school districts to small competitive business firms. Willett (1971:20) questioned whether the resemblance was more like individual utility companies, which are regulated monopolies.
4. Students as an "input" can best be thought of as pertaining to their socioeconomic background. (See Burkhead—1967:85.) School "output," for this study, refers to cognitive achievement only. Theoretically, the higher a student's socioeconomic background, the lower should be school costs for his/her education. In practice, students from higher socioeconomic backgrounds receive "enrichment" of curricula.
5. The institutional (and/or legal) arrangement(s) in the society is (are) also involved to a greater (or lesser) degree.
6. An unpublished Ph.D. dissertation by J. Alan Thomas, entitled *Efficiency in Education: A Study of the Relationship Between Selected Inputs and Mean Test Scores in a Sample of Senior High Schools,* was accepted at Stanford University, School of Education, in 1962.
7. Burkhead does not define "effective" as used in this context; however, he next discusses "efficiency" as an economic concept where "outputs are maximized in relation to inputs" (1967:4).
8. This difficulty is overcome if we concentrate on *total factor* (or input) *productivity,* conversely stated as *total unit cost movement.* In an industry such as education, this is logical because the output of education, as currently defined, is not readily quantified, or "priced."

9. Average expenditure in the United States in 1973-74 was $1364 for each public elementary and secondary school student (Grant and Lind, 1976:71).
10. For further verification, Katzman cites Finis Welch, "Measurement of the Quality of Schooling," *American Economic Review*, *56*(2), May, 1966, pp. 379-391.
11. All decisions are made "at the margin," i.e., where the questions are asked: Should I? Should I not? One course of action always precludes a substitute course in situations where resources are limited.
12. The same problem is encountered in many other public services, e.g., national security, foreign policy, transportation facilities, health care, etc.
13. That "patron saint" of economics, Adam Smith, also considered certain sectors of the economy (e.g., the army) as unproductive and therefore parasitic to the rest of the economy. Baumol has since reconsidered.
14. Edding points out that certain educational outputs are "rarely considered in examinations . . . knowledge of how to learn and eagerness to continue learning; ability to cooperate, to take the initiative, to make decisions under conditions of uncertainty; and virtues like tolerance, honesty, self-control, and creativity . . ." (1969:24).
15. "Instruction or discipline (Webster)."
16. "*Logic.* A form of inference in which it is reasoned that if two (or more) things agree with one another in one or more respects, they will (probably) agree in yet other respects. The degree of probability will depend upon the number and importance of their known agreements (Webster)."
17. Planning, programming, budgeting systems (PPBS); cost-effectiveness analysis; combinations of the two (such as the COST-ED model, a name currently being used for a systems approach to traditional education by a private consulting firm, Education Turnkey Systems, Inc., 1030 Fifteenth Street, Washington, D.C., 20005); and performance contracting.

Chapter III
THE LUDDITE MENTALITY:
Anti-technology and Education

For rationality in choice is nothing more and nothing less than choice with complete awareness of the alternatives rejected (Robbins, 1946:152).

Much has been written, with little consensus reached, concerning social change. Scholarship has yet to produce rigorous theory to explain what causes change to occur, although there is quite general agreement that, at least within limits, change does occur over time. One of the ingredients of change is some form or type of *innovation,* which Barnet (1953:7) defines "as any thought, behavior, or thing that is new because it is qualitatively different from existing forms." He further comments:

Many individuals are prepared to accept new ideas because they have not dedicated themselves irretrievably to a custom or to an ideal of their society ... The greatest number of individuals in this category are children (1953:385).

37

In their earliest years, children exhibit little fear. It is only as experiences cumulate that varying degrees of fear are apparent in the onset of maturity. Several decades ago, Ogburn pointed out:

> The element of fear is another psychological factor in human beings that tends to cause them to resist changes . . . perhaps anxiety is more accurate, or the degree of fear found generally in uncertainty and in ignorance (1964:190).[1]

Fear of change thus appears to be functionally related to uncertainty, which is also often associated with ignorance, defined as "lack of knowledge" concerning the reality of the change(s) proposed and the effect(s) which will result. Frequently, some segment of a society will conclude that certain perceived effects of a change will extrapolate to 100 percent disaster, while another segment of the same society may consider the change to be 100 percent benefit. In general, the actual effects of any change tend to lie between these two extremes, and usually can be adequately estimated by the techniques of benefit-cost analysis or its derivative, cost-effectiveness analysis. Where the innovation is more experimental, pilot-models are of assistance in confirming the original relationships.

Perhaps the anxiety concerning change which is the most difficult to allay is the one which is related to a contradiction of an ideological consensus with reference to some institutional arrangement in the society. A case in point was the resistance to the centralization of the small common school districts in the United States over the past fifty years. The tradition surrounding the "one-room schoolhouse" with its recurrent supply of youthful teachers became deeply ingrained in the American consciousness, especially in rural areas. Since the United States was predominantly agrarian until about 1920, the concern of rural parents over larger, centralized schools was a *real* concern.

The change to mass education was at least precipitated by the transformation of America into an industrialized economy. Denison (1972) attributes 14.1 percent of the growth rate of the American economy between 1929-1969 to increased education per worker.[2] Pushing educational levels above literacy required new techniques which mass education provided with reasonable adequacy until the end of World War II, although, in 1940, Morrison was beginning to question "discontinuous learning," as evidenced in the terms elementary, secondary, and post-secondary schools.

Since World War II, the pressures for change in education delivery systems to cope with the technology of a post-industrial society are meeting the same resistance to change which accompanied the move from rural to centralized schools. The "new" culprit in the minds of those desirous of preserving traditional methods of education is "the machine."

The Luddites

In the early days of the industrial revolution (England, *circa* 1800), workers had difficulty in comprehending the *change in the goal* of the production process. Whereas under the cottage industry then prevalent the objective had been to supply individual and family needs through home production (plus the sale of family skills at home as opportunities were presented), the factory system viewed its goal as mass production in one place at low cost and high profit. Thus, some workers came to view any machine as their enemy. Their solution was simplistic: *destroy the machine.* Historically, people with this attitude toward higher levels of technology have come to be known as "Luddites,"[3] after a leader of the movement.

In this century, people who have been conditioned by the educational arrangements prevalent since 1920 have a similar difficulty in recognizing the *change in the goal* of education from that of developing a minimal level of literacy in the society to that of meeting the much more sophisticated requirements of a knowledge-based, post-industrial world. While a competency level of literacy is still a necessary ingredient of the output demanded of education, an increasing percent of the human expectations relating to learning is concerned with the intelligent and rational application of knowledge to human problems.

The Luddite mentality, today, tends more toward *obstruction* than destruction. It accepts the *fact* of technology, but decries, and seeks ways to limit, its use. As long as those who desire to see change in education push the idea that *change in itself* is a panacea, the result will be continuing polarization between those who favor and those who oppose incorporating modern educational technology into integrated man-machine learning systems.

The Specter of Unemployment

The Luddites of 200 years ago *did* see their fear of large scale unemployment realized. From today's perspective, this was due *only in the short run* to technological change. In the long run, the real cause was the fact that the population of Western Europe doubled between 1800 and 1900, a trend noted (1803) in the famous population essay of Thomas Malthus. This gave rise to "optimum population theory," which suggested that, given the state of technology, there was some upper limit to the amount of population which could be supported at a given standard of living. Derived from this notion is the "lump-of-labor" idea, which assumes that at any given moment there is only so much work available. To maintain the status quo of income distribution, the available work must be shared; thus, any innovation which appears to reduce employment should be resisted. Whether the labor displacement is short run or long run is not examined. As Mansfield (1971:103-104) states, "social attitudes contributed to the fear of and resistance to new techniques" . . .

> In the late 1800's and the early part of this century, the prevailing attitude was 'sink or swim.' Little or no help was available to displaced workers.

One hundred years after the original Luddite movement came the massive unemployment of the 1930's during which the dreaded word was "technocracy." In the 1950's and 1960's, the scare term was "automation," and for scholars of the phenomenon, the current term is "cybernetics." When used negatively, all of these infer technological unemployment.

Is there any truth to this fear of long run, technologically-induced unemployment? Is there a direct cause and effect relationship between the rate of increase of technological change and the amount of increase in total (or aggregate) unemployment in the society? Must we dread the future? In education, would large numbers of teachers be permanently displaced, having no jobs available to them, if capital-intensive learning were a reality?

Mansfield replies (1971:106):

> Contrary to much popular opinion, the answer is no. Changes in aggregate unemployment are governed by the growth in the aggregate demand for goods and services and the growth in the labor force, as well as the growth in output per man-hour [i.e., productivity]. If the rate of increase of aggregate demand equals the rate of increase of productivity plus the rate of increase of the labor force, there will be no increases in aggregate unemployment, regardless of how high the rate of increase in productivity may be. Although there will be increases in some types of jobs and decreases in others, the total number of unemployed will not be affected.

Mansfield continues:

> The important thing is that the government increase aggregate demand at the proper rate.

This means neither "too slowly," increasing unemployment, nor "too rapidly," which can result in inflation.

A superficial reaction to the above would be to assume that in the case of a major technological shift in producing education by capital-intensive arrangements the final answer concerning unemployment in the educational sector is that it would rise or fall with the movements of government policy. This would not be true, however, unless the government abdicated its present bipartisan agreement (spelled out in the Employment Act of 1946) to maintain an adequate level of aggregate demand through appropriate fiscal and monetary policies. Based on the seeming reasonableness that this will not occur, the specter of unemployment in education as the result of a movement to capital-intensive learning systems is not valid for three reasons: (1) adequate aggregate demand policies by government assure the purchasing power to the consumer to acquire more, not less, education; (2) the increase in productivity from capital-intensive modes of education will release resources (in both monetary and real terms) which then become available for the further stimulation of aggregate demand in other sectors of the economy; and (3) whatever portion (of the released resources) society deems necessary *can be allocated in advance* to cushion the short run labor displacement which could occur in the early stages of the development of capital-intensive education production functions.

In calling for a modernization of American public education, increased productivity is only one of many motivating concerns. Looking ahead at the projected demands, the system simply will not be able to respond as it is presently organized. While the traditional school age population is experiencing a slight decline, calls for life-long education are being heard around the nation. Preschool education has become well established during the past decade—in the public sector for poor children and in the private sector for middle class children. Now, federal legislation has started the process of providing learning opportunities for those in the "post-school" years. Federal legislation has also required public schooling for children previously excluded, the physically and emotionally handicapped.

But an expanded clientele is the least of the challenges facing the schools. Far greater are the growing public expectations, including: preparing children to keep pace with the knowledge explosion; coping with social and technological changes; developing saleable occupational skills; and assuming, at least for some children, responsibilities formerly provided by the family unit. To meet these challenges, to the extent that society determines it is appropriate for schools to do, will require the best and most sophisticated thinking and creative arrangements our society can develop.

An anti-technological attitude is not what has brought the United States to its present eminence. Our 200 years of independence have seen tremendous increases in productivity as a result of the application of real capital while at the same time accommodating an increase in the civilian labor force from approximately 1.5 million in 1775 to over 95 million today. This same rise in technological sophistication has made possible the present high levels of educational attainment of our citizens. Total productivity increases could have been even greater had we understood the need to use portions of the increases to assist labor reallocations which could not be accomplished individually. Attitudes of indifference to technological unemployment in the short term are disappearing. Solomon Fabricant, senior staff member of the National Bureau of Economic Research, writes[4] in Shapiro and White (1977:47):

> Whether or not the difficulties suffered by workers in adjusting to changes in the labor market are greater now than they were in earlier times, most of us would agree that the suffering should be alleviated. The solution, it must be stressed, is not to impede capital formation or technological development, or the other factors that make for higher productivity . . . Instead, arrangements must be made whereby society as a whole helps shoulder the problems of adjusting to the rising productivity—to see to it that the problems do not fall only on the backs of those immediately affected.

As this problem pertains to education, the assumption of technologically induced unemployment follows only when one assumes that there is a fixed amount of work to be accomplished.

The function of technology is truly to free human resources for work that rising expectations demand be done in order to improve the quality of life. For education, as for all fields, problems litter the landscape because there is simply not enough material and human resources available to attend to them.

One should not assume that technology will result in a need for fewer educators, although it would result in a need for fewer teachers to do the work that is now being done. The work that needs to be done but can't be accomplished within the constraints of limited resources precludes unemployment in the ranks of professional educators. Undeniably, a shift in functions would occur. Nor would this imply a waste of investment. The return on investment of the educational dollar would likely increase with new ability to make people employable and with greater satisfaction of human needs.

The large monetary savings from capital-intensive modes of education, which are detailed in Chapters VIII and IX, can fully offset any temporary or permanent loss to educational personnel as the result of a change to man-machine learning systems. Once this fact is fully understood by both parents (taxpayers) and educators (tax recipients), there remain no valid reasons for the retention of a Luddite philosophy toward the fullest use of the available technology in the revitalizing of American education.

The Efficiency Cult

In speaking of "man-machine systems," "inputs," "outputs," "production functions," "efficiency," and "effectiveness" with respect to education, it is very easy for modern Luddites to confuse proponents of capital-intensive instruction with the much maligned "scientific management" movement of the early part of this century. While the contemporary proponents undoubtedly share some of the same concerns which motivated what Callahan (1962) termed "The Cult of Efficiency," there are important distinctions. Callahan labeled the consequences of this "Cult," for American education and American society, as "tragic." Acknowledging the importance of efficiency and economy (p. 263), he describes the essence of the tragedy as "adopting values and practices indiscriminately (from business and industry) and applying them with little or no consideration of educational values or purposes" (p. 244).

The person generally credited with creating the system of industrial management (*circa* 1900), known as "scientific management," was Frederick W. Taylor. His purpose was to reduce the amount of discretionary judgment on the part of individual workers and to replace it with standardized rules and formulae developed out of a comprehensive job analysis. The analysis would include time and motion studies of each process and an evaluation of the adequacy of the tools and machines involved. Taylor urged the establishment of tasks for each worker (not too dissimilar from the contemporary "management by objectives") and close supervision of workers through foremen. Finally, he was an early proponent of planning assigned to a specific department which would make the analyses and develop the rules and formulae. Scientific management did result in phenomenal gains in productivity and profits for many companies embracing its principles, and it became a model for evaluating all enterprises with little concern as to the appropriateness of it as a model. Schools were particularly vulnerable because many on their governing boards were drawn from the managerial ranks of industry (Tyack, 1974).

Guthrie (1977) has identified five conditions affecting private sector endeavors which are not immediately similar for schools. These include:

- almost unanimous agreement upon the desired outcome (to make a profit);
- a straightforward means for measuring a firm's successes or failures (a financial balance sheet);
- a basic technology to guide production;
- control over the qualities of raw material used in production; and
- motivation to comply with consumers' preferences.[5]

"To varying degrees," Guthrie (1977:4) claims, "America's public schools do not exhibit these five characteristics."

> There is not widespread and intense public agreement regarding the objective of schooling. Techniques for measuring school outcomes are primitive and imprecise. There is little scientifically derived knowledge regarding the best way to instruct in any particular subject. Schools have almost no control over the quality of "raw material," students, with which they must work. The monopolistic nature of public schools erodes substantially the incentives for schools to respond to the tastes of clients, students, and their parents.

The issues raised by Callahan and Guthrie cannot be ignored. The private sector, especially business and industry, operates under conditions which differ in part from the public sector. In adapting procedures and principles from one sector to another, the process must be guided by an understanding of the unique nature of the recipient. At the same time, however, there is much similarity in the two sectors:

- both sectors must attempt to achieve their respective objectives within the constraint of limited resources;
- both sectors secure their purchased inputs from the same resource and product markets; and,
- both sectors use widely similar line and staff organizations in managing the productive process.

In the face of the mounting crises in American education, it would be foolish for public strategists to disregard the accumulated experience—good and bad—of the private sector.

Contributing to the confusion is the common misunderstanding of the terms "output" and "productivity." Any careful review of the growing volume of literature since 1950 on the general question of "what is wrong with American education?" reveals an almost pathological preoccupation with attempted definitions of "educational output" (product). Yet, for over 100 years, it has been an economic axiom that the consumption of a good or service (and therefore the demand for same) is *not* a function of its quantitative (therefore objective) measurement, but of its "utility," that is, the satisfaction obtained (obviously subjective). Economic theory thus contradicts the present myopic focus on "cognitive achievement" as the output of education. The *true utility* of education—the *real* output—is the opportunity for each learner to become what that person is capable of becoming. The tragic fact that society, consciously or unconsciously, often allows the institutional arrangements of education to block full attainment of this true utility of educational output does not change the accuracy of the definition.

When this correct definition of educational output is accepted, it is clear that the demand (or price) side of the equation, price = cost, is not a problem of production, but of distribution, which involves the political and social aspects of the society as well as the economic. If anything could forcefully demonstrate the *half truth* of Say's Law[6] (that a supply of something creates its own demand), it should be the *supply of schooling* in America. Were the consumption of schooling to a certain age not mandated, far less would be demanded as the "product" is presently constituted for consumption.

Related to this misconception of educational output is a misconception concerning productivity (or efficiency) in the process of supplying the utility (or satisfaction) from education to those who are entitled to it, whether that entitlement is voluntary, or involuntary. Productivity *increases* if the *cost* of supplying the output (however defined) *decreases*. This aspect of productivity has no dependence on whether the output created is objectively measurable. Those who maintain that the technical-industrial model of efficiency cannot be adapted to public sector services such as education are only correct insofar as they are discussing an increase in the quantity or the quality of the *output*. Where the *input(s)* is (are) concerned, *any* rearrangement which lowers total cost, *without changing the perception of the utility of the output by the consumer,*[7] is an increase in productivity. Any such decrease in total cost is *ipso facto* a decrease in the amount of real resources (human and nonhuman) the society must commit to that particular public service, say education.

These two misconceptions—the true nature of educational "output," and the dual definition of productivity (both public and private)—contribute much to the resistance to change in the necessary restructuring of the educational system to meet the challenges of the imminent 21st century.

The term capital-intensive education brings to the mind of many people visions of inhuman, mechanical procedures such as described in Aldous Huxley's *Brave New World* (1932). This certainly is a possibility, but fortunately not the only one. Technological devices, integrated into a total learning system, and combined with the talents of skillful educators, can provide children with a virtually unlimited variety of learning experiences. Schooling can take on a new vitality and relevance. Most important, with the assistance of technological devices, the educator can efficiently prescribe, monitor, and evaluate a far greater number of variables and thereby truly individualize the learning experience of each child. A happy by-product of the capital-intensive school is that it can make the job of the teacher far more demanding, challenging, and inherently rewarding.

Notes

1. Original edition copyrighted in 1922.
2. Another 31.1 percent relates to "advances of knowledge and changes not elsewhere classified," such as: more work done (excepting the effect of education)—28.7 percent; more capital—15.8 percent; and improved resource allocation—10.0 percent.
3. Commenting on this tendency, the Carnegie Commission (1972:7) stated: "We see no need for academic Luddites. But, on the other hand, 'program or perish' should not replace 'publish or perish'."
4. "Perspective on the Capital Requirements Question."
5. As shown in what follows, there is a need to understand consumer

preferences in education if the motivation to acquire education is to be developed and maintained.
6. Named after Jean Baptiste Say, a French economist of the 18th century.
7. Consumers of education can be thought of as primary (students) and secondary (parents). Society is the contingent beneficiary.

Chapter IV

MAN-MACHINE SYSTEMS IN EDUCATION:

Individualization

... I have declined to allow myself to be governed by the limitations of what is at present feasible ... (Morrison, 1940:viii).

Future historians of education may depict the 20th century as an age of transition in teaching methodology. World War II might be taken as the dividing line between the traditional teacher-*lecture* approach, and the mid-century teacher-*plus* (audio-visual aids) arrangement.[1] And those same historians may record that finally, *circa* 2000 A.D., the step was taken to a new plateau known as *man-machine* systems of education to accomplish the goal of individualized learning.

At present, the change from traditional teacher-lecture methods to technologically sophisticated man-machine systems in education as foreseen by many visionaries has stalled in a transitional teacher plus audio-visual equipment phase. The reasons for the standstill are numerous; however, it is not within the province of this book to analyze their implications. It is sufficient to predict that sooner or later pressures will rise to the point where the step to integrated man-machine systems of education *must* be taken.

A significant contribution toward such a movement was made by Kiesling (1970:983-85) in a paper prepared for the Commission on Instructional Technology. He suggests 12 "strategies" for teaching "basic elementary school subjects." All of the strategies are essentially teacher-*plus* methods. What he describes as his most "capital-rich" approach would employ "heavy use of ITV, films, programmed instruction" for groups of 100 pupils, but would provide for the average pupil to see "a classroom teacher during 42% of his total instruction time."

In his conclusion, Kiesling comments on the need to increase productivity in American education by substituting more capital for labor due to the upward pressure of wages in education as a result of wage increases in other sectors of the economy. (In the long run, *all* wage increases occur because of improved productivity.[2]) Kiesling's opinion is that "we should expect to see a much greater use of capital in American Education in the next fifty years (1970:993)."

Any substitution of capital for labor in American education is not likely to come about in sufficient amounts to influence educational productivity in the foreseeable future unless a real effort is made to break away from the traditional teacher-lecture method and the teacher plus audio-visual approach. This can be done with present technology if man-machine systems of education are adopted.

A recent Carnegie Commission report refers to the research of Eric Ashby (1967) who

> has identified four revolutions in education. The first occurred when societies began to differentiate adult roles, and the task of educating the young was shifted, in part, from parents to teachers. . . . The second, which in some places antedated the first, "was the adoption of the written word as a tool of education". . . . The third revolution came with the invention of printing. . . . The fourth revolution is portented by developments

in electronics, notably . . . radio, television, recorder, and computer (1972:9).

While radio, TV, and recording equipment are all essential components of any man-machine system of education, the most versatile electronic adjunct of this "fourth revolution" is the computer, which can be used as a laboratory tool, as an instructional management device, and as a direct instrument of teaching. In addition, it can provide almost infinite (relative to human demand) storage of information, and can act in four modes pertaining to individualized learning: conceptualization; drill and practice; tutorial; and testing (with immediate feedback).

The Carnegie report continues:

> if electronic communications have generated a fourth revolution in education, the growing abundance of information is certainly generating a fifth. The director of libraries for MIT is credited with the observation that "the worldwide outpouring of printed words is going up 8 to 10 percent a year". . . . Jack Belzer (Tickton, 1970:126) has written that "The proliferation of published materials, the storage, retrieval, dissemination, and communication of recorded knowledge can retard our cultural progress, curtail scientific advancement, and drive us to economic disaster". . . . It is at the confluence of the fourth and fifth revolutions that these movements have their greatest momentum and power (1972:29).

Learning as a Continuous Process

The concept of individualized learning that is now made possible by capital-intensive education production functions allows a student to learn as a *continuous* process thus avoiding the necessity for artificial distinctions between learning stages—distinctions which have been incorporated, and solidified, in mass education. The lack of continuous learning in American education was ably pointed out by Morrison:

> . . . it would be a great help if the schoolmaster could

> permanently rid himself of the notion that elementary school, the
> several divisions and kinds of high schools, and junior colleges are
> things in themselves. . . . We are ordinarily very sensitive as to
> how much time will be required for any kind of program.
> It ought to be borne in mind that the issue is part of the
> ideology of the discontinuous school system and of the estab-
> lished practice of reckoning educational progress in terms of time
> spent rather than in terms of learning acquired. The old American
> Common School had no such preconceptions . . . (1940:664 and
> 666).

Education as a continuous process has always been available to
those fortunate enough and/or affluent enough to have a tutor. As
the demand for more universal education spread, a demand which
could only be supplied (it was thought) by direct intervention of
the public sector, the tutorial method became prohibitively
expensive where the teacher was the primary vehicle for information transmission. Both public and private schools were forced to
adapt certain mass-production techniques to the production of
education as a means of coping with the demand for education
within the limits of the resources which a developing economy
could allocate to training its citizens. This led inevitably to the
present system of discontinuous schooling.

Two developments since World War II have brought back into
the realm of possibility the concept of education as a continuous
process. The first of these has been the emphasis on programmed
learning, which in some respects might be thought of as a form of
self-tutoring. The second development is the modern "teaching
machine," which can be a simple, hand-operated device for
presenting in sequence—"frames" of material—or a sophisticated
computer console with a cathode ray screen for display of
instructional content.[3]

When a learning *program* is combined with a teaching *machine,*
the result is supervised self-instruction.[4] This can add to education
a dimension not recently possible, but one first seen in embryo in
the American Common School (an institution known affectionate-
ly in our folklore as the ungraded one-room "Little Red

Schoolhouse)—a dimension of student(s) and teacher(s) learning together. As Morrison identifies it:

> ... what course comes first and what second ... in sequence depends upon their ideational sequence and not upon any assumed process of organic mental development (1940:665).

The primary benefit obtained from automated programmed learning is response (or feedback), which is the same benefit of the tutorial method. Uttal (1962:172) feels that "we have the opportunity to bring back a large degree of interaction to the instructional process." He adds:

> The success of teaching machines will depend largely, I believe, on the degree to which they provide feedback to the student and are responsive to the student's learning needs. The desired relationship between student and teaching machine may be termed conversational interaction (1962:172).

Silberman (1962) did an early survey of the research to that date on programmed instruction.[5] He suggested that the literature fell into three groups: popular surveys, programming experiments, and field studies:

> The popular literature is optimistic, the experiments on programming are pessimistic, and the field studies hover between these poles. One thesis ... is that this apparent conflict is resolved by distinguishing between a *science of programming* and a *technology of education* (1962:13) [italics added].

Learning theorists should concentrate on developing programming to a science, and curriculum specialists should encourage innovative technology, says Silberman (1962:20).

Hughes (1963), reporting on a seminar attended by "representatives from a number of companies and other organizations interested in programmed learning," indicated that the results of programmed instruction were generally favorable.

The application of more sophisticated technology to the use of programmed instruction, for example, educational television, and closed-circuit television, has had considerable experimentation on a national scale. The conclusions tend to agree with those described by Gordon:

> ... in most cases, under controlled experiments, students taught by television did about as well—sometimes worse, frequently better—as students taught under normal conditions. . . . This appeared to hold true under an enormously wide range of conditions: whether the subject matter was abstract or concrete . . . concepts or skills . . . in grade schools, in high schools, in colleges, or in universities (1968:83).

Luskin *et al.* (1972) specifically investigated the present prospects for the computer as a tool of instruction. While not optimistic about how soon computer-assisted instruction will be in widespread use, none of the educational institutions where it is being used have any concerns regarding its ability to transmit information as well or better than traditional means. Luskin says that "in general, the literature seems to imply that the instructional applications of the computer have, to this point, experienced mixed success (1972:13)." A 1967 computer-assisted instruction project in McComb, Mississippi is a case in point:

> The constraints placed on the project to determine its practicality were these: (1) that it be offered to all children (of the proper instructional level) in the school district; (2) that teacher training problems be minimal; (3) that the technology be easily manageable at the local district level; (4) that it create no severe administrative difficulties; (5) that it could be eventually financed by local funds; and (6) that it make a difference in the individual educational training of students.
>
> The superintendent of schools of the McComb public school system reports that after two years experience, the results . . . are encouraging. He states that CAI is a viable educational system but contends that the future is clouded by obstacles (1972:11-12).[6]

The obstacles cited are financial, or operational, or both: "expense of hardware, lack of compatible hardware, lack of sufficient programs in instructional areas," etc. The optimistic note is that "industry is becoming increasingly involved in CAI."

It should be noted that there are pessimists. Their concerns are adequately dealt with by Oettinger and Marks (1969), who argue that "contemporary instructional technology can lead to genuine improvements in education provided it is not force-fed, oversold, and prematurely applied (1969:vii)." In their view, the prime obstacle is the present structure of the school system which "seems ideally designed to resist change (1969:ix)."

> The prevalent mode of public elementary and secondary education aims primarily at *universal goals:* Its processes are created primarily by mass production. They are applied uniformly to groups selected primarily for homogeneity of chronological age. *This is the system which individualization aims to reform* (1969:133) [italics added].

In addition to a resistant educational system, there are also the problems of designing equipment to stand hard use, the novelty (or Hawthorne) effect which the use of computers can engender, and the hourly costs of computer use. Oettinger and Marks conclude:

> ... every attempt to introduce technological change into education has revealed how profoundly *ignorant* we still are (1969:221).

Other proponents of a "go slow" approach to CAI echo this concern about "ignorance" with such comments as "not in touch with current developments about CAI," and question "operational reliability." Meanwhile, in 1974, the largest manufacturer of computing equipment commissioned a study to determine whether "justification of instructional use of computers can be made . . . by relating *added* inputs involved with the computing to *added* outputs due to the computing," with the ultimate goal of increasing instructional computer use as an "add-on" to present instructional costs, or as a preventive of increased-labor-intensiveness in instruction. Their investigator concluded affirmatively (Willey, 1975:14).

What both the optimists and the pessimists tend to overlook in the ongoing discussion about CAI is that the computer is *not* a medium for instruction.[7] Instead, the computer is the integrating core of an *instructional delivery system* combining three components: display, response, and feedback. The first two of these are usually duplicated in other ways. *Display* can be accomplished through books, pictures, or audio devices. *Response* occurs through writing (or typing), or giving verbal expression to, some answer(s) which grow out of the display function. What is productive about a computer-coordinated instructional delivery system is the *feedback* component, which can tirelessly "talk back" to the learner time after time, and in a differentiated fashion that is matched to the learner's own responses. From a level of feedback which can be simply coded, CAI is now moving toward a more sophisticated level which can approximate human responses to the learner's answer(s). In addition, CAI research has now progressed to the point of using the computer to actually generate concepts. As McMullen describes it:

> What developers of CAI have gradually realized is that the power of a computer demands a new frame of reference, one that is oriented toward what a computer does best: executing procedures. Instead of a succession of programmed frames, the computer requires a framework for programs . . . The distinction is not unlike the distinction between associative learning, based on a system of stimulus-response pairings, and structural learning in which elements of a cognitive structure are tested and manipulated so as to transform input into acceptable output (1973:1).

This generative use of the computer involves four components. These are illustrated in Figure 4.1 and further described by McMullen:

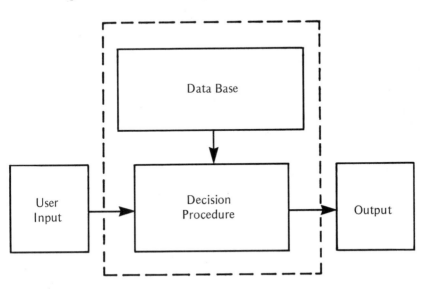

Figure 4.1: McMullen's computer framework for programs.

The user represents a configuration of behaviors, attitudes, interests, and capabilities from which information is introduced into the system. The data base also supplies information, but from elements configured by the system. The decision procedure is the funnel through which both types of information flow merge and undergo transformation into output that is then processed by the user according to his own cognitive structure. . . . System output that is followed by user input may be called a *transaction* since each party has generated a response to the other. Transactions are the central events in teaching, whether the system is another human being (Smith, 1960) or a machine (Stolurow, 1965) (1973:2).

The crucial, or in McMullen's words, "the climactic," phase is the *transaction*, which is the phase that has usually received the most attention, often to the neglect of the *initiation* phase done by the teacher, and the *production* phase which converts the "authored materials into a form suitable for student interaction with the system." The final phase is *evaluation*, which

> may call into operation other phases within the generative process
> in order to develop materials and transactions appropriate to the
> evaluation task. The principle of formative evaluation (Bloom,
> 1971) is in part a recognition that phases of instruction are
> recursive . . . That is, evaluation calls other phases as well as more
> evaluation into operation when the aim is to guide decisions (e.g.,
> revision or remediation) rather than only to reach summative
> conclusions (1973:5).

In pointing out earlier in his paper that the system being described
is "only one of many ways to develop generative CAI," McMullen
adds a statement which is not only applicable to his own project,
but which also describes an attitude the authors of this book feel
must be overcome if any breakthrough into the effectiveness and
efficiency of man-machine systems of education is to take place:

> Educators, like programmers, often lose sight of other options
> and conclude too quickly that theirs is the one way to do a task
> (1973:4).

A few *avant garde* schools are recognizing that to wait until the
"experts" are convinced that CAI is a proper tool for coordinating
learning and instruction will necessitate a great deal of "catching
up" to do when the facts of the "real world" finally penetrate the
educational establishment and the legislative chambers (local or
state) of the society. Two approaches are described in *Curriculum
Product Review* (February, 1974:16). In Wayne, New Jersey,
Wayne public schools and Fairleigh Dickinson University formed
the Instructional Computer Cooperative, Inc., to reduce the costs
of time-sharing. The wholly-owned 64-terminal system, charging
$2000 yearly for full-time use by a member of the cooperative,
performs a variety of teaching tasks in mathematics, the physical
and social sciences, and in business and remedial courses, from
elementary through college level. The second project was set up by
Fayette County Schools in Pennsylvania as a time-sharing consor-
tium and includes telecommunications capability. In addition to
teaching tasks for grades 10-12, the computer handles the clerical

work of reporting marks, class scheduling, ranking, and such listings as honor rolls. It also makes allowances for students who have "trouble learning one subject but are above average in others." It does this by "assimilating test scores" and as a result students are scheduled "more appropriately and more homogeneously than was possible manually."

The popular press has also noted the potential of computer-assisted instruction. *Newsweek* described a new computer approach at MIT to teaching mathematics at the elementary level. The article credits Professor Seymour A. Papert with the concept:

> Instead of using computers to 'program' children by drilling them in such subjects as math, Papert turns the electronic tables and gets the kids to program the computer.... The underlying objective ... is to establish a learning 'environment' that allows pupils to work things out in their own way (August 13, 1973:70).

A *learning environment* is the real potential which capital-intensive education represents; its ultimate goal is to ascertain the optimal combination(s) of human and nonhuman media for the individual learner to absorb the knowledge available.

Stolurow (1967) emphasizes that "programmed instruction and teaching machines were developed explicitly for education." He then adds this important observation:

> The research results have not revealed a high positive relationship among all the desired learning outcomes when a specific method of instruction or instructional program is used. Rather, the studies show that a program that produces maximum learning does not also produce maximum retention or transfer. *It seems necessary, therefore, to think of optimizing a set of outcomes rather than of maximizing each outcome. . . . It indicates that we need to know how to combine methods to produce optimal results* (1967:192) [italics added].[8]

Rawls *et al.* (1971), in a comparison of the college lecture method with "an individual programmed instructional method utilizing a programmed textbook," claims corroboration of "the findings of earlier investigators (Lumsdaine and Glaser, 1960; Hughes and McNamara, 1961; Roe, 1962; McNeil, 1964; Goldberg *et al.*, 1944; Welsh, Antionetti, and Thayer, 1965) that individuals utilizing programmed instructional methods learn as well or better than those using conventional procedures."

The thrust of automated programmed instruction has been outlined by Glaser (1965:771-772). After pointing out that "the work on teaching machines and programmed learning has been one response to education's growing demand for a scientific and technological base," he suggests that the marriage of behavioral science and educational technology comprises four essential tasks: (1) an analysis of the behavior desired, and a specification of the performance necessary to attain that behavior; (2) a description of the characteristics of students who are to be taught; (3) the construction of procedures to guide the student in the development desired; and (4) the provision of suitable evaluation criteria. Glaser concludes:

> By and large the educational profession will show an increasing trend toward professionalization so that the teacher will have to be provided with tools and procedures designed on the basis of scientific research and development; the most effective use of these new designs will be influenced by the personal artistry and skill of the practitioner (1965:805).

In essence, Glaser has described in technical terminology what is practically referred to in modern education as individualized learning. The relationship between the science of programming, the technology of education, and the concept of individualized learning is given by R.S. Dunn:

> ... it becomes very clear that a youngster must be diagnosed in terms of his academic achievement, potential ability, perceptual strengths, interests, motivation, and self-discipline before a program of learning can be appropriately prescribed for him. ...

The student must be permitted to achieve his instructional objectives through the media with which he can most easily relate (1971:28).

This is confirmed in "A Report by the Commission on Instructional Technology":

Individualized instruction does not mean the end of group instruction. It means shaping instruction to the needs and styles of the learners and the requirements of the subject matter. Instruction geared to the individual calls for many different arrangements, from independent study to large-group instruction (Tickton *et al.*, 1970: 17-18).

What the Commission is stating somewhat abstractly is given pragmatic substance by Dunn and Dunn:

WHAT DOES "INDIVIDUALIZATION" REALLY MEAN?

That each child in your group may:

- assume some responsibility for his own learning . . .
- become an independent learner . . .
- learn at a pace . . . comfortable for him,
- learn through materials which are related to his perceptual strengths, . . .
- learn on a level which is appropriate to his abilities,
- learn in accordance with his own learning style (alone, in small groups, through media, at night, etc.),
- be graded in terms of his own achievement and not in comparison with others,
- feel a sense of achievement and thus be able to develop self-esteem and pride . . .
- select options from among a series of alternatives and participate actively in the decision-making areas of the learning process (1972:47).

What About Achievement?

In the preceding discussion of individualization and its relationship to technology, the student has been considered in rather abstract terms. His role is that of a *learner*, but his success or failure in that role is rated on the basis of *cognitive achievement.*

Based upon some set of "norms" (e.g., percentile rating), cognitive achievement is the only generally-agreed-upon measure of educational output in present-day education. For the purpose of this book, that definition must be accepted, even though there are many possible (and valid) reasons to question the usefulness of the "cognitive yardstick" as the sole measure of educational outcomes.

In terms of cognitive achievement, then, what can be said about the use of technology in the promotion of individualized learning? Is learning improved? Is learning reduced? Or is there no appreciable change in either direction?

Kiesling (1970:992-994) presents "A Representative Sample of Experimental Findings: Audiovisual Techniques." This covers a wide range of subject matter taught with a variety of media and compared with control groups using traditional instructional methods. Of the 21 "samples" Kiesling selected, only two indicated any significant difference. In one (Carner: TV instruction, fifth and sixth grade reading), only the superior students did more poorly than under traditional instruction. In the other (Curry: TV instruction, seventh grade mathematics and sixth grade science), the superior students showed no difference, while the average and poorer students did worse than under conventional instruction. Since there are many variables which could explain these "exceptions," the negative effects observed can be considered minimal. What is important about such studies is that, even with our presently limited knowledge of how to most effectively employ a multimedia approach to learning, so many experimental efforts should conclude that *no statistically significant reduction in learning takes place* (Averch *et al.*, 1971:155).

It should be clearly understood that a multimedia approach to learning does not eliminate traditional teaching methods. What it does do is focus on learning, rather than teaching. This focus permits wide experimentation to determine the most effective, least expensive method or combination of methods (including traditional teaching) for the facilitation of individualized learning on the part of the student.

The sample educational designs for multimedia learning which are discussed in Chapter V assume that there is no *one* optimal procedure which is the answer to a student's individual learning accomplishment. Instead, various content areas will be best comprehended by the student through some "mix" of media, including face-to-face instruction. At the moment, learning theory is not sufficiently advanced to accurately determine what each optimal mix should be; neither should it be assumed that if we presently *could* designate the optimal mix of media for each subject area that this mix would be fixed for some predictable future. There must be an allowance for change, if such change indicates improvement can be obtained either in learning, or in cost reduction, or in general acceptability by the learning/teaching community. However, society can no longer afford the luxury of waiting until *all* the learning-theory research has been completed.

These sample designs to follow also assume that continuous, rather than discontinuous, learning can be most productive for all concerned with the learning process. For this reason, the basic environmental unit is a relatively small "learning center," where a maximum of 1200 students, K-12, learn together in a modern version of the American Common School or Little Red Schoolhouse. Multimedia learning techniques are supplemented by frequent intermingling during the learning process, and the limited number of students per learning center allows for mutual assistance, recognition, and respect—that is, a microcosm of life. George Richmond comments:

> Primary schools of tomorrow should foster learning environments in which children create miniature societies of their own. . . . The central thrust of such mini-societies will be toward engaging young people in institutional processes, not to be thwarted by them (1972:45).

Notes

1. Future historians might designate this audio-visual "teacher assistance" as pseudo-technological.
2. It should be noted that wage-*productivity* bargaining (as opposed to *cost-of-living* wage bargaining) is now growing in American industry. By the time this becomes established in the business sector, the supply-demand situation in education may have changed sufficiently to make it a necessary component of public sector bargaining. Meanwhile, the increasing strength of teacher unionization will insure pressure for "parity" between wages in industry and wages in education.
3. Skinner (1968:30) gives credit to S.L. Pressey for developing the basic idea behind the teaching machine in the 1920's but Skinner comments: "Pressey's machines succumbed in part to cultural inertia; the world of education was not ready for them." In the words of Skinner, "A teaching machine is simply any device which arranges contingencies of reinforcement (1968:65)."
4. In the text following, the word "programed" is also optionally rendered "programmed." This is permissible dictionary usage.
5. His bibliography is filed as Document No. 7126 with the ADI Auxiliary Service, Library of Congress, Washington, D.C.
6. Specific reference to the McComb experience can also be found in Peter T. White, "Behold the Computer Revolution," *National Geographic, 138*(5), November, 1970, 594-595, 611-612.
7. See Gagne, 1970:7-8.
8. The problem of integrated learning is a primary concern of Chapter VI.

Chapter V

AN ALTERNATIVE—
CAPITAL-INTENSIVE INSTRUCTION:

Samples of Possible Designs—The Future Today

Each significant shift in cultural values or perceptions over the centuries has led to new theories of knowledge and learning and to new methods of instruction (Saettler, 1968:12).

An environment for individualized learning, rather than a set of operating conditions for lock-step mass teaching, requires a new mind-set on the part of all those who desire to envision the possibilities.

New assumptions must replace old assumptions.

1. Each student requires an individualized prescription for learning, beginning at as early an age as possible, revised recurrently, and open-ended as to termination.

2. Education is a function of all life experiences, not only those which take place in the formal atmosphere of a classroom; cognitive achievement is a function of the time and effort devoted to the development of specific skills.

3. Since learning prescriptions will have commonalities, group

instruction will result in many situations. Individualized learning does not eliminate group instruction, but indicates more clearly where learning in groups is to the advantage of all concerned. The emphasis is on group instruction as a multimedia technique to fulfill desired learning objectives.

4. Face-to-face instruction is only *one* technique among a spectrum of techniques, and is done exclusively by those educational personnel (professionals, or paraprofessionals, or student assistants) who have demonstrated specific talent in the performance of this media approach.

5. Pupil-teacher ratios are understood to be irrelevant except where they can be shown to contribute to greater efficiency in the learning process.

6. The physical space of the learning environment is flexible. *Within* a learning center, space will range from the minimum required for a study carrel to the maximum necessary for a large-group presentation. It is also granted that space *outside* a learning center, where adaptable to the learning experience, is just as acceptable.

7. Educational staff members (professionals, paraprofessionals, and student assistants) act in varied roles: advisors, diagnosticians, facilitators, helpers, motivators, resource personnel, and technical assistants. (They are *not* commanders, directors, leaders, etc.) While professionals will be responsible ultimately for the accomplishment of learning objectives, their role activities will consist primarily of the higher order tasks, with the middle and lower order tasks being performed primarily by paraprofessionals and student assistants.

The Future Today—Introducing the
New Learning Environment

If the preceding assumptions are accepted, and others which are obviously implied, it becomes possible to consider a learning environment which integrates people and technology. Such an environment would include not only enlarged specialization of roles for educators, but revised concepts of space requirements[1] and physical facilities.

These assumptions could be brought into a schooling framework in one of two ways: (1) time-phased, or (2) non-time-phased—designations which pertain, respectively, to either an evolving man-machine system, or to a completely reorganized educational system.

A time-phased approach would introduce man-machine systems gradually, allowing students already in the educational channels to complete their studies under the traditional, or pseudo-technological, methods now being used. Allowance would thus be made for the "receiving areas" (that is, the vocations and continuing-education centers) to adjust for the eventual influx of students trained under increasingly sophisticated methodology. If due consideration is given to the willingness for social change, and the sociological and political accompaniments of such change, the economic implications of time-phasing are extremely difficult to isolate and quantify. While the time-phased process may very well be the way in which the real world will adjust reluctantly to the present revolution in educational technology, the specific impact of truly new designs in education cannot be adequately compared to the cost-structure of present education production functions under a time-phased framework. Thus, for the purposes of evaluating the model herein developed, the time-phased approach is considered as an entirely separate area of research, and will not be discussed further.[2]

By using a research arrangement which is *not* time-phased, the comparison of education production function costs between traditional methods versus man-machine systems can focus on the microeconomic aspects of each system without the distortion of other variables. While this procedure can be faulted as purely a laboratory exercise, it is extremely important to view the economic components of any production function in their basic relationships before the effects of political and sociological circumstances "institutionalize" the constituent parts. It is recognized that the cost data of traditional education production functions have already been institutionalized. To some extent, adjustment for this can be made, but there will admittedly be an error factor in the comparisons to follow which cannot be avoided completely or correctly estimated. If in the mind of the reader this detracts from the objectivity of the research, it should be pointed out that the *degree* of lack of objectivity can be only a subjective judgment which is as questionable as the complaint.

This non-time-phased approach now can be more simply sub-titled: the future today. The sample designs which illustrate this present "future" of education production functions are only representative of the great variety of schema which could be used to employ the capital equipment now available for performing the necessary but tediously repetitive task of information transmission in education.

The designs which are used in this model broadly distinguish three maturation stages whose merging into each other, consecutively, are difficult to discern. In conventional jargon, these stages are: childhood, pre-adolescence, and adolescence. Present education production functions translate these stages into distinct periods of learning: elementary (or primary), middle (or junior), and secondary (or senior). Such current terminology is used here only as a means to the end of comparing traditional and pseudo-technological education production functions (both of which are labor-intensive) with new, man-machine production functions, which are capital-intensive.

Special Consideration for Capital-Intensive Designs

The largest monetary input in present education is the cost of labor for instructional purposes. It was shown earlier that about 83 percent of the total expenditure for instruction in public elementary and secondary schools in the United States is paid out for the labor of instructional personnel. This labor input can be reduced by the use of capital-intensive methods, and the amortization of the cost of new capital equipment (both hardware and software) can be accomplished from the reduction in monetary payments to labor.

While the preceding, at first consideration, may seem improbable, or overly optimistic, a simulation by McCusker and Sorensen (1967:211ff) convincingly shows that the latitude of planners in varying allocation of resources within a constrained budget is far greater than is commonly believed or exercised. They report:

> In our exercise, we examined the effects of varying selected system characteristics while certain others were held constant. Specifically, we varied the following: (1) the average annual salaries of both professional and subprofessional personnel; (2) the ratio of professional to subprofessional personnel; [and] (3) the fraction of the instructional budget to allocate to salaries or, conversely, to supplies and materials. The following were held constant: (1) the total annual budget; (2) the portion of the total annual budget for instruction; and (3) the number of pupils in the system. . . . The data . . . suggest . . . that the educational planner may have considerably more latitude for varying resource allocations than he might realize.

In conclusion, these researchers suggested that

> The most important implications to be drawn . . . appear to be the following: (1) For any given budget allocation or salary pattern, the number of subprofessional or ancillary staff may be increased considerably without exerting radical influences upon the overall ratio of students to staff. . . . (2) If one conceives of subprofessional staff as including educational technicians and auxiliary specialists who assist directly in instructional functions . . . then more favorable student/staff ratios can be obtained by increasing the number of ancillary personnel in relation to professional staff.

In the first portion of their experiment, McCusker and Sorensen compared student per *professional staff* ratio, and student per *total staff* (professional and paraprofessional) ratio, under various staff compositions (ranging from 7:1 down to 1:1, professional to paraprofessional). With professional/paraprofessional salaries of $12,000/$5,000, respectively (1967 salary levels), and total instructional budget held constant, *and with only 60 percent of the instructional budget committed to salaries,* a 3:1 professional to paraprofessional ratio produced a 48:1 student to total staff ratio, while a 1:1 professional to paraprofessional relationship dropped the student/staff figure to 38:1.

In the second portion of their simulation, McCusker and Sorensen indicated the number of students per *total staff* which would occur at (1) varying ratios of professional to paraprofessional staff, (2) varying salary levels for professional and paraprofessional staff, and (3) varying percentages of the instructional budget committed to salaries versus materials. Two conclusions pertinent to the present study appear: (1) there is limited flexibility in rearrangement of the *labor* component of education production functions, particularly in increasing the number of paraprofessionals, *unless* this is accompanied by a significant increase in the capital component; and (2) an increase in the capital component and an increase in the number of paraprofessionals can be accomplished without additional strain on monetary resources or large increases in student/staff ratios.

Bolvin (1970:459-461) calls attention to 23 "duties and responsibilities of teachers under present conditions" which are identified by Denemark (1966), and points out that six of the most time-consuming duties are eliminated with the use of individualized, capital-intensive instruction. Those are: (1) maintaining cumulative student data files; (2) developing reading lists, outlines, study guides, visual material, etc.; (3) maintaining files to correlate learning materials with desired learning outcomes; (4) preparing and grading tests; (5) typing and duplicating tests and other materials; and (6) supervision of homeroom, study hall, lunch room, playground recess, etc.

Bell (1970:435-436) points out that in a multimedia, man-machine teaching system "the number of professional teachers is reduced substantially from those required in the traditional system." His estimate of 45 or 50 students to one professional teacher is not supported by any specific data, and might well be either too low or too high, given the present state of the art of multimedia instruction. He uses a figure of 27 to 1 as conventional under traditional educational systems and remarks that in multimedia systems "the new staffing structure will provide more personnel of varying levels of ability to make it possible for new technologies to help to individualize the instruction for each one of the pupils in the unit."

Saettler (1968:280-281) is even more emphatic:

> It is important to realize that the *majority* of the instructional system staff should be non-teaching members. The non-teaching instructional system staff will assist the teaching members in specialized functions: graphic art, film and television production, photography, secretarial, engineering, programming, etc. Other personnel . . . might include counselors, psychologists, curriculum consultants, research workers, librarians, audiovisual or communications specialists, and instructional technologists.

He adds that, just as in medicine, the difficult task is *diagnosis*. (To this, the authors add, *prescription*.) What follows diagnosis and prescription does not require the highest level of professional training. This highest level should be reserved for the more important aspects of education, which include not only diagnosis and prescription but motivation, evaluation, re-evaluation, and revised prescription, to the point of desired educational attainment. For these functions, there is no substitute for the trained, professional teacher and/or counselor.

Earlier, it was pointed out that man-machine systems of instruction should not be compared with traditional instruction in terms of pupil/teacher ratios. This is so for two reasons: (1) under a man-machine system, the professional teacher is available to the student *as needed;*[3] and (2) the arrangement for instruction under a man-machine system is *planned* and *supervised* by professionals, but the procedures for learning by nonhuman devices are implemented by paraprofessionals, who can also carry out drill, practice, and repetitive segments of instruction.

Thus, a pupil/instructional-staff ratio in a man-machine system is important only to the extent that individualized learning is taking place in the most efficient way which up-to-date learning theory indicates should occur. The number of staff involved in a man-machine system is a function of (1) the complexity of the task and (2) the degree of specialization developed as well as (3) the ratio of professional to paraprofessional personnel and (4) the salary levels used. In traditional educational systems, task complexity is only rewarded at the administrative level, and specialization in the teaching/learning process is limited—especially at the elementary level. At the secondary level, where there is a greater degree of specialization, coordination among specialists is almost nonexistent. Under a man-machine system of learning, the *professional* teacher becomes a specialist in diagnosis, prescription, facilitation, interaction, motivation, and evaluation within the context of one or more subject or skill areas. The *paraprofessional* also specializes, but in those areas requiring less broad or rigorous training, although primarily focused on instructional activity.

While the McCusker-Sorensen demonstration was done within the framework of a present-day teacher-plus-audio-visual approach to education, it indicates the possibilities that await the use of a properly-structured man-machine system of learning. McCusker and Sorensen have dealt with the ideology that only professional teachers can assist students in the learning process. As more and more multimedia procedures for learning are employed, the emphasis shifts to *assisting* rather than teaching the learner. In a properly prescribed individual learning experience, such assistance can be adequately rendered, and often better rendered, by paraprofessionals or student assistants who have been carefully trained to specialize in some specific aspect of the instructional program. This is discussed in more detail later.

McCusker and Sorensen together with the other above cited studies have given new insight into the possibilities which exist for a reallocation of resources in education between labor and capital. The usual response to pleas for drastically increasing the capital component is to call attention to already stretched educational budgets. This response is no longer valid. The monetary resources are available within existing budgets, provided the educational community faces two present realities: (1) the use of multimedia is a viable approach to instruction; and (2) in a multimedia approach, paraprofessional personnel can be 50 percent, or more, of the total instructional staff. To this should be added: (3) an integrated, man-machine system of learning multiplies the outcomes of a multimedia learning approach because it is coupled with the specialization of labor which such a system makes possible. To the economist, this is a result of a higher level of technology.

Toward New Roles in Education

Contemporary teacher-lecture and teacher-plus-audio-visual methods cast the teacher almost solely in the role of the transmitter of information. Under present educational arrangements, the actual amount of time a teacher can spend in transmitting knowledge is a residual—that is, the time remaining after all of the other "chores" of managing a class of 20 or more pupils have been completed. One of the most time-consuming of these chores is discipline, or control, an activity that continues during, and thereby often interrupts, the process of information transmission. The reason so much time must be consumed on the control function is that to be at all economical, lock-step information transmittal requires the attention in unison of the greatest number of pupils possible. When the control function consumes a large percentage of class time, information transmission is greatly reduced.

Hughes (cited in Sullivan, 1962:59-74), in a study of elementary school teachers in Utah, identified seven major categories of teaching activity: controlling functions, imposition of teacher, facilitation functions, functions that develop content, functions of personal responses, functions of positive affectivity, and functions of negative affectivity. In approximately two-thirds of her observations, Hughes found that functions of control exceeded 40 percent of all teaching acts.

Other studies have confirmed that actual instruction time by teachers is a residual. The Bay City study (Sullivan, 1962:22) determined that a combination of activities, not all of which required professional ability, consumed from 21 to 69 percent of a teacher's day. It also noted that the employment of paraprofessionals, such as aides, allowed teachers to spend 23 percent more time on instruction-related activities. Christenson (1956) found that, out of a total day, teachers average 25 minutes on individual work with pupils.

The fact that learning does take place, whether in or out of school, would seem to happen all too often *in spite of* what teachers do, or do not do. This is not to imply that teachers are underworked or overpaid. Carter (1962:4-6) lists six "educational-system goals" other than "subject-matter training"; they are: "thinking and creativity . . . skill development . . . attitude development . . . socialization . . . physical development . . . child care." Concerning each of the seven, he asks, "Is an adult required?" For subject-matter training and physical development the answer is "No." For thinking and creativity the answer is "questionable." For the other four goals, the answer is "yes," but expressed with some uncertainty, even with reference to the goal of child care. But of these five, three stand out: skill development, attitude development, and socialization. None of these take place properly without adult leadership. Carter concludes with

> . . . a word about automation and the teacher. . . . The teaching machine will largely change the role of the teacher, so that the teacher will have time to take on different activities, such as those having to do with the socialization of the child and with the transmission of attitudes rather than with content transmission. . . . It seems that this role will be one that true professionals will welcome (1962:11-12).

By providing each student with an individualized program of subject-matter training complete with the necessary mechanical aids for the transmission of information, much of the time consumed in discipline, clerical tasks, and other duties only indirectly related to instruction, can be more productively used to encourage the whole learning process.[4] "Individualized learning" requires a restructuring of the roles and functions of those who staff educational establishments. Greater reliance on educational technology through man-machine systems has the effect of changing the "mix" of professional and paraprofessional personnel to a much greater degree than at present. The prime purpose of such change is to use more effectively (people-wise), and more efficiently (cost-wise), the human and mechanical resources of a given educational system. In addition, it becomes possible to use the talents of students in (1) assisting other students, and (2) developing the skills and attitudes of learning by working as apprentices with professional and paraprofessional adults in the educational enterprise.

The roles of the personnel to staff centers where individualized learning through man-machine systems could take place would, in general, continue to be categorized as professional and paraprofessional. While more descriptive titles might come into use in the future, the *professional* roles are identified as: (1) administrator, (2) special service, and (3) teacher. The most numerous professional role is that of teacher, but the functions of this role only occasionally will include information transmission *per se*.[5] Instead, teachers would perform: *diagnosis* of student weaknesses and strengths; curriculum *prescription;* personal *response* (that is, interaction, discussion, encouragement); *facilitation* (including supervision of a student's learning program and progress); and *evaluation* (in terms of both student achievement and feedback into the diagnostic and prescriptive process).

Paraprofessional assignments are: (1) business/personnel manager, (2) health officer (or nurse), (3) technical supervisor, (4) adult assistant (or aide), and (5) student assistant. The technical supervisor would work closely with the teaching staff to supply and maintain the hardware, that is, the machines employed for information transmission. This position would also involve the preparation of recommendations for the procurement of new and replacement hardware, and the revision of usage of such hardware in curriculum prescription, as appropriate to changes deemed advisable from ongoing educational research. The *adult* assistants would tend to fall into two groups: (1) those specializing in administrative, clerical, and technical duties; and (2) those, who by natural qualification and training, could best perform as instructional aides. *Student* assistants would be drawn from the secondary learning level for their predilection toward either of the "assistant specializations" above. They could be remunerated by curricular and/or extracurricular credit, or by wages, or with some combination of the two.

The Role of Professionals

The intelligent and logical direction for a man-machine system depends upon the professional educators associated with the system. They are the experts in: (1) learning theory, (2) curriculum design, (3) motivational techniques, and (4) developmental procedures.

A man-machine system permits greater specialization among all professionals than is at present possible. Not all professionals would work on a day-to-day basis with children, although many would. For example, while still a primary *objective* of the learning center, information transmission would no longer be a primary *function* of a "teacher" in a classroom. Instead, there would be a variety of prepackaged learning experiences for the achievement of that objective.

The development of these prepackaged experiences could be done for the most part outside the confines of the learning center by specialists working in both the public and private sectors. Existing textbook and teaching aid publishers could serve as the nucleus of a vastly expanded industry employing numerous professional persons expert in learning theory, developmental psychology, subject matter, curriculum theory, prescription, and evaluation. The private educational "software" industry could become to education what the pharmaceutical industry is to medicine today.

In the public sector, any economically logical grouping of learning centers could, for minimal cost, support a District Media Center where a team of specialists would provide software "on demand" either for experimental purposes or to fill "gaps" in existing private sector material. At the county, regional, state, or national levels, further groups of media specialists could conduct experimental research in software design, as well as advancing planning for coming refinements in hardware applications. At *all* levels in the public sector, citizen input, i.e., consumer advocacy, could make possible the desired oversight which parents and taxpayers deem to be necessary.

In the present study, the authors have incorporated only the cost estimates for District Media Centers, but from the figures presented, it is easy to estimate the types of additional public sector services which could be provided to stimulate and supplement the private sector at minimal public expense. Curricular decision-making by local and state authorities would thus be strengthened through public sector: (1) leadership in curriculum research and development; (2) "pilot model" contracting with the private sector; and (3) interaction with citizens, parents, private producers, teachers, and educational experts. The employment created in both private and public curriculum design and production would (1) tend to offset jobs eliminated in traditional education, and (2) be financed out of the savings which division of labor and specialization has always made possible.

At the learning center level, the educational professional would correspond to the general practitioner in medicine. The "teacher" would have highly developed skills in diagnosing the strengths and weaknesses of individual students with respect to various intellectual and social skills and backgrounds. For the most part, this would be done on a one-to-one basis. Through an instructional management system (see Chapter VI), the "teacher" would be fully aware of the available prepared learning experiences and their expected outcomes so that appropriate prescriptions could be made for each student. Should the "teacher" find it necessary to actually design such experiences, the District Media Center would be readily available.

All of these roles, whether at the developmental or delivery stage, would require the best that the educational profession has to offer. The professional could concentrate on those activities for which professional preparation had been made, rather than using such skills haphazardly, if at all, as in present, traditional education. As noted above, various studies have shown teachers spending up to two-thirds of their classroom time on non-instructional activities, and · their instructional activities are devoted primarily to information transmission. By reorganizing the teacher's role, and by supplementing the teacher with paraprofessionals and student assistants to carry out those functions which do not require professional training, the teacher can serve more children more effectively, and at a much lower cost per student.

The Role of Paraprofessionals

Gartner (1971:19-39) has compiled the results of research on the effectiveness of paraprofessionals in education.[6] He quotes Pearl (1967) as identifying "three types of staffing patterns": (1) "the plantation system"—where paraprofessionals are a subclass of workers who do not advance; (2) "the medical system"—where roles are distinguished but there is advancement within the role; and (3) "the new careers design"—where in-service training allows upward role-mobility. According to Gartner, the Lancaster system of education exemplifies the plantation system, while the Bay City, Michigan model used the medical system. Summarizing the Bay City experiment, Gartner writes:

teachers with aides spent more time on instructional activities;

> there was little objective evidence bearing on the quality of instruction in classrooms with teacher aides as opposed to those without; teacher aides facilitated better deployment of teachers and experimentation with staffing,[7] although there was no noticeable change in teaching methods;[8] the program had little effect on overall costs; and many of the aides were potential recruits for teaching . . .

The negative reactions, says Gartner, "focused on the fact that aides were not replacements for teachers and that the use of aides could not be a justification for larger classes." It should be noted that both of these adverse comments relate to job benefits under *existing* education production functions—that is, the issue of teacher replacement concerns job security, and the issue of larger classes relates to working conditions. In the capital-intensive education production function which a man-machine system makes possible, job security is *enhanced* because of greater opportunities for professional and paraprofessional specialization, while working conditions are restructured so that no adult educator is forced to handle alone all the functions of control, information transmission, facilitation, motivation, technical assistance, monitoring, evaluation, clerical and physical chores, etc., now almost exclusively the sole responsibility of the teacher.

Again, a comment is worthwhile regarding the bleak professional outlook for the average teacher. The routine of the teacher's day is unchanging. Only the faces of the students change. This does not mean that the teacher cannot learn new things or does not have much to learn. But the basic circumstances of the job remain constant; the classroom itself limits growth possibilities. A new technology would expand "career potential" and possibilities of job enrichment.

Gartner also deals with the effect of paraprofessionals in relation to student achievement and teacher behavior. He writes:

> . . . to assess the role of the paraprofessional on pupil learning, we must seek a variety of methods and sources, and even so, express

results with some caution. The data[9] ... were collected from many sources, came to the issues from different vantage points, and sought answers to varying questions. We believe that together they do what no single study does or can do, that is, make a persuasive, although assuredly not final, argument that *paraprofessionals through their direct impact on students positively affect their learning.* And, beyond this ... there is data as to effect on teachers—changes in the allocation and use of their time and their behavior *which allow for greater attention by the teacher to pupils* (Gartner, 1971:24) [italics added].

Finally, evidence is advanced by Gartner that the use of paraprofessionals (1) encourages the teacher in "more preparation at home," because there is "another adult in the classroom,"[10] (2) serves "as a catalytic force in the development of new roles for all the parties in the school system,"[11] and (3) may have a synergistic (or multiplying) effect on allied programs.[12]

The picture which emerges is one of guarded optimism of the possibilities for improved delivery of educational output, at manageable cost, *within present education production functions,* by the use of paraprofessional personnel. If these benefits of the use of paraprofessionals are cumulated with, and used to enhance, the information transmission gains of a *capital-intensive education production function,* the results, even from an extemely conservative viewpoint, should be worth noting.

The Role of Student Assistants

It is only in the contemporary period that the value of "children teaching children" has come into question—probably a function of smaller families and deferred adulthood. Yet even in our highly sophisticated society, there is much that can be taught well—perhaps even better—by children. This is especially true of the types of skills and concepts which are developed in elementary and secondary schools. In primitive societies, older children still play a very important role in the rearing of their younger siblings. The same could be said for the few large families still to be found in our modern society.

In the one-room schoolhouse of a half-century ago, student tutoring was an essential characteristic of the instructional process. Similarly, summer camps, Scout troops, Boys Clubs, etc., are presently staffed around the notion that, as a child matures, greater responsibilities for the instruction of others can be assumed. Fortunately, after a long period of disuse, there are indications that student assistants are again becoming acceptable in some schools.

Gartner, Kohler, and Riessman (1971) have made a survey of the literature on children and youth teaching their peers. They state:

> Properly designed, there can be developed a mutually rewarding relationship between the child requiring individual attention to stimulate and guide his learning and the young person needing to undertake responsible work of recognized importance (1971:x).

An example cited is a project of System Development Corporation:

> For the teaching of reading-readiness concepts to first-grade Mexican-American students in 1967/68 . . . The principle investigators, Newmark and Melaragno, had fifth- and sixth-graders tutor first-graders, as well as first-graders tutor each other. Newmark and Melaragno concluded that tutoring, to be maximally effective, should be extended *to create a "tutorial community" in which everyone is a learner and a teacher* (1971:33-34) [italics added].

In another example, about 500 students participated in a student assistant program at Woodrow Wilson High School, Portland, Oregon. The principal says:

> activities in which they were involved included large group presentations, small group presentations, individual tutoring, correction of homework, secretarial help in the office, operation of the Closed Circuit Television equipment, etc. (Gartner *et al.,* 1971:46).

An indicator of its growing acceptance is that Phi Delta Kappa, a professional honorary fraternity, has published a monograph in its "Fastback" series on the subject, *Students Teach Students*. Its author, Peggy Lippitt (1975, p. 41), concludes:

> The programs mentioned here are only a few of hundreds that are going on. They give an inkling of the power and scope of the help kids can offer other kids in the process of growing up if they have a little help themselves from their "olders" (older children). They do not need to be especially brilliant. Often their experience with learning difficulties themselves makes them exceedingly patient and resourceful in helping others. However, the closer olders are to the age of the youngers they teach, the more expertise they need in the subject matter.

Student assistants, as well as paraprofessional adults, are thus considered an essential component of the man-machine systems which are presented in this study. The roles of both paraprofessionals and student assistants are arranged to complement, and supplement, the roles of the highly trained professionals who have the prime responsibility for individualizing student learning as that is now made possible through educational technology.

The use of these two ancillary groups results in distinct advantages to the professional personnel involved in such an arrangement: (1) each professional can specialize in the areas of expertise to which that individual is best suited by personality and training; (2) the required "omniscience in the classroom," assumed under the present system as necessary for the professional, is relaxed. A "community of learners" becomes a viable option.

The Question of "Time in School"

There is a renewed awareness that the amount of time spent in school, that is, the traditional classroom, is not highly correlated with cognitive achievement although the amount of time spent developing a specific skill is.[13] Historically, this was demonstrated in the early part of this century by, among others, the "Gary Plan," the "Dalton Plan," and the "Winnetka Plan."

As Bourne (1916:35) has stated, the Gary Plan aimed "to form, with its well-balanced facilities of work, study, and play, a genuine children's community. . . ." Devised by school superintendent William Wirt[14] as a radical reorganization of the schools of Gary, Indiana, the plan lengthened the school day to eight hours, and handled many more children per day by alternating them between small groups in classrooms, laboratories, and workshops, with large groups in auditorium, gymnasium, and playground. The flexibility of the Gary Plan not only recognized individual differences in students, but also sensed that the amount of direct information transmission which could be absorbed by each student in one day fell within some reasonable limit, probably not exceeding four hours per day. Students in each Gary Plan school were from levels K-12. Older students assisted in maintenance and repair work, and in cafeteria meal preparation, under supervision, as part of their total learning experience.

The Dalton Plan, so named because of being first introduced in Dalton (Massachusetts) High School, was pioneered by Helen Parkhurst, a teacher who spent a year in 1914 in study with Maria Montessori in Italy. Parkhurst's "laboratory plan" envisioned classrooms as laboratories where students worked at their own learning projects under a teacher/advisor who was a "specialist" in that subject content. Group contact was present along with individualization, since many students would tend to follow similar interests. Student projects were divided into month-long "contracts" of study in each subject area chosen. As Potter (1967:450) summarizes it:

> The Dalton Plan was a compromise between the traditional subject-oriented curriculum and the concern of the Progressives for pupil interest. It provided for the kind of flexible school facilities and scheduling that is central to more recent proposals for "team teaching."

Neither the Gary nor Dalton schemes contained much that would, today, seem to imply the techniques of programmed learning, which can be seen to an interesting degree in the Winnetka Plan. According to Potter (1967:450-451), the Winnetka Plan grew out of experiments, beginning in 1912, by President Frederick Burk of San Francisco State Normal School "with ways of individualizing assignments so that each child could work at his own speed." Burk's monograph, "Remedy for Lockstep School- ing," attracted a teacher named Carleton Washburne to work for Burke from 1914 to 1919. When Washburne went to Winnetka, Illinois in 1919, as superintendent (continuing through 1943), he introduced the concepts there. In the words of Washburne (1926:19), as quoted by Potter:

> One of the characteristic features of the practice materials is that they are written directly to the child as if they were to constitute a series of correspondence lessons. They lead the child step by step ... from the elements he knows to the elements he is to learn. The child practices on each step until he masters it. Then he goes on to the next.

More recently, several national[15] and international[16] studies have suggested that time spent in the classroom *per se* may not be as important in cognitive growth as other factors, such as ideational background, socioeconomic level, and natural ability.[17]

The designs for capital-intensive schooling to be proposed adopt the viewpoint above. Attention is focused on the instructional system as an integrated whole. First, the time spent in learning is seen as both *individual* and *group*. Second, it is seen as *programmed* (to achieve certain levels of cognitive behavior). Third, it is seen as *time-specified* (to adapt to the input-rate of information absorption which is peculiar to each student). The result is that "time in school" is viewed as a means to an end—learning—rather than an end in itself—schooling.[18]

Notes

1. Finley (1970:490) points out that "As we individualize and introduce technology, we will need less space in order to achieve more. All children will not have to be in classes nor come to school at the same time, therefore saving the need to build more buildings and space."

2. A time-phased, or evolutionary, process of incorporating the new educational technology may not be as mild or effective as it first appears. The techniques for a complete interdisciplinary approach to gradual educational change are as yet far from sufficiently developed to cope with the non-economic aspects of the problem.

3. In the traditional classroom, the teacher's attention is largely diffused over all the students rather than focused on one student at a time. Under a man-machine system, where the teacher is relieved of most of the information-transmission function, students can receive a substantial amount of individual attention as their individual learning diagnosis and prescription require.

4. This implies not only skill and attitude development, and socialization, but also motivation, decision-making, and the ability to conceptualize on the part of students.

5. Information transmission will undoubtedly still take place to some degree in the teacher's performance of the functions of personal response and facilitation, but it is not the *prime* function of the teacher.

6. He also discusses paraprofessional roles in mental health, social work, health, and law enforcement.

7. Under a man-machine system of education, "experimentation with staffing" becomes "specialization of function."

8. Teacher-lecture and teacher-plus-audio-visual approaches to education are locked in a methodology which is focused on the teacher/learning situation. Re-focusing on learning/teaching, as in man-machine systems, greatly increases the alternatives of the methodology.

9. *A Study of Selected Programs for the Education of Disadvantaged Children* (Palo Alto, CA: American Institutes for Research, 1968); Bennett, William S., Jr., and R. Frank Falk, *New Careers and Urban Schools* (New York: Holt, Rinehart, and Winston, 1970); Dady, Milan B., *Director's Report: Institute for Support Personnel* (Morehead, Ky.: Morehead State University, 1970); Anastasiou, Nicholas, J., *An Evaluation of the Kindergarten Teacher Assistant Project* (Palo Alto, CA: Palo Alto Unified School District, 1966); Ireland, V.M., *Evaluation of the Teacher Aid Program* (Atlanta: Atlanta Public Schools, 1969); *Utilization of Paraprofessional Personnel in Intensive Remedial Reading, End of Project Report* (Hammond, Ind.: The School City of

Hammond, 1970); *Programmed Tutoring Follow-up* (Muncie: The Reading Center, School of Education, University of Indiana, 1969); Pope, Lillian, "Blueprint for a Successful Paraprofessional Tutorial Program," *American Journal of Orthopsychiatry*, XL, 2 (March, 1970), 299-300; Davis, Donald A., "The Fennville Teacher Aide Experiment," *The Journal of Teacher Education*, XIII, 2 (June, 1962), 189.

10. Gartner (1971:30). The study is: Erickson, E., *Summary Report: Teacher and Teacher Aides Studies* (Grand Rapids, Michigan: Grand Rapids Educational Studies Center, 1968).

11. Gartner (1971:30). The study is: Bowman, Garda W., and Gordon J. Klopf, *New Careers and Roles in the American School: A Study of Auxiliary Personnel in Education* (New York: Bank Street College of Education, 1967), p. 5.

12. Gartner (1971:30-31). The study is: *Public Education in New York City* (New York: First National City Bank, 1969, p. 22).

13. Husen (1972:32) writes: "One of the most widely accepted assumptions in education has been that exposure to teaching is highly related to student learning—and in a linear fashion. . . ."

14. Thus, the Gary Plan is also known as the "Wirt Plan."

15. For example, Coleman (1966) in the United States and the Central Advisory Council for Education (1967) in England. The latter is frequently referred to as the "Plowden Report" after the Council's chairwoman, Lady Bridget Plowden.

16. For example, International Association for the Evaluation of Educational Achievement Report (1967).

17. For a recent discussion of this problem at the international level, see Husen (1972:32-35).

18. Schooling is commonly associated with teaching children to conform to existing social "norms." The concept of learning as used here does not reject the idea of socialization, but looks upon the process of education as a careful cultivation of the urge to learn what is worth learning, which includes societal responsibility.

Chapter VI

A MANAGEMENT SYSTEM FOR INDIVIDUALIZED INSTRUCTION:

Coping with Complexity

One of the criticisms of the present system is that too frequently the student is forced to fit the school (Swanson and Willett, 1977:27).

Changing the configuration of men and machines in a school will not, by itself, lead to an improvement in the quality of education. Such action merely increases the potential for improvement. By using technology, overall costs *could* be reduced; machines *could* be used for both instructional and management purposes; and, therefore, teachers *could* apply themselves to tasks which would make education more effective. But the mere reallocation of resources will not assure these gains; they only make them possible.

It is not the mix of technological and human resources, by itself, that makes the critical difference. It is the ways in which they are used and the ends toward which they are directed. To be effective, resources must be coordinated into an overall system which implements the best concepts of educational design. But what are these concepts? What are the critical tasks toward which a man-machine system or any educational system must be directed? And why, as the authors persistently maintain, can these tasks be realistically accomplished only through greater use of technology? This chapter addresses these questions and proposes one of many ways in which technology offers vehicles for solving those problems which educational theorists claim to be the most important.

Design Concepts Derived from the Functions of Education

Educational theorists have attempted to distinguish between the role of the teacher as a transmitter or source of information and the more complex role as a "manager of instruction." These distinctions are useful in defining the functions which the overall system must encompass and the roles which technology can play. For purposes of this discussion, those educational functions which involve the storage, retrieval, and transmission of information which is used in instruction will be grouped into an "Instructional Media System." More broadly, the media system will provide the learning experiences which implement educational plans. Those tasks involved in the development of educational plans will be considered part of instructional management.

The functions of instructional management parallel the functions of any management system, i.e., planning, control, staffing, and coordination. Such functions may be directed toward the operations of instruction, in which case they can be called an "Instructional Management System." Or they can be directed toward the system as a whole, in which case they can define a "General Management System." But theorists who stress the instructional management functions of educators imply something more. They suggest that teachers should have the capability of assessing or diagnosing *each individual's* needs, and from this information, develop educational plans which capture his uniqueness and which maximize his potential for further growth and development. Such a conception of instructional management does not necessarily follow from the general management functions. Something more has been added, and that something is often referred to as individualized or personalized instruction.

Given the most complete evidence on individual differences, however, it is unlikely that the empirical facts would resolve the issue of whether individualization is a necessary component of educational systems, or if an instructional management system should have the capability of individualizing educational plans. Ultimately, the decision to individualize depends on a value judgment. A society may choose to subordinate individual differences and strive for uniformity or sameness. Complex societies which seek to develop the maximum potential of their human resources eventually find it necessary in some degree to recognize and exploit the talents and capabilities that are unique to each individual. In a democratic society which measures the quality of life in terms of both social and individual good, individualization is both an economic and ethical necessity. The authors support the concept of individualization in education for all the reasons cited. However, because of the mistaken notion that individualization implies permissiveness or a subordination of the common good to individual whim, it seems necessary to define the concept in less value-loaded terms.

For purposes of this discussion, the concept of individualization can be equated to system flexibility. It means the ability of the system to manage and respond to the diversity and complexity which follow when individual differences are recognized and the system seeks to develop the maximum potential of each individual. The critical issue then becomes one of the system's capacity to recognize and accommodate those factors which influence and produce variation in the learning process. This should hold true whether the differences are traced to genetic inheritance, cultural background, traumatic events, disabilities, or mental illness. With these modifications, it can be asserted that the quality of education improves to the degree that it can recognize and respond to the diverse needs of individuals.

From the foregoing discussion, it is possible to diagram the major concepts in Figure 6.1 as a preview of the system to be proposed. At the center of the system is the interaction between the student and the teacher. This has always been the focal point in the educational process, and it likely will continue to be. All that has been added is the notion that a new capability for developing individualized educational plans will emerge as a consequence of using technology. To support this capability, information technology can be used in two ways. On the right side of Figure 6.1, an "Instructional Media System" has been envisioned in which technology relieves the teaching staff of routine functions of information storage and retrieval. Such a system does not preclude the use of human resources in providing learning experiences for students, but it provides for the transfer of functions to information technology whenever possible.

On the left side of Figure 6.1, the concept of management information systems is represented including an "Instructional Management System" to be used by teachers in planning and controlling educational experiences for students, and a "General Management System" for use by administrators in insuring the most efficient use of human, financial, and physical resources. This latter system will receive no further attention in this chapter.

Practical Constraints to
Individualized Instructional Management

While individualization has sparked a great deal of controversy, the arguments for the most part have not been over the principle of accommodating individual differences but over the *practicality* of doing it. In the individualized interpretation of instructional management, the process begins with an assessment or diagnosis of individual differences and needs. Supposedly, what will emerge is a description of the individual's strengths and weaknesses, goals and interests, cognitive style, pace of learning, and a variety of other

Figure 6.1: Major components of an individualized
man-machine instructional system.

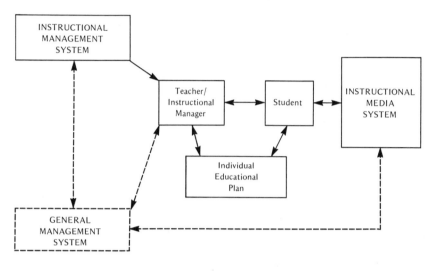

factors which seem to multiply as research expands our understanding of human beings. With such information available from
the needs assessment process, the teacher is in a position to
develop an individualized plan containing different learning
objectives, and different learning experiences for their attainment.
Finally, in some unspecified way, the teacher is envisioned as
being capable of working with students individually as they
proceed to study different subject matter, at different rates of
speed, and using different media of instruction.

But how and where is all this to take place? Will it be in the
simple classroom with which generations of Americans are
familiar? Empirical studies of teacher behavior in traditional
classrooms, such as described in Chapter V, suggest that the
realities of the teacher's day fall far short of the described ideal.
But if all possible criticisms of teachers were to be examined and
all claimed faults were to be corrected, one unpleasant fact would

remain. The ideals of individualization exceed the capability of labor-intensive education and its human resources. Any teacher who is sensitive to the differences in students accepts the demands of the personalized ideal *in principle*. But, under existing conditions in which teachers are confined to classrooms filled with rows of desks and 20-30 students, the concepts are rejected as impractical, if not ridiculous.

Many teachers have attempted to "individualize," but in a survey of such programs, Gibbons (1971) found that ". . . the term *individualized instructional program* is used to describe such a varied assortment of curricula that it is no longer a useful, restrictive (sic) category of instructional methods. It likely never was" (p. 2). Some teachers used programmed textbooks and "individualized" by allowing students to proceed at their own pace. At the other extreme, some programs provided open classroom environments and a general participative role for students in planning their own education. The student had a choice in the selection of materials for study, the methods of studying them, and choice in a variety of factors that would normally be decided by the teacher. However, individualized instructional programs were not characteristic of education in general. In no case was the theoretical range of individual differences captured in an organized system of needs assessment or in a flexible arrangement of instructional patterns which could accommodate those differences.

While recognizing that the rejection of individualization by many practicing teachers is justified under existing conditions, it is nevertheless maintained that the ideals are attainable if new capabilities of technology are used and if certain constraints imposed by the existing structure of education are relaxed. Many practical changes which could improve flexibility were presented in Chapter V. These designs greatly increase the number of program elements which are available to students and which must be monitored by the professional educator. The law of combinations and permutations suggests that the program capability of a school will increase geometrically as the program elements are reduced in size and recombined according to student needs. The capability for making such changes is assumed in the individualized system to be discussed.

Growth and Development as a Central Concept
in Information Systems Design

Any system of education evolves from the assumption it makes regarding human behavior and the processes involved in learning. This holds true for both labor-intensive and capital-intensive systems. When the teacher perceives students as potentially self-directed, responsible decision-makers, learning experiences are designed to improve self-knowledge, rational processes, and decision-making skills. When students are regarded as essentially passive beings or blank pages to be written upon, learning experiences emphasize acquiring the adult-provided facts of experience, and reinforcing the proper rules of behavior.

If such differences of opinion were merely historical curiosities, the problem would not constitute a barrier to systems design. But, in fact, these differences exist in most school systems today. One could attempt to resolve these differences by precisely defining what is to be meant by such terms as "individualization" or "needs." But two observations more clearly define the barrier to systems design. First, despite the ambiguity of such terms as needs, individualization, and even individual differences, the intuitive message is clear. The better one knows the student, the more effective one can be in planning educational experiences. Consequently, the foundation of any management system for education is the portrayal of information about the student. Second, such a system must do more than capture the range of individual differences which affect learning. It must also accommodate the diverse opinions of educators as to what needs to be known, and what needs doing; e.g., one cannot construct the system on a humanistic picture of human behavior and expect the stimulus-response behaviorist to find it useful.

The concept of growth and development has the advantage of being able to transcend conflicting views of human nature. The perspective it presents of the person is a total one. One immediately locates infancy at one end of its continuum and maturity, even old age and death, at the other. It is the entire person who is developing. To speak of part of the person, it is necessary to speak of the aspects of physiological development, intellectual development, emotional development, and so forth. No one argues with it; however, relative to our current understanding of human behavior, the concept of growth and development is like an outline map of uncharted territory. Biological and psychological research have filled in only sections of it. It is imperfect; yet, it is on the map of human development that the progress of education must be plotted.

While few would disagree with this view, there is one conflict that adoption of the growth and development perspective cannot resolve. It is the *difference* between people that leads some to probe unexplored territory, and others to live in areas that have been safely charted. In educational theory, this difference might be described as the conflict between the "Holists" and the "Behavioral Objectivists." While the map of growth and development is shared by both, their dispute has an immediate impact on deciding what amount and kinds of information are necessary to the proper conduct of education. It also affects the feasibility of using the growth and development perspective as the basis for educational information systems.

The Dispute Between Holists and Behavioral Objectivists

Behavioral objectivists have claimed that educators are too vague in formulating their goals and objectives. They should become skilled at specifying what they want to accomplish and at stating their objectives in terms of the observable and measurable behaviors that the student is to demonstrate upon completion of instruction. Advocates of criterion-based objectives go even further and claim that an objective should be stated in terms of the criterion of performance, or standard, by which accomplishment will be measured. They want educators to be specific in regard to their goals and skilled at measuring achievement. Their ideas have been extended to the problems of accountability in education and the development of competency-based education. Their philosophy might be compared to the use of management by objectives (MBO) in business.

Behavioral objectives are useful. Thousands have been written. Some have been published in books for specific academic disciplines, such as physics. They have been used in curriculum guides. Most computer applications in instruction use the objective as a basis for developing instructional modules. Goals and objectives have often been taken as the starting point for curriculum construction, although most theorists will point out that the process really begins with the identification of needs. Albeit, having identified the needs and specified the objective, it is a simple matter to develop a list of learning experiences which can meet the objective and a set of criteria that will measure its accomplishment. Taken together, a learning module or mini-instructional unit is formed which can easily be stored on a computer. Such packages are needed if the flexibility to support individualization is to be attained.

On the other hand, a serious problem exists in the use of behavioral objectives. Combs (1972:12) expresses it well:

> The general tendency of the behavioral objectives approach is to attempt to break behavior down into smaller and smaller fragments capable of more and more precise measurement. This attempt must be resisted, for the process of fractionation destroys the very goals sought. Intelligent behavior is a gestalt—an intricate pattern of parts in which genius resides, as in a symphony, not in the notes but in the composition, in the way the elements are put together. Such behavior is expressed in action in global, holistic terms. That fact cannot be ignored just because it is inconvenient. If intelligence is exhibited in holistic behavior, we shall simply have to define our objectives in these terms and, thereafter, find ways to assess it. Measuring what we

know how to measure is no satisfactory substitute for measuring
what we *need* to measure.

Both the holist and the objectivist positions have validity, and the
usefulness of any information system designed to support needs
assessment depends on finding a balance between them. It is
necessary to be specific about educational objectives and to
measure their accomplishment. But if the objectives become
fragmented and disorganized, or adopted without awareness of
their relevance to the total person, the very essence of education is
lost.

It is in the context of this problem that the concept of growth
and development offers a potential solution. If one can use the
dimensions of growth and development to portray a picture of the
whole person developing over time and, within that framework,
specify and organize the multitude of behavioral objectives
relevant to the growth process, the conceptual framework for an
information system might be established.

Dimensions of Growth and Development

A growth and development perspective contains at least two
general dimensions. First, it portrays some long-range continuum
to account for the individual's growth over time. Second, it
contains specifications as to what aspects of the individual are
involved in growing. Both are necessary to maintain a perspective
of the total person.

As societies grow more complex and are subject to increasing
rates of change, education is forced to shift its perspective from
merely teaching young children how to read and write to meeting
the needs of adults for dealing with mid-career changes and the
needs of the elderly for adjusting to retirement years. The notion
of the lifelong continuous learner is changing from an idealistic
concept to a practical necessity. While this challenge will continue
to lurk in the background, one need not address it to recognize
that a continuous record of progress is a necessity for educational

planning. One need merely ask how it is possible for young people to spend 12 years in an educational system and graduate without the capability to read or to perform simple arithmetic tasks.

One might argue that traditional education has viewed the process of development in terms of courses and grade levels. That is, the student develops by enrolling in units of instruction called courses, and progresses in terms of grade levels extending from kindergarten through twelfth grade and beyond. In this framework, the problem of organizing and measuring progress is addressed by "articulating" the connection between courses and grade levels. The emphasis is on drawing relationships between the various offerings of the schools, rather than on measuring the actual growth of the individual.

Does developmental theory offer alternative frameworks which are more viable? Given the current state of research, the answer seems to be both yes and no. One set of theories attempts to divide the life cycle into conceptual stages of development which are useful for theoretical purposes, but not for organizing the specifics of learning. Buhler (1961) has discussed the various life stages, and psychologists in general have recognized such periods as infancy, early childhood, adolescence, middle age, and old age. Such stages do not seem to have any advantage over the grade level perspective. Another set of theories can be related to the specific tasks of learning, but they apply only to limited aspects of development. Piaget (1973), in presenting his theory of intellectual development, proposed the concept of stages which were distinguished by the emergence of a new capability which did not exist before. Erickson (1963) distinguished stages of personality development around critical tasks, or life crises, which every person meets.

Comparison of these theories leads to the conclusion that no single set of categories exists by which the longitudinal growth of the total person can be predicted and mapped. On the other hand, categories do exist for establishing relationships between tasks involved in various aspects of growth, such as intellectual, emotional, and physiological maturation. In view of this, the strategy recommended in the design of an information system is to simply leave room for recording the cumulative capabilities acquired by students, and to organize specifics within the different aspects of development for which frameworks do exist.

In dealing with this problem, Havighurst (1972, 3rd Ed.) proposed the concept of the developmental task. It is interesting to note that he derived his position in an attempt to escape the conflicts in educational theory.

> The developmental task concept occupies middle ground between the two opposed theories of education: the theory of freedom— that the child will develop best if left as free as possible; and the theory of constraint—that the child must learn to become a worthy, responsible citizen through restraints imposed by his society (p. vi).

Havighurst's solution was to specify the precise tasks which a person must face or perform in the process of growing and developing and to use these tasks to organize the activities of the educational system. To this end, he began construction of a taxonomy of developmental tasks grouped around recognizable periods of development, such as infancy, early childhood, middle childhood, adolescence, early adulthood, middle age, and later maturity. Within each stage, he attempted to define the biological, psychological, or cultural basis for the task.

Havighurst's concept does not constitute a theory of growth and development. The developmental task is a pragmatic device for organizing educational processes when knowledge is incomplete about what truly goes on in the process of growing. It is consistent with behavioral objectives, but maintains reference to a broader developmental perspective. The attempt to trace each task to its biological/psychological source was not entirely successful. It seems likely that the more detailed research of Piaget in intellectual development and comparable research in emotional development will provide a firmer foundation for organizing the tasks involved in the various aspects of growth.

Cognitive, Affective, and Psychomotor Aspects of Growth

The "holists" maintain that educators must deal with the whole person. In the design of an information system, this translates into the problem of specifying the aspects of human growth to be recorded. But is education concerned with, or responsible for, the development of the whole person? Can it be effective without considering the complexity of the entire personality? What is the responsibility of the school, and what functions must it perform? To resolve these questions before proceeding with a design of an information system might delay the project indefinitely. To ignore them assumes too much about the potential utility of the information system.

Since education was recognized as a societal function, there has been concern for three aspects of learning: the acquisition of knowledge or intellectual development; the formation of values or ethical development; and the acquisition of skills relevant to life experiences. In the early days of public education, the major concern was literacy for the poor and scholarship for those who wanted it and could afford it. Later, the elimination of class distinctions led to the educational goal of scholarship for all. In the early 1900's, the demands of industrialization for manpower development created an emphasis on learning skills useful in earning a living. Dewey (1929, 1938) challenged the entire intellectual base of educational theory by examining the relationship of knowledge to action and demonstrating that meaningful learning only took place when verbal knowledge was related to experience. More recently, the research of Piaget has lent support to his views.

Throughout this period, major responsibility for moral development was left to the family and/or church. Since that time, social mobility has increased, stable family structures have deteriorated, and society in general has entered into what May (1967) and others have called a value crisis. Today, educational literature is filled with concerns over gaps in the education of the total person. For now, it may be concluded that society and education have entered the age of complexity, and the path is probably irreversible. It seems more reasonable to design an information system with the capability of addressing the new concerns which abound in educational literature, rather than to limit the capability to the traditional and still dominant emphasis on cognitive development alone. At worst, the greater capability will lie unused. At best, the system will be capable of addressing challenges which may be inescapable in the coming decades.

The threefold aspects of human behavior provide well-established categories for organizing the specifics of learning, whether they be called behavioral objectives or developmental tasks. The research of Piaget in intellectual development and of Erickson in personality development has been noted. Educators have already constructed taxonomies of educational objectives which are consistent with the framework. The work of Bloom, Krathwohl, and their associates deserves consideration in conceptualizing the framework of the information system to be proposed.

Their taxonomy of educational objectives divides behavior into three domains: the cognitive, the affective, and the psychomotor. The cognitive deals with intellectual or rational aspects of behavior and is structured along a continuum of simple to complex tasks. The affective deals with "objectives which describe changes in interest, attitudes and values, and the development of appreciations and adequate adjustment" (Bloom *et al.*, 1956, p. 7). The psychomotor deals with the area of manipulative behavior or motor skills.

Since 1956, the terms cognitive, affective, and psychomotor have been widely used in educational literature. In retrospect, the very existence of the three-part framework presented an open, and as yet unanswered, challenge to educational practice. There has been no serious denial of the claim that public school education has been almost exclusively cognitive; and within the cognitive, major effort has been expended on only the more elementary processes. With the information explosion, educators were faced with a dilemma. It seemed desirable that young people be exposed to the growing complexity of their world and be made aware of the increasingly diverse classifications of knowlege. Schools responded by providing a greater variety of courses. But when the limited resources available are spread over a wider variety of tasks, the student learns less and less about more and more. Cognitive activity is increasingly limited to the tasks of learning terminology and the elementary techniques for organizing and classifying data. There is little opportunity for mastering the more complex cognitive processes, such as analysis and synthesis.

At first, this pattern raises the question of what it means to learn cognitively. Is the educated man to be described by the variety of facts at his disposal? Or, is he to be judged by the depth of his thinking processes? Whitehead (1929) described the "merely well-informed man" as the "most useless bore on God's earth" (p. 13). Whitehead decried *that* educational practice which emphasized the reception of "inert ideas" without training the child to test them, use them in practice, or integrate them with other aspects of knowledge. If integrated learning takes time, and not all subject matter can be covered, then it is better that one learn a few facts well than many superficially. More recently, Bloom (1968) and others (Block *et al.*, 1971) have also advocated a departure from pushing on from one subject to another and pushing students along through grades. Their primary complaint, however, is that failure to take the time required to master each step in the learning process prevents the student from mastering tasks at the next level. Gentile, Frazier, and Morris (1973:35) comment:

> This last point of *moving on to new material before prerequisite materials have been mastered is probably the greatest single failing of educational systems.* If a student has not mastered a skill that is prerequisite to mastering a higher-order skill, it should not be surprising when he falters at the next level. Yet the lock-step process of much of education moves all students at the same rate through a curriculum, plotting each person's performance against that of his peers or against some national norm.

Though such comparisons may be useful for some purposes, they
are irrelevant to the individual's actual progress, which depends
on his own mastery of each component of the skill being learned.

At first glance, integrated learning can be interpreted as the
ability to synthesize knowledge and place it within a broader
cognitive perspective in which one element becomes related to
another. A second glance reveals that more is involved. Integrated
learning involves the interrelationships between knowledge and
values, and knowledge and action. One not only knows, but also
appreciates the relative value of that knowledge. One not only
knows, but also applies that knowledge in the conduct of life. In
short, mastery and integrated learning involve the total human
process and a judicious mixture of cognitive, affective, and
psychomotor learning.

Designing a "Foundation" Matrix of Information

Theoretical demands for an information system which captures
"holistic" or "integrated" learning probably exceed the requirements of a public school system that emphasizes elementary
aspects of cognitive activity. Nonetheless, in order to anticipate
future requirements, prevent early obsolescence of the system, and
to enable assimilation of research yet-to-come, it is assumed that
the most appropriate base for an instructional management system
is the most comprehensive portrayal of human learning that
theory can support.

Using the concepts previously discussed, Figure 6.2 is used to
structure one possible portrayal of growth and development. The
ordinate of the figure divides behavior into the three components
of cognitive, affective, and psychomotor learning. No categorical
scheme is recommended for the horizontal dimension of the
matrix. The appropriateness of any one of the many schema which
exist must be evaluated relative to the aspect of human growth
and learning which one intends to describe. An advantage of
maintaining separate longitudinal frameworks for each aspect of

Figure 6.2: An information matrix for needs assessment.

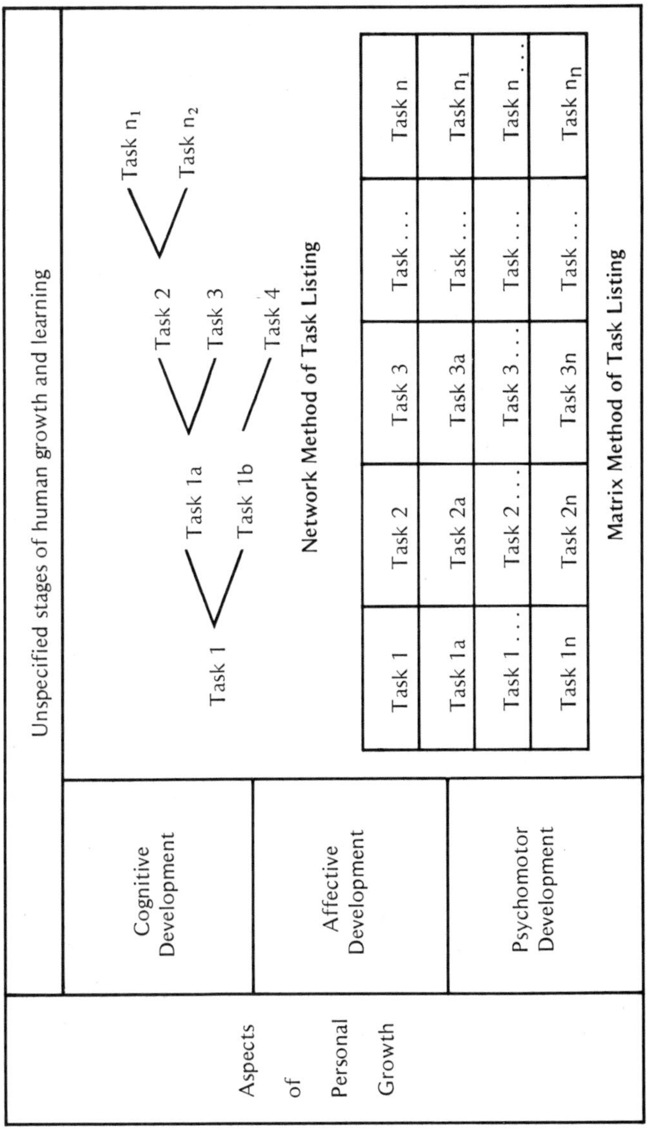

development is that most often growth does not proceed in each dimension at the same rate. Emotional development may lag cognitive development, or vice versa. If this is true, a single longitudinal division of growth would prove unworkable. As previously noted, Piaget's stages of intellectual development seem valuable in delineating the emergence of new cognitive capabilities. Erickson's "life crisis" concept identifies crucial turning points of affective development. Gagne's (1970) description of learning hierarchies and sequences seems valuable for describing the sequential flow of tasks involved in mastering complex concepts and areas of subject matter. All of these schema can be subsumed by the intent of Havighurst's developmental tasks. Quite simply, the design of the information matrix rests on an increasingly precise specification of the tasks which must be encountered in the process of learning and growing, along with a definition of their relationship to other tasks in the overall matrix.

Figure 6.2 suggests two ways of organizing the developmental tasks. The first involves a grouping of tasks involved in the educational process into a matrix. The grouping may be governed by some notion of grade levels, developmental stages, or other concepts most appropriate to the aspect of individual development involved. A second method of organization might be called the network technique. While compatible with the matrix organization, the conceptual difference is important. Logical analysis suggests the existence of so-called critical tasks which have implications for further development. Two such implications are immediately apparent. First, the accomplishment of some tasks are necessary conditions to the accomplishment of some tasks in the growth and development process. A simplified example is the need to grasp the concept of literal numbers as a prerequisite to learning algebra. Failure to master the task precludes further learning of what is to follow. A second kind of critical task does not halt development, but changes its direction. Erickson's concept of basic trust is an example. In this case, the failure to develop a sense of trust not only blocks the development of desirable human relationships, but also implies the alternative path of mistrust which leads to an entirely different pattern of learning. Similar examples can be found in the adoption of epistemological assumptions which lead to the tradition of rationalism and/or the tradition of empiricism. One such assumption concerns the relative validity of sensory observation. The empiricists tend to believe that only data obtained by sensory observation can be admitted to the bank of knowledge called valid. The rationalist tends to believe just the opposite. Depending on what assumptions are adopted, the cognitive style and general approach to knowledge and learning will vary.

The ability to move from merely listing and grouping developmental tasks in a matrix, to arranging them in a network which illustrates causal connections and outcomes depends primarily on the state of knowledge which exists regarding human psychology. It is one matter to agree that a certain task should be included as a function of the educational process. It is another matter to understand the causative relationships between tasks and their implications for further growth and development. Ultimately, the latter concerns will provide more appropriate criteria for judging the adequacy of new education information systems. But until adequate research is developed to support such an ideal system, one must live with existing capability. For this reason, and to simplify discussion, the application of the basic information requirements of an instructional management system will be limited to the listing and grouping of developmental tasks within a simple matrix.

Instructional Management System

Figure 6.3 illustrates how the concept of growth and development may be used as a foundation for an entire instructional management system. Each of the subcomponents of the system parallels the essential functions which the teacher must perform as an instructional manager. The first tasks are needs assessment and accounting for the progress of the student. Both are combined in one system, for they deal with portrayal of student growth before and after learning. Whether one emphasizes this portrayal as a process of needs assessment or evaluation is relatively unimportant. The important concept is that educational planning requires a comprehensive picture of the student's "growth status" with sufficient information regarding his strengths and weaknesses.

Given this information, the second function of instructional management is to identify the types of instructional resources and/or learning experiences available for accomplishing the developmental tasks. The related computer support system may be called an "Instructional Resource Management System." Again, the concept is a simple one. For each task or objective in the needs assessment system, the resource management system would list the "lessons," instructional packages, or structured learning experiences which the school has at its disposal for providing instruction (shown in the figure as the Instructional Media System). It could include videotapes of outstanding lectures or presentations made by teachers, films, individualized instructional packages, programs for computer-assisted instruction, or a variety of other media that may be developed. The important trend toward using community resources outside the school could also be accommodated. Employers willing to participate in cooperative work experience could be listed, as could available internships or opportunities for youth participation in community projects. One can conceive of the merit badge counselor program, as it operates in the Boy Scouts, being extended to education in general. As the need for affective and experiential learning is recognized in education, it is likely that the limitations of schools will become more apparent.

The result of combining input from the needs assessment and resource management system is to make possible the development of an individualized education plan for each student. But, simultaneously, the individualization of instruction increases the problems of scheduling and control. In existing high school systems, it is typically the task of the guidance counselor to assist the student in the selection and scheduling of the courses to be

Figure 6.3: A management system for individualized instruction.

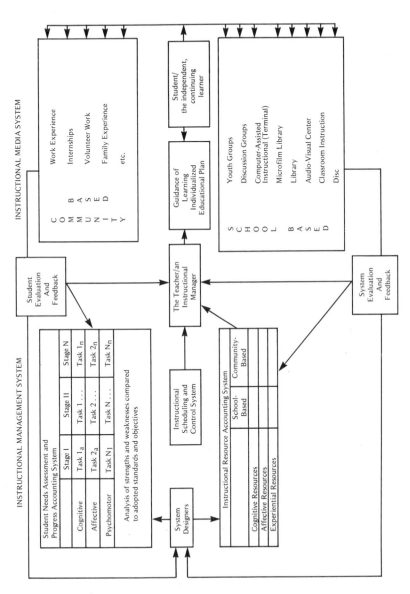

taken. When the teacher assumes the role of instructional manager, as has been more typical of the primary and intermediate levels, the functions of counseling are assumed as well. Means must be devised to build into the system a capability for handling the far greater complexities of scheduling resulting from the use of a variety of resources on an individual basis. The existence of on-line reservation systems for airlines, hotels, and entertainment events suggests that the problem is not insurmountable.

An important aspect of control is to know that activities are being pursued according to a plan. In this sense, the planning capability provided by the needs assessment and resource management systems contribute to the school's control capability. Nevertheless, even greater control capability is necessary; a means must be provided to insure that students actually engage in the learning activities that were scheduled. Whether the unit of study is an individualized learning packet which can be completed in one hour, or a two-week program of instruction on operating a lathe, controls can easily be built into the student progress accounting system. End-of-unit tests or other performance measures are implicit in every unit of instruction. The test results (or other evidence of completion) can be entered by the student aide or teacher as evidence that the activity was completed. A computerized system for comparing projected completion dates with end-of-unit notifications can easily alert instructional managers to difficulties and the need for modifications in the individualized educational plan.

Student Needs Assessment and Program Accounting System

For over 50 years, educators have been consistent in claiming that everything that happens in education should begin with an assessment of the needs of students in the context of their society. But if the concept of individualization is ambiguous, relative to the range of individual differences to be recognized, the concept of needs proves even more confusing. What is a need? Is it a demand imposed by society which must be accommodated by every individual? Is it a deficiency, like hunger, which must be satisfied to preserve health? Is it a tendency in behavior which, having been observed in "normal" people, is assumed to be a requirement for all? Is it an innate characteristic of human functioning which must be fulfilled if growth is to occur? Is discipline a need? Is freedom a need? The major barriers to developing an individualized system of education are found in such questions as these. In advocating individualization, educators have asserted that they know what *ought* to be done. This is not necessarily the case.

Three major tasks must be accomplished before a system of needs assessment and student evaluation can become operational. First, the diverse paths of individual growth and development must be charted. Second, instruments for measuring the changes which occur along these paths must be developed. Third, one must specify the appropriate uses of such evaluative data. Whether one speaks of assessing needs, or evaluating student progress, a technology of assessment is implied. But Comb's (1972:12) comment that "measuring what we know how to measure is no satisfactory substitute for measuring what we *need* to measure" suggests some dangers in over-reliance on the field of evaluation in designing the system. It follows logically that the technology of evaluation receives its purpose from the rationale underlying the educational system it supports and not vice versa. This becomes even more important when the state of the art of evaluation technology is not adequate to measure what needs measuring. There is no agreement that existing instruments measure what they purport to measure and even less agreement as to their proper interpretation or application. Part of the danger, as Combs points out, is to value measurement too highly as an end in itself and fall into the trap of ignoring more critical processes simply because we do not have the capability of measuring them. To avoid this danger, it is necessary to be explicit about the appropriate role of evaluation in education.

Tyler (1942), in Chase and Ludlow (1966:21-22), states four

assumptions underlying the role of evaluation in education that have gained widespread acceptance. These are:

1. Education strives to bring about changes in the behavior patterns of human beings.
2. Educational objectives are statements of the kinds of changes which are sought.
3. Evaluation is a process of determining the degree to which changes are actually taking place in students.
4. The critical aspect of behavior which needs to be measured is the way in which the changes are organized in the student's behavior patterns.

Tyler's further comments on the last assumption deserve repeating.

> There is always the danger that the identification of these various types of objectives will result in their treatment as isolated bits of behavior. Thus, the recognition that an educational program seeks to change the student's information, skills, ways of thinking, attitudes, and interests results in an evaluation program which appraises the development of each of these aspects of behavior separately, and makes no effort to relate them. We must not forget that the human being reacts in a fairly unified fashion; hence, in any given situation information is not usually separated from skills, or from ways of thinking, or from attitudes, interests, and appreciations. ... So that this interrelation will not be neglected, it seems necessary to emphasize as a basic assumption that the way in which the student relates his various reactions is an important aspect of his development and an important part of any evaluation of his educational achievement.

Tyler's fourth and most critical assumption may be held permanently in view by using a broad framework of individual growth and development as the core of the information system. Such a perspective can counteract the tendency to focus on those isolated bits of behavior that we know how to measure. But Tyler's assumptions also imply something about the appropriate uses to which tests and measurements may be put. Ebel (1964), in Chase and Ludlow (1966:26-31), has suggested that most public criticism of the tests and measurement movement has not been based on the nature of the instruments being used, but relate to their faulty interpretation and misapplication. One of the chief areas of misapplication has been to use test results for prediction, classification, and control rather than for improvement of the educational process. Ebel comments (p. 28):

> This means, among other things, that we should judge the value of the tests we use not in terms of how accurately they enable us to *predict* later achievement, but rather in terms of how much help they give us to *increase* achievement by motivating and directing the efforts of students and teachers. From this point of view, those concerned with professional education who have resisted schemes for very long-range predictions of aptitude for, or success in, their professions have acted wisely. Not only is there likely to be much more of dangerous error than of useful truth in such long-range predictions, but also there is implicit in the whole enterprise a deterministic conception of achievement that is not wholly consistent with the educational facts as we know them, and with the basic assumptions of a democratic, free society.

The notion that the central purpose of evaluation in education is to increase the potential for achievement is a critical one. In the system being proposed, a common data base portraying individual growth and development is used to support both needs assessment and student evaluation. This rationale assumes that needs assessment constitutes a "before treatment" view upon which educational planning can be based. Evaluation constitutes an "after treatment" view by which change is measured, which in turn becomes a needs assessment which leads to the prescription of a new treatment. This rationale seems valid so long as all users of the system are concerned with information which portrays the changes which actually take place in students. But other uses of evaluative data are found in educational systems, and they can often be counter-productive.

One might classify the many uses of evaluative data in three groups: (1) to guide teachers and students in the process of learning; (2) to evaluate the many components of the educational system, i.e., its programs, curriculum, and techniques; and (3) to evaluate the effectiveness of the educational system as a whole and to represent it to the community that supports it. It is invalid to argue that only the first use is appropriate. It is valid to argue that only evaluative data which describes changes actually taking place in students is adequate for the three purposes. As Tyler (1942) stated:

> The aims of any educational program cannot well be stated in terms of the content of the program, or in terms of the methods and procedures followed by teachers, for these are only means to other ends. Fundamentally, the purposes of education represent those changes in human beings which we hope to bring about through education. (In Chase and Ludlow, 1966:21.)

To this day, however, it can be justly stated that the type of information needed to truly evaluate the needs of students and the performance of the education system does not exist.

Since traditional and developmental theories of education insist that educational planning begins with assessment of student needs, the lack of information on these needs is appalling. One need not advocate an individualized program of instruction to recognize that improvement in the system of assessment and evaluation should constitute one of the pressing priorities of education.

The Instructional Resource Accounting System

The task of assessing student needs is a first and necessary step in the design of educational programs, whether they are directed at individuals or groups. Given this necessary information, the next step, of selecting the learning experiences and resources appropriate to the objective, is conceptually routine. In practice, however, the complexity of the task grows as the number of individual differences to be accommodated increases. In general terms, the function of the resource management system is to provide the instructional manager with a listing of the alternative resources the school has at its disposal. However, several advantages derive from computerizing this information as part of the instructional management system.

To appreciate the improvements which are possible in the quality of instruction and the reduction of costs, one should recognize the tremendous duplication of effort that is involved in the process of providing instruction today. Teachers operate essentially as autonomous units within the school. They are given a course description and a curriculum guide which lists the topics to be covered in the course with suggestions as to the sequence in which they are to be offered. Using reading assignments in textbooks and other standardized material available, each teacher throughout the country prepares very comparable lesson plans. There is little sharing of materials, for where a spirit of cooperation makes sharing possible, individual differences in teaching styles and values lead each teacher to make changes which he or she feels will result in a "better" presentation. Unfortunately, "better" presentations do not always emerge. Through national curriculum networks, or by other means, different presentations of material could be developed by experts, each suited to anticipated differences in student learning styles, and made available through the proposed learning resource centers in each school.

A more important aspect of instructional improvement, however, probably lies in the capability to match instructional resources with variations in individual learning objectives. Under existing conditions, the teacher is faced with 20-30 students in a single classroom. Assuming that a needs assessment system provides the teacher with information about individual needs, it is still necessary to select learning experiences appropriate to those needs and possibly implement 20-30 separate plans of instruction. In Figures 6.2 and 6.3, the task of providing instruction has been assigned to the Instructional Media System. However, the selection of appropriate resources remains the task of the instructional manager in creating an individualized plan.

If the Instructional Resource Accounting System is to be effective, it must be correlated with variations in student needs. Each developmental task or instructional objective in the needs assessment system was organized with reference to a related stage and/or aspect of development, i.e., cognitive, affective, or psychomotor. Instructional resources would be similarly organized with reference to the instructional objectives in the needs assessment system. The data presented to the instructional manager would be the student's developmental profile with a listing of objectives, and a correlated list of alternative resources suited to those objectives.

One other potential benefit of the resource accounting system deserves mention. It concerns the capability of the school to provide the types of learning experiences needed by people in a complex, modern society. It has always been true that schooling is not equivalent to education. The education of children has always been a responsibility shared by schools, family, and the community as a whole. But since the turn of this century, dramatic changes have taken place in American society. Educative functions formerly assumed by agencies outside of the school have been neglected, and the school has been called upon to accomplish more and more. It has become increasingly clear that children need more experiences that can be provided *only* outside the school walls. In anticipation of a growing concern for community-based learning experiences, the Instructional Resource Accounting System diagrammed in Figure 6.3 has been divided to provide for school-based and community-based resources.

The concept of taking children into the community is not new, and current trends are moving in this direction. A national network of Industry-Education Councils is providing schools with lists of thousands of volunteers from business and public agencies and with a description of the services they are willing to offer individual students and schools. They include cooperative work experiences and internships as well as guest speakers and field trips. That members of the community are concerned and willing to cooperate with school districts has been demonstrated in hundreds of projects throughout the country. The resources yet to be tapped are innumerable.

Instructional Management in Perspective

The instructional management system proposed in this chapter was designed to be constantly modified and changed as research provides new understanding of what goes on in the process of growth and development. But three design concepts provide a framework for the system which seems to be viable for the foreseeable future. First, the foundation of the system, and its constant focus, is that set of processes in reality by which the individual grows and develops in interaction with society. Knowledge of the reality processes is still imperfect, but if the system loses this focus, it loses its claim to being educative. Second, the system assumes that fundamental processes are common to educational systems everywhere. They include needs assessment, specification of learning experiences and resources, and their combination into educational plans. Third, if the human personality reflects complexity and diversity, then it follows that learning will be more effective when it is individualized, and educational systems will be more effective when they become flexible enough to handle complexity and diversity.

One might puzzle over the discrepancy between the rhetoric of education which has developed and affirmed these concepts over the past few decades and the practice of education which seems to ignore them entirely. The many problems of effecting change will be discussed in Chapter X, but for now, one important consideration should be emphasized. The ideals of needs assessment and individualization are beyond the capability of labor-intensive systems, at least within realistic cost constraints. One might argue that teams of human tutors could more effectively individualize than a man-machine system, but even this is questionable when it is realized that a man-machine system can draw upon the talents of experts world-wide and duplicate that capability by reproducing programs. But even if a team of human tutors were to be more effective for small numbers of students, who could *afford* them? Realization of the ideals of instructional management seems possible only through the use of capital-intensive systems.

Development of an instructional management capability is one of two tasks to be performed. The other is to reconceptualize the entire educational system so that having identified individual differences, it is capable of responding to them. Traditional education has been organized to respond to people in terms of standardized programs. Its focus is on mass education and production systems rather than individual differences in growth. People do not grow uniformly in terms of the school's structure of grade levels. Nor do human brains and hearts have neat compartments labeled language skills, social studies skills, and physical education which can be gradually filled by visits to classrooms for 40-45 minutes. People can and have adjusted to schools, but many are unhappy with the results. It is time to design institutions so that they can be adjusted to people. In place of structured classrooms, this study speaks of open learning centers which incorporate the resources of the community. This is based on the assumption that the design of educational systems begins with knowledge of the student.

Chapter VII

CONCEPTUAL MODELS OF
A MAN-MACHINE SYSTEM:

Reallocating Scarce Educational Resources

People most directly involved in education must be convinced that there is no other way out of the crisis . . . that educational systems must themselves become equipped with the means for innovation . . . (Coombs, 1968:167-168).

In designing capital-intensive models of schooling, it is assumed that the natural resource—students—is held constant, and the product—defined as learning as measured by standard cognitive achievement tests—remains unchanged. Thus, capital may be substituted for labor up to the point where the marginal rate of substitution[1] of capital for labor declines to one. Such revisions of the capital and labor inputs going into an education production function can be thought of as a range of isoquants, or constant-product curves.[2]

It then becomes possible to conceptualize and select one or more isoquants, or constant-product models, for the production of educational output. Two such capital-intensive "representative" models are herein developed to illustrate the rearrangements of capital-versus-labor components possible in man-machine education production functions. These models are designed as: (1) the five-day (or transitional) model and (2) the three-day (or future) model. The balance of this chapter outlines their general characteristics. Subsequent chapters will describe the models and their projected costs in considerable detail.

The Learning Environment

Structuring capital-intensive education production functions requires certain changes in traditional thinking about the learning environment. Some of these changes have been discussed, or inferred, particularly those which appear to involve ideological change. There are additional changes which are primarily structural in nature, although some changes may qualify as both ideological and structural. The changes which seem necessary to implement the five-day and three-day designs are summarized in Table 7.1.

1. The term "school" becomes "educational center," or "learning center," or just "center."[3]

2. The clientele of each learning center consists of a balanced socioeconomic mix.[4]

3. Instructional and/or learning time encompasses a maximum of three to four hours per day per student, including art and music.

a. In the five-day design, the standard school day also includes two to three hours per day per student for planned activities, plus physical education. Some activities are optional, especially in the case of elementary-age students.[5] Older students participate in group organizations in art, music, and physical education.[6]

b. In the three-day design, the standard school day is replaced by four half-days for instruction and/or learning only.[7] Both morning and afternoon sessions are scheduled to handle up to double the number of students in each learning center as in the five-day design. This does not imply a doubling of the educational

Table 7.1

Five-Day (Transitional) and Three-Day (Future) Designs:
Summary of Descriptive Features

Five-Day (Transitional)	Three-Day (Future)
• Building/some nonhuman media: leased when feasible	• Same
• "School" becomes "Learning Center"	• Same
• Clientele has socioeconomic balance	• Same
• Time in Learning: per day—3 to 4 hours per week—15 to 20 hours	• Time in Learning: [a] per half day—3 to 3-½ hours per week—12 to 14 hours
• Each student five days	• Each student four half-days
• Extra-curricular and curricular activities: each day	• Extra-curricular and curricular activities: one separate day per week
• Students per day per Center: 800-1200	• Same (per half-day)
• Total staff per Center: 30 (Tables 8.2 and 8.3)	• Total staff for Center: 40 to 50 (Tables 9.1 and 9.2)
• Traditional lunch periods for all staff and students	• No lunch periods, except: (1) for staff, daily (2) for students, on activity day
• Instructional Television by Cassette; Educational Television as available	• Same
• Dial-Access Information Retrieval district-central or commercial	• Same
• Computer-Assisted Instruction, district-central or commerical	• Same
• Students from all program levels intermingled in each learning area	• Same
• Mix of media	• Same

[a] The smaller amount of hours per week for "learning time" in the three-day design still provides equivalent time for development of academic skills, since extra-curricular or co-curricular activities are scheduled on a separate day.

staff. Some increase in staff is necessary to insure adequate personnel levels for human efficiency; however, concentration on instruction/learning, only, for four out of five days of the week eliminates overlapping duties of an extra-curricular nature. Such duties occur on a fifth, "all-school activity day," perhaps in mid-week, when organized groups of both a co-curricular and extra-curricular nature are scheduled, and when other activities, such as remedial or make-up instruction, field trips, and faculty planning sessions, take place. (The four half-days plus one full-day result in a total of three equivalent school days, or the "three-day design.") Especially at the secondary level, the three-day design also allows the arranging of other learning activities, including work experience, either in, or out, of the learning center environment.

4. Lunch periods in the two models differ.

a. In the five-day design, traditional lunch periods are scheduled, except that elementary-age children may be excused as indicated above.

b. In the three-day model, lunch periods for most students occur outside of school, or are optional at school, except on the all-school activity day. On instruction/learning days, lunch periods are arranged for staff, and those students remaining to work as student assistants.

5. Instructional television (ITV) is by videotape cassettes, supplemented, as available, by educational television (ETV) broadcasts.

6. Dial-access information retrieval (DAIR) is obtained from a district-central system, or from available commercial systems, on a time-sharing basis.[8]

7. Computer-assisted instruction (CAI) is from a district-central system, or from a regional system, or may be contracted to commercial suppliers.

8. Technological facilities for individual learning and instruction are so arranged that students from all program levels intermingle to some degree during the instruction/learning time.

This permits efficient use of technical and paraprofessional staff, and student assistants, since much of the work of ancillary staff concerns the nonhuman instructional media being employed.

9. The "mix" of media, both human and nonhuman, for instruction/learning activity, is related to identifiable student variables: ideational background; age; interests; personality profile; and possible work experience.[9]

Size and Organization of Learning Centers

Both the five-day and three-day model are assumed to be located in hypothetical school *districts* composed of similar five-day and three-day models. Each district is assumed to comprise student populations between 12,000 and 24,000 from the learning levels now designated elementary and secondary.

The size of hypothetical districts has been chosen to approximate the estimated optimal size (as determined by the number of students) for regional school districts. Use of this size district for illustration does not imply that districts which have larger or smaller student populations should not employ capital-intensive education production functions. With reference to most educational technology, such as computers, television, and multimedia-preparation staffs, district size is meaningless. All, or any, of these technological developments can be shared by whatever is a sufficient number of districts to make the technology financially feasible, provided the "will to share" is present.

Under the most traditional learning conditions now in use, Swanson (1961) demonstrated that there is a relationship between school district size and potential district efficiency. After studying a national sample of school districts, where the *community size* ranged from 1000 to 1,000,000 people, he determined that:

> the most favorable conditions for achieving good school quality exist in *communities* from 20,000 to 50,000 in population. Below and above this range, special arrangements are necessary in order to achieve the best possible quality of education.[10]

In a summary of later studies on this subject, James and Levin (1970:253) suggested that there appeared to be "either no relationship or a negative one between student enrollments and the level of educational output."

What appears more important than district size is the size of the individual learning center (or school). Again, under traditional learning conditions, Swanson (1966:39) pointed out that:

> in the small schools, professional personnel are almost exclusively classroom teachers. In more adequately organized districts, the new personnel are not necessarily classroom teachers, but are more likely specialists such as reading teachers, librarians, guidance counselors, psychologists, music teachers, art teachers, science consultants, etc.

Using data showing the "sparsity corrections"[11] in New York State in selected years, 1949 through 1962, Swanson found:

> at the elementary level there has been a decline in the needed correction for school districts of 200 Average Daily Attendance and over. At the secondary level there has been a general decline in the needed correction for all Average Daily Attendance categories.

The meaning of this trend is that where the more adequately staffed schools have developed a heterogeneous group of professionals, the smaller schools have had to settle for a homogeneous grouping of staff with a minimum of specialization, minimum division-of-labor, and higher per student per year cost for comparable quality of program.

Capital-intensive models, such as the five-day and three-day designs of this study, make heterogeneous staffing a reality for every learning situation. Heterogeneous staffing, or specialization, along with educational technology, is a prerequisite for developing individualized learning. Under traditional systems, as Swanson has shown, heterogeneous staffing is found in larger schools. Smaller schools must expect teachers to be "masters of everything."

With this background, the five-day and three-day designs in the present study establish in each school district a given number (10 to 30) of "learning *centers.*" It is assumed that the enrollment at each center would range from 800 to 1200 pupils.[12] Approximately ten "learning *areas*" are envisioned in each learning center. Thus, the number of students in each "area" of learning is not likely to exceed 120 except under extreme (and hopefully temporary) conditions. Each area is to include a cross-section of the total student population, that is, some students from *each* learning level designated K-12 (as cognitive levels are currently measured). The management of each learning area in the learning center is supervised by a professional, who qualifies not only as a teacher, in the best sense of that word, but who is also a resource person in a specific body of subject matter.[13] Students at all learning levels move in and out of the learning areas, individually, or in large or small groups, as the demands of their individual programs require. All learning areas are completely equipped with nonhuman multimedia resources as the needs of that area determine, and all learning areas have access to special all-learning-center space, such as lecture halls, conference rooms, physical education space, etc., for large- and small-group instruction.

This concept of relatively small learning centers containing relatively large learning areas has as its rationale two criteria which have already been discussed in some detail: (1) the need (and present technical capability) for individualized learning on the part of the student; and (2) the benefits which are derived from a systems approach to learning at all cognitive levels.

With reference to the first criterion, individualized learning was demonstrated very early in the history of American education in the so-called Common School. In spite of the much greater number of students today and the infinitely larger store of knowledge, such learning is again technically possible through the proper use of modern educational technology in a multimedia universe (human and nonhuman).

The second criterion, the systems approach, becomes necessary in order to properly integrate the human units (learners and educators) with the machine units (crude or sophisticated). Each learning center is made up of ten or so[14] sub-systems, which comprise the core subject matter areas, such as: reading and native language skills; foreign language(s); mathematics; natural sciences; social sciences (including history); art; music; and health/physical education. The basic professional staff must cover these areas adequately.

Traditional, mass-education systems were forced to sacrifice the old Common-School individualization concept in order to provide adequate (sometimes only minimal) staffing at an affordable cost in public funds. While modern technology makes individualization again affordable, it is only possible provided the funds for nonhuman media can be obtained by reducing the monetary input for human media. This necessitates determining an *optimum,* or most-efficient, size of each learning center (or school) in terms of both nonhuman and human media. Research on the size of student population in a single learning center which would meet the dual stipulation of individualizing learning while minimizing the costs of same is at present nonexistent. However, as will be demonstrated later, the per student per year cost of nonhuman media is less than for human input. Thus, the decision on the optimum number of human staff versus student population continues to be crucial. As will be shown in the next section, the figure of 800 to 1200 student population represents an estimated balance between the relative "smallness" to best promote individualized learning and the relative "largeness" to obtain adequate, but not over-adequate, staffing. In economic jargon, this is the concern for increasing total productivity to the limits permitted by the capital-labor "mix," thus moving down the Average Total Cost curve to its lowest point for that "mix" of capital and labor. (See Figure 8.1 and Figure 9.1, pages 161 and 178, respectively.)

Details Pertaining to Population and Staffing

Having described the general features of the learning environment, we now turn to specific details as to student population, and professional/paraprofessional staffing in each learning center.

1. The number of students per center can range between 800 to 1200, but 1200 is considered optimum. Also, since it is assumed that most centers would use leased facilities for ten-year periods, this range allows for expansion or contraction in student census.

2. The number of staff—professional and paraprofessional—is derived by using the McCusker-Sorensen study, previously discussed, as a basis. Their lowest ratio of professional to paraprofessional staff in a conventional school district was 1:1, which produced a student-to-total-staff ratio of 38:1. The capital-intensive nature of the five-day and three-day designs makes a further reduction of this ratio to 2:3 or even 1:2 feasible, while at the same time assuring each student of much more individual attention from an adult staff member, professional and paraprofessional, than is currently the practice in traditional education production functions.[15]

3. The number of student assistants per center has been arbitrarily determined for this study. It could be varied as conditions warrant. In both the five-day and three-day models, three remunerative options for student assistants may be used. All have imperceptible budget impact.

   a. Instead of monetary compensation, student assistants might receive curricular, or extracurricular, credit, or both.
   b. Monetary compensation at minimum wage rates may be preferable.
   c. Some combination of monetary and non-monetary compensation may seem desirable.

With this overview of two possible conceptions of how capital-intensive schools might appear, it is now in order to consider in detail the quality and quantity of staff and equipment, and to project and to compare their costs with each other and with traditional schooling arrangements. Toward this end, Chapter VIII describes the quality and quantity of resources required for the five-day model, translates these resources into dollar costs, and compares them with the costs of traditional schooling arrangements. Chapter IX describes the three-day model in detail and analyzes its costs. Chapter X concludes the discussion by examining political, economic, and demographic issues which could facilitate or impede the change to more capital-intensive schooling.

Notes

1. The marginal rate of substitution for two factors is defined as "the ratio of the decrement in Y (for example, labor) required to compensate for a unit increment in X (for example, capital) while leaving output unchanged" (Weintraub, 1964:30). Algebraically, this would be expressed: $MRS = -\Delta Y/\Delta X$. In monetary units, this would be stated: P_x/P_y (where P_x is the price per unit of labor and P_y is the price per unit of capital) at equilibrium.
2. An isoquant is a concave curve representing the relations between a given amount of output and alternative arrangements of inputs.
3. Space for urban, and most suburban, centers could be leased for a period not to exceed ten years, but with the option to renew.
4. Procedures for establishing and maintaining such a balance have been excluded from this study. Since both political and sociological considerations are involved, however, leasing of space could minimize certain problems.
5. These students could be excused before lunch if parents desired.
6. Any professional or paraprofessional staff member could assist with extra-curricular activities as talent and time permitted. Some assignments of staff might have to be made to assure coverage.
7. A four-day week is in operation in Unity, Maine. Started as an economy measure, it has become a success as an innovative technique for learning. *Saturday Review of Education*, February 1973, *1*(2), p. 61, reports that "study of achievement scores by the University of Maine found that students were learning more—by going to school less."
8. If private enterprise is interested in bidding for this, or other time-sharing services, educational districts should investigate the relative cost differential. This could become a different version of what is now known as performance contracting.
9. These variables are those which are most clearly identifiable in present learning theory development. The list is not definitive.
10. The community size largely determines the school district student population. Italics added.

11. Sparsity corrections provide additional funds to districts which are so located that consolidation for adequate staffing is not feasible, given the existing state of technology used in education production functions.

12. Under certain conditions, enrollment might go below 800 or above 1200 depending, for example, on whether the center was in a newly settled residential sector, or in a sector which was approaching the time for rearrangement of the constituency from which the student population is drawn. A 1200-student enrollment is considered optimum (or "most efficient").

13. As in the American Common School, the "new professional" will become a *manager of learning*.

14. Foreign language, social science, and natural science might require more than one learning area. Hence, the number of areas could vary in any learning center. In some communities, English should be taught as a second language.

15. Gartner (1971:67) points out that in the health field, the ratio of physicians to nurses prior to World War II was 2.5 to 1. By 1962, "the number of physicians doubled, nurses increased sevenfold, the medical and dental technicians twentyfold."

Chapter VIII

THE FIVE-DAY
CAPITAL-INTENSIVE MODEL:

Description and Costs

It is short-sighted . . . to assume that a suitable pedagogy for the
future school will materialize as a matter of course. We must,
instead, extrapolate from the present . . . (Rubin, 1975:205).

Skinner (1968:229) points out that the "goal of educational
reform has always been to restore the place of the practical
consequences which determine support and policy" for the
educational enterprise. Those who are aware of the history of
educational change recognize that successful reform is generally
gradual in its movement; it is, in essence, a type of *special
education* for the constituency which provides support, focusing
attention on the underlying reasons for the needed change. The
decision models *for* the type of change desired must always move
in tandem with the objectives *of* that change. Only from this
context can a new policy merit ongoing support for the new plans
which can be developed.

One decision model, which current educational research indicates is feasible, retains the traditional five-day school week but restructures it into a capital-intensive mode for instruction. This permits meeting the objective of *no change* in *time in school* while also providing individualized learning, division and specialization of tasks, and reduction in costs of instruction.

Staffing the Five-Day Design

The features of this transitional model correspond closely to traditional education production functions. Since most urban centers still use the five-day work-week, a demand continues for similar educational time-periods for families with children. The format of the "regular" school day and school week, however, should be viewed as only a framework within which a new philosophy prevails for both staff and students. *Learning* is the activity. *Individualization* of instruction is the facilitating technique.[1]

Table 8.1 presents a statistical description of a Transitional educational *district* which can range from 12,000 to 24,000 students.

The size of each learning *center* within the district can range between 800 and 1200. This allows some flexibility for demographic changes within a reasonable period of time, say, ten years. The optimum (or most efficient) size of each learning center is considered to be 1200 students. Beyond that point, the scale of operation (capital and labor) would need to be re-considered. If only 800 or 1000 students are present, however, the per student per year cost is still found to be relatively low when compared with present education production functions.

The total number of staff per learning center is a function of (1) the ratio of professional to paraprofessional personnel selected, plus student assistants, and (2) the actual student population. In Table 8.1, the total staff (professional and paraprofessional plus student assistants) is deemed adequate for up to 1200 students. The ratio of professional to paraprofessional staff is 2:3. If the ratio of professional to paraprofessional were changed to 1:2, six

Table 8.1

Five-Day Design (Transitional):
Description of Educational District

Total Student Population (K - 12)[a]	12,000	to	24,000
Approximate Size of Each Learning Center of K - 12 Students	800	to	1,200
Number of Learning Centers in District			
If 800 Students per Center	15	to	30
If 1000 Students per Center	12	to	24
If 1200 Students per Center	10	to	20
Optimum Number of Students per Center		1200	

Total Number of Staff per Center[b]

If Ratio of Professional to Paraprofessional is 2:3

Professional[c]	12
Paraprofessional	18
Total Adult	30
Student Assistants	22
Total Staff	52

[a] As learning levels are conventionally measured.
[b] Derived from Tables 8.2 and 8.3 where number of staff for each necessary function is detailed.
[c] As indicated on page 68, pupil-teacher ratios are objective data which change only because the learning process is more efficient if they change.

more paraprofessional personnel would be added, plus student assistants as desired.

Table 8.2 details the professional staffing which is estimated for each learning center.[2]

The *administrator* of the learning center should be skilled in human relations, and in instructional maintenance. To the extent that this person has further training in counseling and/or guidance, he/she serves in that capacity as time permits. As required, the role in these areas may be supplemented by a shared district specialist. If the administrator is not especially adept in external public relations, this function may be performed by an adult assistant who is so trained. The overall mission of the administrator is to create and maintain an environment in which individualized learning can take place successfully for the student, who is viewed as both a client and a customer. The Administrator's position also entails necessary liaison with the Educational District Office.

Special Service staff are responsible for curricular, co-curricular, and extra-curricular programs in art, music, and physical education. If a learning center is at the lower range of its population span, special service staff may be able to serve (at least partially) more effectively by rotating their services so as to care for more than one center at a time through the use of adult and student assistants assigned.

The *Teacher-Specialist* personnel play a key role in the learning center. Each is a content specialist in at least one area; some may qualify in more than one content discipline. Diagnosis of each student's needs in each content area, curriculum prescription to match learning processes to those needs, interaction and discussion with individual students and groups of students, general supervision of student programs, and summary evaluation of, and feedback to, the learning processes are all a part of this job specification. Division of labor and specialization within this role are encouraged.

A *Senior* (or Master) *Teacher* completes the professional staff for the five-day model. This person is the leader of the

Table 8.2

Five-Day Design (Transitional)

Calculation of Number of Professional Staff Needed Per Learning Center

Professional Assignment	Number Per Center	Functions Performed
Administrator	1	General Supervision Counseling/Guidance Public Relations: Internal and External Liaison with District Office Supervision of Personnel Hiring (with District Office)
Special Service	3	Art Program(1) Music Program (1) Physical Education Program (1)
Teacher-Specialist	7[a]	Diagnosis of Student Needs Curriculum Prescription Interaction-Discussions Supervision of Programs Evaluation and Feedback
Senior (Master) Teacher	1	Overall Diagnostic and Curriculum Supervision Teacher Personnel Arrangements (including substitutions)[b]
Total	12	

[a] Content areas are: Reading comprehension (native language); foreign languages; mathematics; natural sciences; and social sciences (including history). It is assumed that some teachers (as at present) are reasonably qualified in more than one area so that combinations of specialties will cover the content areas adequately.

[b] Short-term substitutions are not needed in the conventional sense because of the team-approach. Long-term substitutions are arranged through a district office, with assistance of the Administrator.

instructional team, and has overall diagnostic and curriculum responsibility. An additional function is to handle the personnel arrangements for both the professional and paraprofessional staff (including necessary short-term substitutions) in conjunction with the Business/Personnel Manager, who is a paraprofessional.

All the professionals, above, have been trained in: organization and planning; delegation and supervision; and evaluation of both student and staff achievement. Their prime objective is to so manage their portion of the learning environment that it functions without visible manipulation. As Skinner (1968:255) suggests:

> The teacher is a specialist in human behavior, whose assignment is to bring about extraordinarily complex changes in extraordinarily complex material.

Table 8.3 outlines the paraprofessional staffing for each learning center of the five-day design. *The ratio of professional to paraprofessional personnel is assumed to be 2:3.*[3]

Six *Adult General Assistants* and six to eight *Student Assistants* work with the administrative and special service professional staff: *Two* adults perform general secretarial duties in the administrator's area: one of these is available for assignments in any part of the learning center as work schedules permit. *Two adults* are assigned to special service; one of these works full-time with the physical education professional staff; the other works part-time for both the art and music professional staff. *One* adult is assigned full-time to the Technical Supervisor for machine maintenance and minor repair. *One* adult works as full-time secretary for the Senior Teacher. The Student Assistants work as directed.

A *Business/Personnel Manager* carries out specified responsibilities in the areas of ordering supplies and equipment under the general supervision of the Administrator, and assists with paraprofessional personnel arrangements in conjunction with the Administrator and Senior Teacher.

Eleven *Monitors* (or Teacher Assistants) are assigned

Table 8.3

Five-Day Design (Transitional)
Calculation of Number of Paraprofessional Staff per Learning Center
Ratio, Professional/Paraprofessional: 2 to 3

Paraprofessional Assignment	Number per Center Adults	Students[a]	Functions Performed
Assistant to:			
Administrator	2	1	Secretarial Public Relations
Senior Teacher	1	1	Secretarial General
Technical Supervisor	1	3	Machine Maintenance and Repair
Special Service	2	2	Assist in Art, Music, and Physical Education Programs
Business/Personnel Manager	1		Paraprofessional Personnel Arrangements (including substitutions) Ordering of Supplies and Equipment Operation of Building
Teacher Assistants[b] (or Monitors) Elementary School	3	6	Group Drill: Reading, Film, and TV Presentations, etc.
Teacher Assistants (or Monitors) Middle School	2	9	As Above, or as Designated
Teacher Assistants (or Monitors) Secondary School	2	0	As Designated
Technical Supervisor	1	Previously Listed	Issuing and Performance of All Equipment Technical Assistance in Each Level of Learning Technical Liaison with Equipment Suppliers
Health Officer[c]	1	0	Student Health; Attendance Records
Social Work Services	2	0	Family Service
Total	18	22	

[a] Additional student assistants are always useful in a capital-intensive instructional system. Number can be varied as desired with little budget effect.

[b] Number of adult assistants to teachers can vary slightly as student composition changes, but will normally not exceed seven per center. The term "monitor" is a carryover from conventional terminology. A more descriptive term would be "Adult Instructional Assistant." Classification as elementary, middle, and secondary is also a concession to convention.

[c] For the purposes of this study, a ratio of 800-1200 students to one Health Officer is deemed adequate.

to the professional teaching staff. Normally, they will tend to work with all levels of achievement as needed but can be assigned to specific levels as expertise, or occasion, makes desirable.

The paraprofessional *Technical Supervisor* is selected for his technical ability and know-how with reference to the various types of educational technology employed at each learning center. He is responsible for the issuing and performance of all equipment, technical assistance at each level of learning, and technical liaison with equipment suppliers.

A *Health Officer*, probably a registered (or licensed practical) nurse, as regulations may require, is on duty for minor student health problems, school public-health functions, attendance records, etc.

Two *Social Service* personnel complete the paraprofessional roster in the five-day model. They are responsible for family service functions, and work closely with the administrator, the district office, and the usual social service agencies.

Equipping the Five-Day Design

The capital component, in a capital-intensive learning system, also requires certain expendables which have varying degrees of durability, and certain complementary expenditures (depreciation and maintenance) peculiar to the specific equipment.

Two recent studies, Erickson (1968), and Kiesling (1971), have provided valuable data and preliminary cost estimates for structuring capital-intensive designs for learning. Erickson and Kiesling handle the capital component with different approaches. This reflects the fact that each has a separate background and viewpoint.

As a former "science teacher, city director of audio-visual services, school principal, U.S. Navy training aids officer, and finally university professor and audio-visual center director" (1968:v), Erickson is interested in audio-visual equipment: its uses and its costs. From his experience with education for below-college-level students, he is conscious of the need for detailing the types and quantities of hardware for a capital-intensive instructional system.

Kiesling, on the other hand, is a professional economist, who admits (1971:979) that he "has had little direct experience in audio-visual technology," but recognizes that "Education is a public product . . . and the professional economist whose specialty is Public Finance" understands that there is a relationship between "the problem of evaluating educational outcomes with that of evaluating government outputs in general." Thus, Kiesling employs research (which is already a matter of record) concerning the present methods and costs of educational technology. It is interesting to note that one of the major sources of Kiesling's data is a study prepared by Booz, Allen, and Hamilton, Inc., on ITV and CAI, for the Committee on Economic Development (1968:75). Apparently Kiesling overlooked, or ignored, a separate comment in the CED text:

> In many advanced schools, the basic instructional unit has been increased from the customary 30 or so students to 90 or even 120 students. The group is housed in a large, open, carpeted area staffed with a team comprised of assistants, interns, and media technicians, who function in subcenters around a learning center containing various instructional resources. *The certified teacher-to-pupil ratio is increased to 45 or 50 to one . . .* (1968:40) [italics added].

The five-day design is a first attempt to move forward, and as Rubin has suggested, "extrapolate from the present." He notes that the

> overriding research questions are . . . what kind of teaching will the available terminology permit, and what kind of teaching will the school need? . . . What might help us most, in this connection, is a set of contrasting scenarios depicting potential new schools (1975:205-206).

The studies by Erickson (1968), and Kiesling (1971), have

provided valuable cost estimates for structuring capital-intensive designs for learning. Cost calculations presented herein use each of these prior studies as separate starting points. The data are adjusted to yield a per student per year figure for instructional costs, only, of a present-day (or traditional) labor-intensive education production function. In addition to giving a valuable point of initiation for estimating capital-intensive educational costs, the Erickson and Kiesling studies also serve as cross-checks on each other.

Both Erickson and Kiesling include labor input costs which pertain to the hypothetical education production functions that each researcher projects. In the case of Erickson, the labor input cost is given only for the audio-visual media specialist staff. The removal of this labor cost leaves the capital cost, that is, the cost for all nonhuman media in the Erickson model. Kiesling does not mention audio-visual media specialists as a separate labor category.[4] His labor input cost includes teachers, paraprofessional personnel, principals, supervisors, and secretarial assistants. The Kiesling model (1971:985, 996) used here was earlier referred to as his most "capital-rich" strategy, although including considerable labor cost. In estimating costs for the five-day and three-day models, Kiesling's labor costs have been eliminated leaving only the cost of the capital component. (See Appendix P.)

Erickson does not specifically discuss pupil/teacher ratios as conventionally understood. Erickson's model envisions a 1600-student middle school with 92 teaching stations and a staff of 117 teachers. This would be a low ratio of less than 14 to 1. The thrust of the Erickson approach is to demonstrate the very reasonable per student per year cost of up-grading a conventional school for a full multimedia approach. Erickson assumes (1968:545) that if a multimedia program is adopted, the funds will be obtained. Thus, this present study uses only the capital component of Erickson's figures, and, drawing from other research already discussed, estimates the revised labor cost component in a fully integrated man-machine system of education.

Kiesling (1971:989) makes a direct assumption of a 25 to 1 pupil/teacher ratio. This is consistent with his first instructional strategy—teacher only (1971:995), but seems very inconsistent with his twelfth strategy (1971:996), his most "capital-rich" approach, which uses only 42 percent of the time of the professional teacher, and includes "heavy use of ITV, Film, and Programmed Instruction."[5] Kiesling makes no mention of a specific pupil to paraprofessional ratio, but his "Strategy 12" calls for 14 percent of paraprofessional time in addition to the 42 percent of teacher time.[6] This use of professional and paraprofessional labor appears excessive in view of the Kiesling commitment to a capital-intensive education production function. It possibly is explained by Kiesling's comment on "Strategy 12": "There have probably been no experiments where A-V materials are used this heavily" (1971:991).

Since present salary levels for professionals and paraprofessionals are 40 percent (or more) higher than the $8,000 and $4,000 figures used in the Kiesling study, the cost for labor input for instruction becomes crucial. In spite of lessened demand for (and thus greater surplus of) professionals for below-college-level teaching, public employee organization tends to offset the otherwise normal downward pressure of market forces on salaries. This, in turn, limits the resources which can be diverted to educational technology. In addition, present collective bargaining by teachers focuses on maintenance of job status with seemingly little concern for competence or function. The CED report (1968:49-50), referred to above, observes:

> Both individual teachers and teachers' associations . . . should recognize that in the long run the compensation of teachers would be greatly increased if the teacher's pay were effectively geared to his competence and function.

Having established the Erickson and Kiesling studies as the basis for the capital cost portion of the present research, and having explained the reasons for removing from both the Erickson and Kiesling models the labor input costs originally incorporated, the next step is to construct a per student per year cost for the total amount of nonhuman media, as adjusted to present (1976-77) dollars. This per student per year cost of the nonhuman media in a man-machine system of education then becomes the estimated true cost of the greatly increased capital component of a capital-intensive education production function.

The third step is to incorporate this per student per year cost of educational technology into the five-day and three-day designs.

It then remains to determine the per student per year cost of labor inputs necessary for both the five-day model, and the three-day version, estimated in 1974-75 dollars,[7] and add these costs to the costs of the capital components of each design.

The result should be an aggregate *instructional cost,* only, per student per year (capital plus labor) for a man-machine, capital-intensive learning system.[8]

What Is Included in Instructional Cost?

To establish a uniform basis for instructional cost comparisons between capital-intensive and labor-intensive educational arrangements, it is useful to list those items of expenditure which are specifically included as instructional cost. Since labor-intensive education production function data are from western New York State, those items which are designated as for "Instruction" by the State Education Department, State of New York have been chosen.[9] (Western New York staffing and financial norms generally rank somewhat above the national averages.) These items are as follows:

Supervision, Principals
Supervision, Others
Teaching
Co-Curricular Activities[10]
Interscholastic Athletics
Textbooks

Guidance, Psychological, and Social Work Services
Attendance Services
Health Services
Teaching Equipment, Supplies, and Materials

With the exception of Attendance Services and Health Services, the items above are also substantially the same as those categorized under "Instruction" in school district accounting on a national basis.[11]

What Is Included in Capital Cost?

To adapt the Erickson (1968:544 ff.) research to the present study for the calculation of the capital component costs, the following procedures have been accomplished:

1. Revised lists of media service needs (see Appendices A through I) have been prepared. These detail hardware, software, supply, maintenance, repair, and depreciation costs to equip an 800- to 1200-student learning center for what Erickson terms "adequacy level," plus the estimated necessary additions by this study for individualized learning requirements.[12]

2. Erickson's labor input cost for a *media specialist staff* at the learning center level has been removed. This is re-inserted at the district level with proper adjustment to bring salaries to 1974-75 dollars (Appendix J).

3. The new total for capital outlay has been amortized over a five-year rather than eight-year period, since Erickson points out that *some* of the equipment wears out in five years, and *all* of the items are subject to rapid technological improvement (Appendix K).

4. There has been added an estimated capital outlay for Art, Music, Physical Education, and Science. None of these are included in Erickson's figures (except for audio-visual equipment), but would be part of the cost of equipping a learning center as envisioned in this study (Appendix E-1).

5. Print-media (i.e., textbooks), omitted by Erickson, have been added as an option at the current figure (1974-75) expended by western New York schools (Appendix E-2).

6. Computer-Assisted Instruction is treated as a separate option, at a later point in this study, for both the five-day and three-day learning center designs.

The integrated results of these adaptations of the Erickson calculations are detailed in Appendices I and E, and summarized in Table 8.4. All figures have been converted to 1976-77 dollars.

The Capital Outlay for educational technology required by the five-day design, based on the Erickson study, is seen from Appendix I to be $655/student, on a basis of 800 students. This figure drops to $524/student for 1000 and $436/student for 1200 students.

To the Capital Outlay for educational technology, there has been added from Appendix E-1 (and included in Appendix I) an amount of $90 per student ($18 per student per year for five years) to cover the equipping of an 800-student learning center with the capital facilities for art, music, physical education, and science. This figure would also be reduced to $72 and $60 ($15 and $12 per student per year over five years) for 1000 and 1200 students, respectively.

Thus, the total Capital Outlay of $596,000 comes to $745 per student for 800 students, or $596 each for 1000 students, and $497 each for 1200 students. Amortized over five years, this is $149, $119, and $99 per student per year. If a longer amortization period were used, the per student per year cost would be reduced accordingly. *These figures do not include interest.*[13]

The inclusion of these per student costs for the capital outlay for equipping an 800- to 1200-student learning center provides a marked contrast to the costs which are generally associated in the mind of the public for something "new" in the production of education. Under present educational arrangements, the largest single cost for establishing an educational unit is for the "bricks and mortar," i.e., the building.

It is a generally accepted fact in previously cited educational research that there is no significant correlation between buildings and learning achievement. This infers that what *is* important in any study of the cost of education is an examination of those inputs in education production which can be rearranged to affect cost with no reduction in learning achievement. Space, for

Table 8.4

Five-Day Design (Transitional)

Summary of Instructional Hardware and Software:
Equipment, Maintenance, Repair, Replacement,
and Supply Costs (Based on Erickson)

Stated in 1976-77 dollars per student per year[a]

Erickson Study	Total Per Student		Per Year: First Five Years[b]	Per Year: Year Six and Following
Capital Outlay[c]				
Nonhuman Media, No CAI	$655	÷ 5 =	$131	0
Art, Music, Physical Education, and Science	90	÷ 5 =	18	0
Annual Recurring Cost				
Nonhuman media, No CAI: Replacement of Equipment				$ 73
Supplies, Spare Parts, Maintenance, and Repair[d]				18
			Sub-total	$ 91
Other Equipment				
Art, etc.: Replacement				10
Sub-Totals	$745	÷ 5 =	$149	$101
Addition for				
Print-media and Miscellaneous Instructional Materials			$ 51	$ 51
Totals			$200	$152

Refer to Appendices I and E for details.

[a] Totals in Appendix I have been divided by 800 students, but are deemed adequate for up to 1200 students.
[b] All equipment is amortized during the first five years.
[c] The Capital Outlay Cost is included in these calculations for two reasons: (1) to derive the proper amount for Annual Recurring Cost; and (2) to point out that the *total* Capital Outlay per student for a capital-intensive system of education is less than many present school districts have spent on "Instruction" per student in any given year to date.
[d] Original capital outlay covers spare parts, supplies, maintenance, and repair, for the first five years.

learning, is an input which can be rearranged. Whether it is more economical to accomplish such change by renovating old buildings, constructing new buildings, or leasing space, is not directly related to the present study except for the need to call attention to the *relatively small cost* for equipping learning centers with constantly up-to-date educational technology as compared to the *relatively high cost* of building construction. The business of the education industry is to create an environment for learning.

Once the modest initial Capital Outlay for up-to-date non-human media has been made[14] (which implies the willingness of a community to reallocate funds for capital inputs), the Annual Recurring Cost for the new technology is minimal even when compared to the labor input which would still be required. Based on the Erickson study, this figure is put at $101 per student per year for 800 students ($83 and $71 each for 1000 and 1200). (See Appendix I.)

As an option in the five-day design, there is included a per student per year figure for print-media (i.e., textbooks) and miscellaneous instructional materials of the conventional type. The allowance for this is $51 each per year (Appendix E-2). In a highly developed capital-intensive system, however, textbooks may become increasingly less a part of instruction.

* * *

Adapting the Kiesling (1971:977 ff.) study to the present research presents a slightly different problem than the Erickson study. Kiesling assumes (p. 985) a school district of 20,000 students (approximating the student population in our model educational district). While not specifically stated, the cross-section of experimental findings on audio-visual learning techniques which Kiesling cites (pp. 992-994) suggests the students considered are below-college-level.

The "capital" inputs which Kiesling uses are "closed circuit TV, films, and programmed instruction (computer or teaching machine)." He adds (1971:985):

> ... the estimates obtained are merely approximate, although I feel they are reasonable interpolations of what I have found in the available literature on costs. The two most important single sources used were the detailed study by the General Learning Corporation ... for all the major audio-visual media and the Booz-Allen-Hamilton estimates of the cost of instructional television and computer-assisted instruction which were prepared for the Committee on Economic Development.

The Kiesling calculations are structured in ten percent blocks of instructional time (p. 989), and are stated as a per student per year cost.[15] Because of the method of calculation, the cost of the capital component can be computed directly without removing any labor input, as was necessary in modifying the Erickson study.

Referring to Kiesling's Table 1, Item 12 (p. 996), the cost per student per year for each of these inputs in his "Strategy 12" has been calculated in Appendices P and Q, and summarized in Table 8.5. All of the studies from which Kiesling distills his figures include a complete package of hardware, software, and annual upkeep for same.

Instructional television tends to be the lowest cost nonhuman medium. The Hagerstown figures cited by Kiesling (p. 986) came from actual experience, and when adapted to ten percent blocks of instructional time in the Kiesling model, actually cost out at $10.67 for each 10 percent. Hagerstown produced its own programs. (See Appendix P.)

The General Learning Corporation ITV estimate used by Kiesling (p. 986) came to $32.92 for a similar ten percent of instructional time. Hence, Kiesling's $20.00 figure appears reasonable, and his estimated reduction to $10.00 for the second, third, and fourth blocks of ITV instructional time also seems in order. (See Appendix P.)

Film costs could no doubt be reduced if films were identified as a capital purchase and amortized over several years.

Teaching machines other than CAI are also relatively expensive at present, according to Kiesling (p. 988), although one system not

Table 8.5

Five-Day Design (Transitional)

*Summary of Instructional Hardware and Software:
Equipment, Maintenance, Repair, Replacement, and
Supply Costs (Based on Kiesling)*

Estimated[a] to Be in
1974-75 Dollars Per Student Per Year

Kiesling Study (Appendix P)	*"Strategy 12"* Cost Per Student Per Year	*If Percent of Instructional Time Is Doubled*
Type of Media		
ITV	$ 16.60	$ 25.90
Films	15.00	30.00
Teaching Machine[b]	49.80	99.60
Total (No CAI)	$ 81.40	$155.50
Kiesling, UNIVAC, and Urbana Studies		
Optional CAI (Appendix Q)		
CAI[c] (Kiesling) Estimated (1970)	$166.00	$332.00
CAI (Chicago-UNIVAC) Estimated (1973)	180.00	360.00
CAI (Urbana-PLATO) Estimated (1974):		
@ $ .50/hour	45.00	90.00
@ .35/hour	31.50	63.00

Refer to Appendices P and Q for details.

[a] Because of the way in which the Kiesling figures are developed, there appears to be ample provision for any inflation since 1970. See text for further comment.
[b] Programmed Learning.
[c] Computer-Assisted Instruction.

presently in use has been estimated to cost as low as $22.00 per year per student for ten percent of the time as compared with the $60.00 figure Kiesling used for the Auto-tutor.

The preceding discussion appears to suggest that, except for some minimal inflation, costs for nonhuman instructional media other than CAI are not apt to increase, and may well be lower than those being used for comparison in this present study.

Computer-Assisted Instruction is as yet in its infancy, though there are a number of experimental programs in use throughout the United States—mostly in college or university settings. In 1972, however, a major program was instituted in the Chicago school system. Quoting William T. Schaefer of UNIVAC Division of Sperry Rand:[16]

> We now have twenty-one schools in Chicago being served by the Computer-Assisted Instruction Drill and Practice System. Each week we provide approximately 9,000 one-hour student sessions. Based on the equipment cost, equipment maintenance cost, modem cost and communication costs, the per-hour, per-student session figure works out to be less than two dollars and fifty cents.
>
> It should be noted that the $2.50 figure will be reduced as we bring on more schools. This is true because the central computer, a UNIVAC 418-III, is now large enough to support at least thirty-two schools without the addition of other components.

Translated into a per student per year cost for 3.3 percent instructional time (36 hours of a possible 1080 hours per year), the Chicago experience would result in a $90.00 per student per year total.[17] If the cost were to drop to $2.00 per student per hour, the annual cost for 3.3 percent instructional time would be reduced to $72.00 per student per year. Adjusting this to Kiesling's 8.3 percent of instructional time (at $2.50 per hour, for 90 hours of instruction out of a possible 1080 hours in a 36-week year), the amount is $225.00 per student per year. The Chicago rate would only have to drop to $2.00 per student per hour (a 20 percent reduction) to result in a cost per student per year of $180.00 for 8.3 percent of instructional time.[18]

Thus, Kiesling's figure of $200.00 per student per year for ten percent of instructional time (or $166.00 for 8.3 percent time), using CAI, does not seem at all unreasonable. What *may* make Kiesling's calculation high, however, is his assumption in "Strategy 12" (p. 996) that 8.3 percent of instructional time is actually required. *Experience*, such as that in Chicago, may well see per student per year cost for CAI much lower than currently being estimated if (1) less than 8.3 percent of instructional time is required, or (2) lower operational costs become practical, or (3) both were to occur.

It is interesting to note that Oettinger (1969:193), quoting figures from a 1967 study, indicated a cost per hour for CAI using time-shared terminals ranging from a "low" of $24.00 to a "high" of $43.50. The actual 1972 figure of $2.50 per hour given by UNIVAC, above, is therefore, a drastic reduction in the hourly cost in just five years, giving further credence to the probability that CAI costs may continue to decline. With mini-computers and even micro-computers entering into greater use, the cost decline may be quite substantial, if not startling indeed, during the next five to ten years, while teacher salary costs will continue to rise.

This tendency toward declining CAI costs where time-sharing is possible is further confirmed by the Computer-Based Education Research Laboratory (CERL) at the University of Illinois in Urbana, which has developed the PLATO (Programmed Logic for Automated Teaching Operations) system. As described in *Education USA*, "PLATO[19] allows each student to work at his own pace in an individualized way." It can be adapted "to students of any age (three to 70 years old)." In addition to response time to student input of less than one-fifth of a second, CERL also allows random access to both audio and visual material. The cost?

CERL officials estimate that up to 4,000 terminals may be added by 1974, and that mass production of the terminals could bring the cost of computer-assisted instruction down to about 35 cents

to 50 cents per student per hour . . . with access by students to
about 250 lessons at any one time (1971:53).

Converting the $.50 per hour per student to Kiesling's per student
per year cost of CAI for each ten percent instructional time, gives
a figure of $54.00 per student per year. If the per hour cost went
to $.35, the per student per year cost for each ten percent
instructional time would further reduce to $37.80 (see Appendix
Q).

In the foreseeable future, computer-assisted instruction thus
becomes a viable capital input for education production functions
along with television, films, and teaching machines (other than
computer-controlled) for programmed learning. When CAI is
coupled with the curriculum-information and control functions
for which computers are now being used in education, further
rearrangement of the labor input can occur; that is, fewer, but
highly trained professionals, working with more trained paraprofessionals and student assistants.

Comment on Summary Tables

Tables 8.6, 8.7, and 8.8 are first used to summarize the
adaptation of the Erickson Study to obtain the new capital input
for a capital-intensive education production function under the
five-day design. This is combined with the new labor input
(professional, paraprofessional, and student assistant) which the
capital-intensive arrangement makes feasible. The tables do not
include computer-assisted instruction, or traditional textbooks,
although a figure for textbooks based on present expenditures, for
the reference group, has been calculated in Appendix E-2, and
offered as a footnote in each table.

One important distinction among the tables is in the labor input
cost per student per year. This is noted as follows:

1. The professional and paraprofessional staffing (from Tables
8.2 and 8.3) is deemed adequate, under the capital-intensiveness of
the five-day design, to handle up to 1200 students. The labor

Table 8.6

(Erickson Study) Five-Day Design—800 Students
SUMMARY OF ESTIMATED PER STUDENT PER YEAR INSTRUCTIONAL COSTS
FOR A CAPITAL-INTENSIVE MAN-MACHINE SYSTEM OF INDIVIDUALIZED EDUCATION
BELOW COLLEGE LEVEL (Stated in 1974-75 Dollars)

MODEL DISTRICT SIZE: 12,000—24,000 Students	Learning Centers of 800 Students			INPUT:	FOR COMPARISON: W.N.Y. State Traditional (Plus Audio-Visual Instruction) [b]		
	High	Median	Low		Third Quartile	Median	First Quartile
INPUT: (No CAI and no TEXTBOOKS) [a]							
Staff							
Professional (Appendix L-1)	$343	$297	$251	Labor Costs:	$ 991	$ 932	$ 867
Paraprofessional (Appendix M-1)	$224	$193	$162				
Student Assistant (Appendix N) [c]	47	47	47				
Sub-Totals	$614	$537	$460	Sub-Totals	$ 991	$ 932	$ 867
Instructional Facilities							
Annual Recurring Cost (Appendix I)	101	101	101	Teaching Materials:	Included in above. See Appendix R.		
District Instructional Expense							
Media Service Staff with fringe benefits (Appendix J)	13	10	7	Other Costs:	Included in sub-totals above.		
Media Service Equipment and Supplies (Appendix K)	2	1	1				
Fringe Benefits for Personnel in Learning Center (Appendix O)	170	136	114	Fringe Benefits:	223	205	188
TOTALS	$900	$785	$683		$1,214	$1,137	$1,055

[a] If textbooks are used, add $51 per student per year. See Appendix E-2.
[b] From Appendix R. See categories of labor costs.
[c] Based on a minimum wage of $2.50 per hour. If this were to rise to $3.00 per hour, add $53 instead of $47.

Table 8.7

(Erickson Study) Five-Day Design—1000 Students
SUMMARY OF ESTIMATED PER STUDENT PER YEAR INSTRUCTIONAL COSTS
FOR A CAPITAL-INTENSIVE MAN-MACHINE SYSTEM OF INDIVIDUALIZED EDUCATION
BELOW COLLEGE LEVEL (Stated in 1974-75 Dollars)

MODEL DISTRICT SIZE: 12,000–24,000 Students INPUT: (No CAI and no TEXTBOOKS) [a]	Learning Centers of 1000 Students			INPUT:	FOR COMPARISON: W.N.Y. State Traditional (Plus Audio-Visual Instruction) [b]		
	High	Median	Low		Third Quartile	Median	First Quartile
Staff							
Professional (Appendix L-2)	$274	$237	$200	Labor Costs:			
Paraprofessional (Appendix M-2)	$179	$154	$130				
Student Assistant (Appendix N) [c]	47	47	47				
Sub-Totals	$500	$438	$377	Sub-Totals	$ 991	$ 932	$ 867
Instructional Facilities					$ 991	$ 932	$ 867
Annual Recurring Cost (Appendix I)	83	83	83	Teaching Materials:	Included in above. See Appendix R.		
District Instructional Expense							
Media Service Staff with fringe benefits (Appendix J)	13	10	7	Other Costs:	Included in sub-totals above.		
Media Service Equipment and Supplies (Appendix K)	2	1	1				
Fringe Benefits for Personnel in Learning Center (Appendix O)	147	117	98	Fringe Benefits:	223	205	188
TOTALS	$745	$649	$566		$1,214	$1,137	$1,055

[a] If textbooks are used, add $51 per student per year. See Appendix E-2.
[b] From Appendix R. See categories of labor costs.
[c] Based on a minimum wage of $2.50 per hour. If this were to rise to $3.00 per hour, add $53 instead of $47.

Table 8.8

(Erickson Study) Five-Day Design—1200 Students
SUMMARY OF ESTIMATED PER STUDENT PER YEAR INSTRUCTIONAL COSTS
FOR A CAPITAL-INTENSIVE MAN-MACHINE SYSTEM OF INDIVIDUALIZED EDUCATION
BELOW COLLEGE LEVEL (Stated in 1974-75 Dollars)

MODEL DISTRICT SIZE: 12,000—24,000 Students	Learning Centers of 1200 Students			INPUT:	FOR COMPARISON: W.N.Y. State Traditional (Plus Audio-Visual Instruction) [b]		
INPUT: (No CAI and no TEXTBOOKS) [a]	High	Median	Low		Third Quartile	Median	First Quartile
Staff							
Professional (Appendix L-3)	$229	$198	$167	Labor Costs:	$ 991	$ 932	$ 867
Paraprofessional (Appendix M-3)	$149	$129	$108				
Student Assistant (Appendix N) [c]	47	47	47				
Sub-Totals	$425	$374	$322	Sub-Totals	$ 991	$ 932	$ 867
Instructional Facilities							
Annual Recurring Cost (Appendix I)	71	71	71	Teaching Materials:	Included in above. See Appendix R.		
District Instructional Expense							
Media Service Staff with fringe benefits (Appendix J)	13	10	7	Other Costs:	Included in sub-totals above.		
Media Serivce Equipment and Supplies (Appendix K)	2	1	1				
Fringe Benefits for Personnel in Learning Center (Appendix O)	124	99	82	Fringe Benefits:	223	205	188
TOTALS	$635	$555	$483		$1,214	$1,137	$1,055

[a]　If textbooks are used, add $51 per student per year. See Appendix E-2.
[b]　From Appendix R. See categories of labor costs.
[c]　Based on a minimum wage of $2.50 per hour. If this were to rise to $3.00 per hour, add $53 instead of $47.

input costs set forth in Tables 8.6, 8.7, and 8.8 are calculated on a basis of 800, 1000, and 1200 students, respectively. With 800 students the student/adult ratio is 27:1; with 1000 students, the ratio is 33:1; and at 1200 students the ratio is 40:1. The ratio derived from the McCusker and Sorensen study, cited in Chapter V, is 35:1.

2. From Appendix R, it can be seen that the labor input in the reference group expenditures for "Instruction" covers the full spectrum of services which are also part of the capital-intensive mode, and are therefore, fully comparable to the estimated figures given for the capital-intensive designs.

3. Labor input cost in the "High" column under "Learning Centers" is a function of (1) maximum salary levels, and (2) minimum student population. Labor input cost in the "Low" column is a function of (1) minimum salary levels, and (2) maximum student population.

A second point to be observed in comparing the tables is the "Annual Recurring Cost" for the new, capital-intensive "Instructional Facilities." There is no comparable figure available in traditional education accounting. The money spent annually for "Teaching Materials" in the reference group includes *minimal* provision for new equipment or the replacement of old equipment, which must be funded on a hit-or-miss basis, as possible. Under the five-day design, not only is the initial capital outlay relatively low (see Appendix I), but the capital nature of the outlay is recognized, and proper budgeting allows for depreciation in a fast-changing technical horizon of five years.

"District Instructional Expense" is the last item appearing in the Tables. This consists of expense for "Media Service," which includes labor, equipment, and materials, and (taken from Appendices 0, V-1, and V-2) the "Fringe Benefits" are displayed for learning center personnel as a per student per year cost.

Tables 8.9, 8.10, and 8.11 incorporate the figures derived from the Kiesling Study into the five-day design. Labor input is the same as in the previous set of tables. The "Annual Recurring Cost"

Table 8.9

(Kiesling Study) Five-Day Design—800 Students
SUMMARY OF ESTIMATED PER STUDENT PER YEAR INSTRUCTIONAL COSTS
FOR A CAPITAL-INTENSIVE MAN-MACHINE SYSTEM OF INDIVIDUALIZED EDUCATION
BELOW COLLEGE LEVEL (Stated in 1974-75 Dollars)

MODEL DISTRICT SIZE: 12,000–24,000 Students	Learning Centers of 800 Students			INPUT:	FOR COMPARISON: W.N.Y. State Traditional (Plus Audio-Visual Instruction) [b]		
INPUT: (No CAI and no TEXTBOOKS) [a]	High	Median	Low		Third Quartile	Median	First Quartile
Staff							
Professional (Appendix L-1)	$343	$297	$251	Labor Costs:	$ 991	$ 932	$ 867
Paraprofessional (Appendix M-1)	$224	$193	$162				
Student Assistant (Appendix N) [c]	47	47	47				
Sub-Totals	$614	$537	$460	Sub-Totals	$ 991	$ 932	$ 867
Instructional Facilities							
Annual Recurring Cost (Appendix P)	156	119	82	Teaching Materials:	Included in above. See Appendix R.		
District Instructional Expense							
Media Service Staff with fringe benefits (Appendix J)	13	10	7	Other Costs:	Included in sub-totals above.		
Media Service Equipment and Supplies (Appendix K)	2	1	1				
Fringe Benefits for Personnel in Learning Center (Appendix O)	170	136	114	Fringe Benefits:	223	205	188
TOTALS	$955	$803	$664		$1,214	$1,137	$1,055

[a] If textbooks are used, add $51 per student per year. See Appendix E-2.
[b] From Appendix R. See categories of labor costs.
[c] Based on a minimum wage of $2.50 per hour. If this were to rise to $3.00 per hour, add $53 instead of $47.

Table 8.10

(Kiesling Study) Five-Day Design—1000 Students
SUMMARY OF ESTIMATED PER STUDENT PER YEAR INSTRUCTIONAL COSTS
FOR A CAPITAL-INTENSIVE MAN-MACHINE SYSTEM OF INDIVIDUALIZED EDUCATION
BELOW COLLEGE LEVEL (Stated in 1974-75 Dollars)

MODEL DISTRICT SIZE: 12,000–24,000 Students	Learning Centers of 1000 Students			INPUT:	FOR COMPARISON: W.N.Y. State Traditional (Plus Audio-Visual Instruction) [b]		
	High	Median	Low		Third Quartile	Median	First Quartile
INPUT: (No CAI and no TEXTBOOKS) [a]							
Staff							
Professional (Appendix L-2)	$274	$237	$200	Labor Costs:	$ 991	$ 932	$ 867
Paraprofessional (Appendix M-2)	$179	$154	$130				
Student Assistant (Appendix N) [c]	47	47	47				
Sub-Totals	$500	$438	$377	Sub-Totals:	$ 991	$ 932	$ 867
Instructional Facilities							
Annual Recurring Cost (Appendix P)	156	119	82	Teaching Materials:	Included in above. See Appendix R.		
District Instructional Expense							
Media Service Staff with fringe benefits (Appendix J)	13	10	7	Other Costs:	Included in sub-totals above.		
Media Service Equipment and Supplies (Appendix K)	2	1	1				
Fringe Benefits for Personnel in Learning Center (Appendix O)	147	117	98	Fringe Benefits:	223	205	188
TOTALS	$818	$685	$565		$1,214	$1,137	$1,055

[a] If textbooks are used, add $51 per student per year. See Appendix E-2.
[b] From Appendix R. See categories of labor costs.
[c] Based on a minimum wage of $2.50 per hour. If this were to rise to $3.00 per hour, add $53 instead of $47.

Table 8.11

(Kiesling Study) Five-Day Design—1200 Students
SUMMARY OF ESTIMATED PER STUDENT PER YEAR INSTRUCTIONAL COSTS
FOR A CAPITAL-INTENSIVE MAN-MACHINE SYSTEM OF INDIVIDUALIZED EDUCATION
BELOW COLLEGE LEVEL (Stated in 1974-75 Dollars)

MODEL DISTRICT SIZE: 12,000—24,000 Students	Learning Centers of 1200 Students			INPUT:	FOR COMPARISON: W.N.Y. State Traditional (Plus Audio-Visual Instruction) [b]		
INPUT: (No CAI and no TEXTBOOKS) [a]	High	Median	Low		Third Quartile	Median	First Quartile
Staff							
Professional (Appendix L-3)	$229	$198	$167	Labor Costs:	$ 991	$ 932	$ 867
Paraprofessional (Appendix M-3)	$149	$129	$108				
Student Assistant (Appendix N) [c]	47	47	47				
Sub-Totals	$425	$374	$322	Sub-Totals	$ 991	$ 932	$ 867
Instructional Facilities							
Annual Recurring Cost (Appendix P)	156	119	82	Teaching Materials:	Included in above. See Appendix R.		
District Instructional Expense							
Media Service Staff with fringe benefits (Appendix J)	13	10	7	Other Costs:	Included in sub-totals above.		
Media Service Equipment and Supplies (Appendix K)	2	1	1				
Fringe Benefits for Personnel in Learning Center (Appendix O)	124	99	82	Fringe Benefits:	223	205	188
TOTALS	$720	$603	$494		$1,214	$1,137	$1,055

[a] If textbooks are used, add $51 per student per year. See Appendix E-2.
[b] From Appendix R. See categories of labor costs.
[c] Based on a minimum wage of $2.50 per hour. If this were to rise to $3.00 per hour, add $53 instead of $47.

for "Instructional Facilities" (see Appendix P) has already been structured in "blocks of instructional time" such that the "Low" figure of $82 per student per year arranges 21.6 percent of instructional time to be accomplished by ITV, Films, and Programmed Learning. The "High" figure doubles this to 43.2 percent of instructional time at a cost per student per year of $156. *It is especially important to note that the "Low" figure of $82 could just as well appear in the "High" column, and the "High" figure of $156 in the "Low" column.* Or, the "Median" figure of $119 could be placed in either of the other two columns. Thus, a district with a high labor input cost might be capable of working out a departmental instruction strategy in each of its learning centers which could accomplish the goals of a man-machine system of learning at a "Low" rate, say $82, or a "Median" rate, say $119, for use of capital.

From the preceding, it can be seen that the five-day design using either the Erickson or Kiesling data as the basis for a capital-intensive individualized system of education reduces both labor input cost and total cost for instruction as compared with traditional education production functions which use audio-visual devices only as "aids."

Comparative Average Total Cost Curves

Traditional education production functions have become so focused on cognitive achievement tests, class size, and student-teacher ratios that the proper concern for an *optimum* (or most efficient) scale for a total combination of educational inputs has been either disregarded or lost. In the language of economics, optimum size of a production function denotes the lowest point on an average total cost curve (ATCC) consistent with some given state of technology and some predetermined arrangement of inputs. The five-day capital-intensive design developed in the preceding pages results in an optimum size learning center of 1200 students.

In Figure 8.1, the relationship between (1) the dollar cost per student per year of the five-day design, and (2) the number of students, is plotted to show the average total cost curves which are based upon the Erickson, and Kiesling capital input data, respectively. It would appear that beyond a student population of 1200, the ATCC should turn upward, since both the capital and labor inputs in the five-day design have been arranged to achieve optimum allocation of these resources at, or near, the determined capacity of each center. While it is possible that these ATC Curves might continue downward, or even move horizontally, as more than 1200 students were accommodated, it is very doubtful if capacity could be increased more than five to ten percent without diseconomies of scale becoming evident.

Figure 8.1 also illustrates how far below the *lowest* expenditure for instruction by the reference group are the instructional costs for capital-intensive education production. Only the upper range of the Kiesling data ATC Curve, with a minimum of 800 students in the five-day design, lies within 15 percent of the First Quartile of the reference group. This occurs only because *all* salary ranges in the five-day design are higher than in traditional education production functions. The average salary of teachers in the first quartile for the reference group, in 1974-75, was $11,214 (Rott, 1976:1). In the five-day and three-day designs presented here, and in Chapter IX, the *lowest* teacher salary is $15,000.[20]

In a day when teachers are in surplus and the cost of living continues to rise, the insights derived from examining the production of education under optimum human and technological considerations merit the serious attention of educators, parents, and the various political entities involved with future policy for the allocation of educational resources.

Figure 8.1: Five-day design—Average total cost curves: Instruction only.

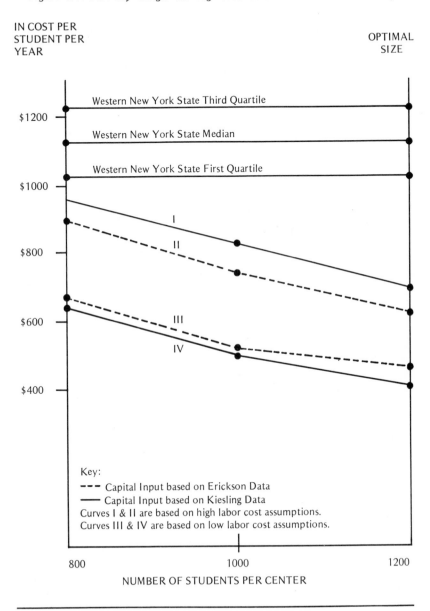

IN COST PER
STUDENT PER
YEAR

OPTIMAL
SIZE

Western New York State Third Quartile

$1200

Western New York State Median

Western New York State First Quartile

$1000

I

II

$800

$600

III

IV

$400

Key:
- - - Capital Input based on Erickson Data
——— Capital Input based on Kiesling Data
Curves I & II are based on high labor cost assumptions.
Curves III & IV are based on low labor cost assumptions.

800   1000   1200

NUMBER OF STUDENTS PER CENTER

Notes

1. "A fundamental guideline," says Postlethwait (1969:1), "which must be given prime consideration is that 'learning is an activity done *by* an individual and not something done *to* an individual.' "

2. An unrelated, but somewhat similar, pattern is found in the operations of a non-profit, privately managed, chain of educational centers, Learning Foundations, Inc. An interview (January, 1972) at a Town of Amherst, New York, location revealed that the instructional personnel (all certified teachers) supervised five students per hour in language, mathematics, and reading comprehension using teaching machines. This converts to a 30 to 1 student-teacher ratio for a six-hour day. Learning Foundations guaranteed a 94 percent success rate, and 22 percent of their clients were children of teachers.

3. See Chapter V for discussion of other possible ratios.

4. It is possible that Kiesling assumes this function is handled within the total professional/paraprofessional staffing provision.

5. Kiesling's dozen instructional strategies are in turn based upon a spectrum of experimental findings from the use of audio-visual techniques.

6. However, if we assume in the teacher-only strategy that 100 percent teacher time is absorbed by 25 students, it follows that in the capital-rich strategy, which consumes only 42 percent teacher time, the pupil-teacher ratio *could* rise to 60:1.

7. These were the latest "actual" figures available on Western New York salaries at the time of writing this manuscript. If these figures are increased by a factor to represent inflation between 1974-75 and 1976-77, and later, the savings of the capital-intensive models would be even greater than those shown in Appendix Y.

8. See the Appendices for the detailed calculations. It should be noted that, while labor costs are for 1974-75 (the latest data available for this study), the costs of the nonhuman media are updated to 1976-77. Since labor costs have continued rising, the comparisons between labor-intensive and capital-intensive education will be even wider than shown in this Chapter and in Chapter IX.

9. See State of New York, Department of Audit and Control, "Uniform System of Accounts for School Districts—Double Entry Basis," 1965.

10. Defined as "allied to, but not integral to, instruction."

11. See U.S. Department of Health, Education, and Welfare, Office of Education, *Financial Accounting for Local and State School Systems— Standard Receipt and Expenditure Accounts: Handbook II,* Bulletin, 1957, No. 4.

12. The Erickson study envisions "future" instructional systems which are

quite individualized (1968:526-528), but Erickson is at the moment concerned with greater use of multimedia in more conventional approaches to learning. Therefore, in the appendices, the Erickson provision for individualized learning has been up-graded to a higher level of adequacy.

13. If interest were added at ten percent of $596,000 on a declining balance basis over five years (principal being reduced by $119,200 per year), the total interest cost would be $178,800 ($59,600 + $47,680 + $35,760 + $23,840 + $11,920). This would increase the *initial* Capital Outlay to $774,800, which is $969 per student for 800 students, $775 for 1000, and $646 for 1200. Over five years this is $194, $155, and $129 per student per year, respectively, after which the per student per year figure becomes only the Annual Recurring Cost of $101, $83, and $71, respectively. (Appendix I.)

14. In man-machine, individualized systems of learning, and especially with CAI, the equipping of large science laboratories becomes unnecessary. See Postlethwait (1969).

15. For example: each 10% block of teacher time is valued at $32 per student per year; each 10% block of paraprofessional time is valued at $16 per student per year. The nonhuman media are priced accordingly: Films—$30 for each 10% of time; TV—$20 for first 10%, $10 each for the second, third, and fourth 10%, $20 for the fifth, etc.

16. William T. Schaefer, National Marketing Manager, Computer-Assisted Instruction, UNIVAC Division, Sperry Rand, 300 N. State Street, Chicago, Illinois 60610, from a personal letter to E.J. Willett, dated December 20, 1972. An update on these figures was requested in 1977, but not received.

17. The Chicago figure of $2.50 per student per hour over a 36-week school year would amount to $90 for 1/30 (or 3.3%) instructional time per year. In order to adjust to the Kiesling format, this is multiplied by three to get 9.9% instructional time per year, costing $270.00 per student per year. Lower *hourly* costs can be translated into 10% yearly instructional time costs, similarly, in order to compare with the Kiesling computation.

18. It is reasonable to assume that a 30% increase in utilization (from 24 schools to 32 schools on the UNIVAC 418-III) could produce at least a 20% reduction in per student per year cost.

19. The PLATO system marketed by Control Data Corporation.

20. See Appendices S-1, S-2, and S-3.

Chapter IX

THE THREE-DAY
CAPITAL-INTENSIVE MODEL:
Description and Costs

Fully qualified teachers should work as masters surrounded by apprentice teachers and assisting personnel in complementary functions at various levels of competence (Edding, 1969:30).

The three-day (or Future) design for a man-machine system of education to promote individualized learning below college level could be structured for either a five-day or a six-day week.[1] As chosen for this study, the format of the five-day week in the three-day design has been previously outlined (Table 8.1) as consisting of four half-days of instruction, totaling 12 to 16 hours per week, plus an all-school activity day of approximately six hours; or, as noted, the temporal equivalent of three days (thus, our "three-day" design).

Tables 9.1 and 9.2 detail the professional and paraprofessional staffing provisions for the three-day design within a five-day week. It should be noted that the ratio of professional to paraprofessional staff is continued at 2/3 to 1. Also, the number of both

Table 9.1

Three-Day Design (Future)
CALCULATION OF NUMBER OF *PROFESSIONAL* STAFF NEEDED PER LEARNING CENTER
RATIO: PROFESSIONAL TO PARAPROFESSIONAL—2/3 TO 1

Professional Assignment	Number Per Center			Functions Performed
	800 Students: (Twice)	1000 Students: (Twice)	1200 Students: (Twice)	
Administrator	1	1	1	General Supervision Counseling/Guidance Public Relations: Internal and External District Office Liaison
Teacher-Senior	1	1	1	Overall Diagnostic and Curriculum Supervision Teacher Personnel Arrangements (including substitutions)
Teacher-Specialist	10[a]	12	14	Diagnosis of Student Needs Curriculum Prescription Interaction-Discussions Supervision of Programs Evaluation and Feedback
Special Service - Coordinator	1	1	1	Coordination of Special Service Programs, and Activity Days
Special Service - Specialist	3	3	3	Art Program (1) Music Program (1) Physical Education Program (1)
Total[b]	16	18	20	

[a] Same content areas as listed in Table 8.2. Three, five, and seven additional teacher-specialists as staff for the 800, 1000, or 1200 extra students handled in a 6-8 hour school day, are added.
[b] Short-term substitutions are not needed in the conventional sense because of the team-approach. Long-term substitutions are arranged through district office.

Table 9.2

Three-Day Design (Future)
CALCULATION OF NUMBER OF *PARAPROFESSIONAL* STAFF PER LEARNING CENTER
RATIO: PROFESSIONAL/PARAPROFESSIONAL—2/3 TO 1

Paraprofessional Assignment	Number Per Center				*Functions Performed*
	Adults			*Student Assistants*[a]	
	800 Students: (Twice)	1000 Students: (Twice)	1200 Students: (Twice)		
Assistant to:					
Administrator	3	3	3	2	Secretarial Public Relations
Teacher-Senior	2	2	2	2	Secretarial General
Technical Supervisor	2	2	2	6	Machine Maintenance and Repair
Special Service	3	3	3	4	Assist in Art, Music, Physical Education
Business/Personnel Manager	1	1	1	1	Paraprofessional Personnel (including substitutions) Ordering of supplies and equipment Operation of building
Teacher Assistants[b] (or Monitors) Elementary (continued, next page)	4	5	6	10	Group Drill/Reading/Film and TV

[a] An increase in student assistants from 40 to 50, if deemed advisable for student population increase from 800 to 1000, would not increase per student per year cost. See Appendix U.
[b] Number of adult assistants to teachers can vary slightly as student composition changes, but will normally not exceed 8 to 14 per center.

Table 9.2 (continued)

Paraprofessional Assignment	Number Per Center				Functions Performed
	Adults			Student Assistants	
	800 Students: (Twice)	1000 Students: (Twice)	1200 Students: (Twice)		
Teacher Assistants (or Monitors) Middle	2	3	4	10	As above or as designated
Teacher Assistants (or Monitors) Secondary	2	3	4	2	As designated
Technical Supervisor	1	1	1	Previously listed	Issuing and Performance of all equipment; Technical Assistance in each level of learning; Technical Liaison with Equipment Suppliers
Health Officer[c]	1	1	1	1	Student Health; Attendance Records
Social Work Services	3	3	3	2	Family Service
Total	24	27	30	40	

[c] If student health service is provided as a District function, another paraprofessional monitor could be added in place of the Health Officer. Using as a base 1 Nurse-Health officer per 1200 students, at an average salary of $10,000 per/academic year, a 6000 student district with 5 nurse-health officers would require an expenditure of only $10 per student per year to accommodate $50,000 in salaries plus $10,000 for fringe benefits. Another $2 per student per year would provide a rotating relief health officer as needed.

professional and paraprofessional staff is increased by one-third, one-half, and two-thirds as the student population *per half-day* rises from 800 to 1000 to 1200. The number of paid student assistants has also been increased from 22 to 40. (For comparison with the five-day design, see Tables 8.2 and 8.3.)

In Table 9.1, it should be noted that one new professional has been added—a Special Service Coordinator. This individual provides needed assistance and supervision in the scheduling, staffing, and implementing of the special service programs: instructional, co-curricular, and extra-curricular activities in each learning center. The time of this person is divided equally between the two half-day sessions.

The Teacher Assistants (or Monitors) listed in Table 9.2, as in Table 8.3, are categorized as Elementary, Middle, and Secondary. This is an arbitrary arrangement which does not imply rigidity in terms of the number of assistants in each category. The number of such adult assistants, as well as student assistants, in each *Learning Area* in a learning center, will tend to vary to fit the requirements of the individualized learning programs in progress. A team approach is the assumed mode.

For the three-day design, one additional Social Worker has also been added, as detailed in Table 9.2.

The implications for labor input costs of these staffing patterns for the three-day design are calculated in Appendices S-V. The Annual Recurring Costs for the capital input, based on the Erickson study, are estimated in Appendix W. Annual recurring capital costs based on the Kiesling Study are the same as in the five-day design. (See Appendix P.)

Tables 9.3, 9.4, and 9.5 bring together the costs for both capital and labor inputs for the three-day design based upon the Erickson Study.

Tables 9.6, 9.7, and 9.8 compile the capital and labor input costs for the three-day design based on the Kiesling Study.

Significant reduction in labor costs occurs in both sets of tables, although professional and paraprofessional staffing has been

Table 9.3

(Erickson Study) Three-Day Design—1600 Students
SUMMARY OF ESTIMATED PER STUDENT PER YEAR INSTRUCTIONAL COSTS
FOR A CAPITAL-INTENSIVE MAN-MACHINE SYSTEM OF INDIVIDUALIZED EDUCATION
BELOW COLLEGE LEVEL (Stated in 1974-75 Dollars)

MODEL DISTRICT SIZE: 12,000—24,000 Students	Learning Centers of 800 Students (Twice)			INPUT:	FOR COMPARISON: W.N.Y. State Traditional (Plus Audio-Visual Instruction) [b]		
INPUT: (No CAI and no TEXTBOOKS) [a]	High	Median	Low		Third Quartile	Median	First Quartile
Staff							
Professional (Appendix S-1)	$224	$194	$164	Labor Costs:			
Paraprofessional (Appendix T-1)	$145	$125	$105		$ 991	$ 932	$ 867
Student Assistant (Appendix U) [c]	85	85	85				
Sub-Totals	$454	$404	$354	Sub-Totals	$ 991	$ 932	$ 867
Instructional Facilities							
Annual Recurring Cost (Appendix W)	69	69	69	Teaching Materials:	Included in above. See Appendix R.		
District Instructional Expense							
Media Service Staff with fringe benefits (Appendix J)	13	10	7	Other Costs:	Included in sub-totals above.		
Media Service Equipment and Supplies (Appendix X)	2	2	2				
Fringe Benefits for Personnel in Learning Center (Appendix V-1, V-2)	110	96	81	Fringe Benefits:	223	205	188
TOTALS	$648	$581	$513		$1,214	$1,137	$1,055

[a] If textbooks are used, add $51 per student per year. See Appendix E-2.
[b] From Appendix R. See categories of labor costs.
[c] Based on a minimum wage of $2.50 per hour. If this were to rise to $3.00 per hour, add $101 instead of $85.

Table 9.4

(Erickson Study) Three-Day Design—2000 Students
SUMMARY OF ESTIMATED PER STUDENT PER YEAR INSTRUCTIONAL COSTS
FOR A CAPITAL-INTENSIVE MAN-MACHINE SYSTEM OF INDIVIDUALIZED EDUCATION
BELOW COLLEGE LEVEL (Stated in 1974-75 Dollars)

MODEL DISTRICT SIZE: 12,000-24,000 Students	Learning Centers of 1000 Students (Twice)			INPUT:	FOR COMPARISON: W.N.Y. State Traditional (Plus Audio-Visual Instruction) [b]		
INPUT: (No CAI and no TEXTBOOKS) [a]	High	Median	Low		Third Quartile	Median	First Quartile
Staff							
Professional (Appendix S-2)	$199	$173	$146	Labor Costs:	$ 991	$ 932	867
Paraprofessional (Appendix T-2)	$125	$108	$ 92				
Student Assistant (Appendix U) [c]	85	85	85				
Sub-Totals	$409	$366	$323	Sub-Totals	$ 991	$ 932	$ 867
Instructional Facilities							
Annual Recurring Cost (Appendix W)	58	58	58	Teaching Materials:	Included in above. See Appendix R.		
District Instructional Expense							
Media Service Staff with fringe benefits (Appendix I)	13	10	7	Other Costs:	Included in sub-totals above.		
Media Service Equipment and Supplies (Appendix X)	2	2	2				
Fringe Benefits for Personnel in Learning Center (Appendix V-1, V-2)	98	85	71	Fringe Benefits:	223	205	188
TOTALS	$580	$521	$461		$1,214	$1,137	$1,055

[a] If textbooks are used, add $51 per student per year. See Appendix E-2.
[b] From Appendix R. See categories of labor costs.
[c] Based on a minimum wage of $2.50 per hour. If this were to rise to $3.00 per hour, add $101 instead of $85.

Table 9.5

(Erickson Study) Three-Day Design—2400 Students
SUMMARY OF ESTIMATED PER STUDENT PER YEAR INSTRUCTIONAL COSTS
FOR A CAPITAL-INTENSIVE MAN-MACHINE SYSTEM OF INDIVIDUALIZED EDUCATION
BELOW COLLEGE LEVEL (Stated in 1974-75 Dollars)

MODEL DISTRICT SIZE: 12,000–24,000 Students	Learning Centers of 1200 Students (Twice)			INPUT:	FOR COMPARISON: W.N.Y. State Traditional (Plus Audio-Visual Instruction) [b]		
	High	Median	Low		Third Quartile	Median	First Quartile
INPUT: (No CAI and no TEXTBOOKS) [a]							
Staff							
Professional (Appendix S-3)	$183	$159	$135	Labor Costs:	$ 991	$ 932	$ 867
Paraprofessional (Appendix T-3)	$113	$ 97	$ 82				
Student Assistant (Appendix U) [c]	85	85	85				
Sub-Totals	$381	$341	$302	Sub-Totals	$ 991	$ 932	$ 867
Instructional Facilities							
Annual Recurring Cost (Appendix W)	46	46	46	Teaching Materials:	Included in above. See Appendix R.		
District Instructional Expense							
Media Service Staff with fringe benefits (Appendix J)	13	10	7	Other Costs:	Included in sub-totals above.		
Media Service Equipment and Supplies (Appendix X)	2	2	2				
Fringe Benefits for Personnel in Learning Center (Appendix V-1, V-2)	89	77	65	Fringe Benefits:	223	205	188
TOTALS	$531	$476	$422		$1,214	$1,137	$1,055

[a] If textbooks are used, add $51 per student per year. See Appendix E-2.
[b] From Appendix R. See categories of labor costs.
[c] Based on a minimum wage of $2.50 per hour. If this were to rise to $3.00 per hour, add $101 instead of $85.

increased. The reason lies in what economists refer to as "volume," or turnover. The capital-intensiveness of the design makes it possible for the adult instructional staff, professional and paraprofessional, to work with double the number of students in the same time period. The staff are able to accomplish this because (1) cognitive instruction time is concentrated and not interrupted for non-cognitive learning, (2) real specialization (or division) of labor is present, (3) information transmission is largely carried out by nonhuman media in conjunction with the human energy of the student which is focused on his/her own program of learning, and (4) integration of man and machine in the learning/teaching process relies on both the human and nonhuman components to do what each is best equipped to perform.

It should be noted in Tables 9.6, 9.7, and 9.8 that the "Annual Recurring Cost" for "Instructional Facilities" is a constant figure of $156. A reference to Appendix P will confirm that this is double the amount of instructional time estimated as necessary by Kiesling in his most "capital-rich" strategy. Thus, the $156 figure also represents double the use of the capital input which is called for in the three-day design. One could argue that the figure should be $164, instead, since this is exactly twice the $82 cost of the Kiesling "Strategy-12" based upon the first ten percent of instructional time for ITV, Films, and Programmed Learning. If the higher capital input figure of $164 is used (ignoring the economies of scale of increased use of ITV), the additional $8 per student per year is minimal and has little effect upon the total costs as developed in the Tables.

Another comment, which could arise out of a consideration of the cost estimates for the three-day design (whether based on the Erickson or Kiesling studies), might concern what to many educators is a cardinal sin: the drastic reduction in the number of adults employed in the instructional process as compared with present education production functions. This will be further considered in Chapter X. However, it can be pointed out here that there is no reason to infer, either from the existing research

Table 9.6

(Kiesling Study) Three-Day Design—1600 Students
SUMMARY OF ESTIMATED PER STUDENT PER YEAR INSTRUCTIONAL COSTS
FOR A CAPITAL-INTENSIVE MAN-MACHINE SYSTEM OF INDIVIDUALIZED EDUCATION
BELOW COLLEGE LEVEL (Stated in 1974-75 Dollars)

MODEL DISTRICT SIZE: 12,000-24,000 Students	Learning Centers of 800 Students (Twice)			INPUT:	FOR COMPARISON: W.N.Y. State Traditional (Plus Audio-Visual Instruction) [b]		
	High	Median	Low		Third Quartile	Median	First Quartile
INPUT: (No CAI and no TEXTBOOKS) [a]							
Staff							
Professional (Appendix S-1)	$224	$194	$164	Labor Costs:	$ 991	$ 932	$ 867
Paraprofessional (Appendix T-1)	$145	$125	$105				
Student Assistant (Appendix U) [c]	85	85	85				
Sub-Totals	$454	$404	$354	Sub-Totals	$ 991	$ 932	$ 867
Instructional Facilities							
Annual Recurring Cost (Appendix P)	156	156	156	Teaching Materials:	Included in above. See Appendix R.		
District Instructional Expense							
Media Service Staff with fringe benefits (Appendix J)	13	10	7	Other Costs:	Included in sub-totals above.		
Media Service Equipment and Supplies (Appendix X)	2	2	2				
Fringe Benefits for Personnel in Learning Center (Appendix V-1, V-2)	110	96	81	Fringe Benefits:	223	205	188
TOTALS	$735	$668	$600		$1,214	$1,137	$1,055

[a] If textbooks are used, add $51 per student per year. See Appendix E-2.
[b] From Appendix R. See categories of labor costs.
[c] Based on a minimum wage of $2.50 per hour. If this were to rise to $3.00 per hour, add $101 instead of $85.

Table 9.7

(Kiesling Study) Three-Day Design—2000 Students
SUMMARY OF ESTIMATED PER STUDENT PER YEAR INSTRUCTIONAL COSTS
FOR A CAPITAL-INTENSIVE MAN-MACHINE SYSTEM OF INDIVIDUALIZED EDUCATION
BELOW COLLEGE LEVEL (Stated in 1974-75 Dollars)

MODEL DISTRICT SIZE: 12,000-24,000 Students	Learning Centers of 1000 Students (Twice)			INPUT:	FOR COMPARISON: W.N.Y. State Traditional (Plus Audio-Visual Instruction) [b]		
	High	Median	Low		Third Quartile	Median	First Quartile
INPUT: (No CAI and no TEXTBOOKS) [a]							
Staff							
Professional (Appendix S-2)	$199	$173	$146	Labor Costs:	$ 991	$ 932	$ 867
Paraprofessional (Appendix T-2)	$125	$108	$ 92				
Student Assistant (Appendix U) [c]	85	85	85				
Sub-Totals	$409	$366	$323	Sub-Totals	$ 991	$ 932	$ 867
Instructional Facilities							
Annual Recurring Cost (Appendix P)	156	156	156	Teaching Materials:	Included in above. See Appendix R.		
District Instructional Expense							
Media Service Staff with fringe benefits (Appendix J)	13	10	7	Other Costs:	Included in sub-totals above.		
Media Service Equipment and Supplies (Appendix X)	2	2	2				
Fringe Benefits for Personnel in Learning Center (Appendix V-1, V-2)	98	85	71	Fringe Benefits:	223	205	188
TOTALS	$678	$619	$559		$1,214	$1,137	$1,055

[a] If textbooks are used, add $51 per student per year. See Appendix E-2.
[b] From Appendix R. See categories of labor costs.
[c] Based on a minimum wage of $2.50 per hour. If this were to rise to $3.00 per hour, add $101 instead of $85.

Table 9.8

(Kiesling Study) Three-Day Design—2400 Students
SUMMARY OF ESTIMATED PER STUDENT PER YEAR INSTRUCTIONAL COSTS
FOR A CAPITAL-INTENSIVE MAN-MACHINE SYSTEM OF INDIVIDUALIZED EDUCATION
BELOW COLLEGE LEVEL (Stated in 1974-75 Dollars)

MODEL DISTRICT SIZE: 12,000-24,000 Students	Learning Centers of 1200 Students (Twice)			INPUT:	FOR COMPARISON: W.N.Y. State Traditional (Plus Audio-Visual Instruction) [b]		
INPUT: (No CAI and no TEXTBOOKS) [a]	High	Median	Low		Third Quartile	Median	First Quartile
Staff							
Professional (Appendix S-3)	$183	$159	$135	Labor Costs:	$ 991	$ 932	$ 867
Paraprofessional (Appendix T-3)	$113	$ 97	$ 82				
Student Assistant (Appendix U) [c]	85	85	85				
Sub-Totals	$381	$341	$302	Sub-Totals	$ 991	$ 932	$ 867
Instructional Facilities							
Annual Recurring Cost (Appendix P)	156	156	156	Teaching Materials:	Included in above. See Appendix R.		
District Instructional Expense							
Media Service Staff with fringe benefits (Appendix J)	13	10	7	Other Costs:	Included in sub-totals above.		
Media Service Equipment and Supplies (Appendix X)	2	2	2				
Fringe Benefits for Personnel in Learning Center (Appendix V-1, V-2)	89	77	65	Fringe Benefits:	223	205	188
TOTALS	$641	$586	$532		$1,214	$1,137	$1,055

[a] If textbooks are used, add $51 per student per year. See Appendix E-2.
[b] From Appendix R. See categories of labor costs.
[c] Based on a minimum wage of $2.50 per hour. If this were to rise to $3.00 per hour, add $101 instead of $85.

literature, *or* from experience in other fields where man-machine systems have been developing, *or* from the experiments already underway in education, that the staffing levels proposed in the three-day design are not adequate to accomplish the educational objectives desired. *What is more probable is that we are so conditioned to labor-intensive schooling that it is difficult to adjust to the concept of a capital-intensive process.*

But savings in the per student per year cost of instruction of up to 50 percent are difficult to ignore. (See Appendix Y.) In Figure 9.1, these savings are graphically illustrated by again comparing (1) the dollar cost of instruction per student per year, and (2) the number of students, ranging from 800 to 1200, in a learning center. The plotted average total cost (ATC) curves lie even further below the First Quartile expenditures of the reference group than did the similar curves for the five-day design. It should be noted, however, that they *are not twice as low*, since the three-day design uses the same equipment and facilities to process double the number of students in a standard school week, and also adds 30 percent more instructional staff. The significant additional savings accrue because both human and nonhuman resources are optimally allocated to take advantage of the productivity increases possible from the use of modern educational technology.

If the savings in the three-day (and five-day) design are thought of as an "income stream" over time, then the "rate of return" as a percent per annum on the initial capital investment for technologically up-to-date schools is sufficiently higher than the market rate of interest (i.e., the cost of financing the initial capital outlay) to make capital-intensive education a most attractive proposition. When there is added *the plus* of individualized instruction, it is difficult to imagine that rational citizens and their elected officials would hesitate to *update the little red schoolhouses* in every community.

There are certainly many students in American school systems who are psychologically "ready" for a learning environment similar to this three-day design. Such students might continue

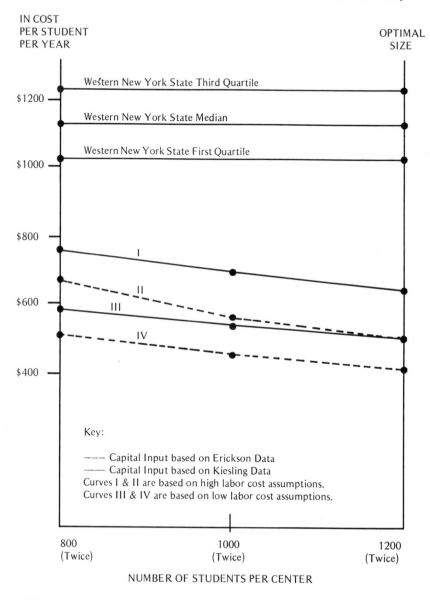

Figure 9.1: Three-day design—Average total cost curves: Instruction only.

IN COST
PER STUDENT
PER YEAR

OPTIMAL
SIZE

Western New York State Third Quartile

$1200

Western New York State Median

Western New York State First Quartile

$1000

$800

I

II

$600   III

IV

$400

Key:

——— Capital Input based on Erickson Data
——— Capital Input based on Kiesling Data
Curves I & II are based on high labor cost assumptions.
Curves III & IV are based on low labor cost assumptions.

800   1000   1200
(Twice)   (Twice)   (Twice)

NUMBER OF STUDENTS PER CENTER

restless and unfulfilled even under the five-day design. This possibility accentuates the need for carefully prepared pilot projects for *both* the transitional (five-day) and future (three-day) models. Only the development of such pilot models can actually confirm (or disavow) what considerable present research appears to indicate: that there *is* a more resource-conserving way of structuring learning environments than is presently in focus.

Note

1. The six-day week would require a different, and perhaps somewhat larger staffing arrangement. A reader interested in this model could easily calculate the revised labor costs from local data using the procedures described herein. Capital costs would tend to remain the same.

Chapter X

CAN CHANGE OCCUR?

Implications for Policy
and Further Research and Development

> ... in the sciences, and in true scholarship, the great advances are
> made by a patient willingness to reexamine what other people
> regard as obvious (Stone, 1977:10).

In presenting some possible ways in which modern technology
can economically and effectively individualize the educational
process for below-college-level students, no pronouncements have
been offered concerning the probable adoption of the capital-
intensive methods advocated. Technological change is but one
aspect of social change. *Resistance to change*—technological,
economic, political, or social—is an accepted fact in the area of
social science research. However, the *willingness to change* is
engendered gradually, by a slow erosion of the resistance to
change through the accumulation of evidence that the change
suggested is feasible and logical.

The preceding chapters have examined a cross-section of this
evidence from its historical and prophetic roots to the present

reality of affording dollars per student per year for capital-intensive education production functions.

The *feasibility* of change to man-machine systems of education is clearly seen in the dollar savings which can be generated as compared with the cost of present educational arrangements, and with no reduction in learning. There are also other absolute advantages: professionalization and specialization for teaching; technological parity for education with the rest of society; and release of monopolized resources of land and buildings for multiple usage.

The *logic* for change is another matter. Until knowledge of the present feasibility of capital-intensive education is disseminated widely, there will be little pressure from parents, or teachers, or taxpayers in general to attempt change. And even if parents become convinced of the benefits of individualization of learning coupled with per student per year dollar savings, the educational establishment represents an entrenched bureaucracy which appears to many as a formidable opponent of any drastic revision of the status quo. Teacher organizations may unconsciously misunderstand the rearrangement of the labor components in any new designs for capital-intensive education production functions, considering the rearrangement a threat to job security and the job market in general. An oversupply of teachers does not increase the probability that capital-intensive methods will be warmly received. Thus, any expectation that the soundness of the logic of moving to man-machine systems of education will achieve quick acceptance by educators should be viewed with reservations. One is tempted to yield to the pessimism which Oettinger voiced (1969:221):

> . . . every attempt to introduce technological change into education has revealed how profoundly *ignorant* we still are.

Lineberry (1967:195) has an interesting comment on the resistance to change which so often impedes the attempts of a society to prevent further erosion of its resources in an outmoded concept. He writes:

> The "antitechnologists" of antiquity were convinced that the book, by downgrading memory, could produce only a race of imbeciles.

Implicit in this illustration is the attitude which appears to represent a large segment of American society in relation to adapting education to 21st century technology. The use of a mechanical device to transmit information in a formal setting is viewed as ersatz, although the same mechanical information transmission in an informal setting is considered recreational, or even educational.

Associated with such antitechnological bias in the society are the personal concerns of educators (as a subculture of that society) with reference to job security and job status should man-machine systems of education become a reality. Perhaps the most poignant reminder of the dilemma facing teaching personnel in the public schools on this point is the sudden change in philosophy by the National Education Association from an idealism about "professionalism" to a pragmatic ideology of teacher "unionism."

Usdan (1963:2), and many others, have argued that "public schools are a political enterprise because *education must compete with other governmental functions for limited resources.*" Thus, in addition to creating improved awareness of the change in the goal of education, there must be structured a "political will" to accomplish the rearrangement of the educational process which is required. This political will involves *all* leadership in *all* sectors related to education—administration, labor relations, and legislation.

The fact that up to this point in time no one has seriously grappled with the economic feasibility of capital-intensive systems of education may indicate no faith in the political probability of such change. It is the course of least resistance to increase monetary inputs for traditional production functions. But as the collective needs of an urbanized society mount, the economic resources become even scarcer. This creates the pressure to find alternative solutions.

Meanwhile, the perceptive social critics reiterate that only drastic restructuring of the educational system can preserve the best of American culture.

It has been the contention of this book that rearranged education production functions represent a reasonable middle ground between what appear as two extremes: (1) deschooling, and (2) growing chaos in the status quo. By moving to the capital-intensive arrangements now possible, distinct advantages can accrue: (1) the savings in per student per year expenditures over present costs can literally "buy us into" the new system;[1] (2) the steady increase in the cost of education will be slowed in absolute dollars, and in further increases as a percent of Gross National Product; and (3) the professionalization of educators through greater specialization can continue, rather than being aborted in eventually futile efforts to preserve an outmoded methodology.

As was demonstrated in Chapters VIII and IX, the five-day and three-day designs, which exemplify the possibilities of capital-intensive arrangements, show sufficient savings in all of the restructured production functions to pay for the new capital equipment *plus* additional salary increments.

When changes in productivity are positive, unit costs fall; when changes in productivity are negative, unit costs rise. In the case of public education, the benefits derived from declining unit costs may be shared by the public in the form of declining or stabilized tax rates and by the employees of the system, teachers and support personnel, in the form of higher wages. These relationships are illustrated in Figure 10.1. While in the short run, the reduction in unit costs is made possible by a reduction in the numbers of professionally trained persons employed, in the long

Figure 10.1: Relationships between productivity, unit costs, wages, and taxes.

Productivity	Unit Costs	Wages	Taxes
↓	↑	↓	↑
↑	↓	↑	↓

run, positive changes in productivity generally result in more employment of people.[2] Such increases might take place in private sector firms producing the hardware and software required by the new system, and/or in the public sector if curriculum development adopted some of the techniques of the modern mass media.

Specifically, where might these savings be employed, and those of even greater magnitude when start up costs have been met, say, after the first five years?

1. Although the salary levels already included in the three-day and five-day designs are higher than presently being paid, there is ample reserve for further increases. These increases could take the form of (a) higher monetary gains, or (b) lower student/adult ratios,[3] or both.

2. Educational personnel not required for the staffing of the new designs could be phased out (through early retirement, or retraining) with no economic loss to themselves or to society.

3. Research and development efforts to further improve the

theory of learning, and its human and technological applications, could be increased. (In the long run, this would result in the creation of even more education-related jobs, either directly, or indirectly through the peripheral businesses which multiply in the private sector to support advanced technology.)

4. Community-related activities, which have the effect of increased socialization of students, could be added, including many special facilities for which funds now become available (with both volunteer and paid labor being used).

5. Reduced public sector expenditures for education could occur while maintaining the quality of services.

If education as a good or service were produced entirely in the private sector of the economy under relatively competitive conditions, rational decision-making today would mandate capital-intensive methods to better allocate scarce resources. Then, why should there be hesitation to change methodology *in the public interest* in the public sector? The OECD's[4] Center for Educational Research and Innovation (CERI) suggests that

> ... the sound and the fury produced at the thought of a change may in fact come from fear of inadequacy in a new situation: when the situation is faced and overcome, a process of identification with the new system begins. (1971:62)

CERI further emphasizes

> that there is no technological miracle in education. . . . Instead, educational technology has to be seen as part of a persistent and complex endeavor of bringing pupils, teachers, and technical means together in an effective way. (1971:7)

In fact, says CERI (1971:21) "factors to be taken into account . . . are likely to be the same whatever the educational system of which the learning system forms a part."

The Costs and the Benefits

If the transition is to be made to capital-intensive education, the principal parties involved (students, parents, the public, taxpayers, and teachers) must be convinced that their personal interests will be protected and possibly enhanced. The costs and benefits are not evenly distributed. What is in it for each party?

"What's in it for students?" The principal benefit to students and parents would be a more stimulating and hopefully a better formal learning experience. The experience would be personalized for each child, reducing the frustration and boredom which characterizes today's schools. The *time in actual learning*, which seems to be the strongest school factor correlated with cognitive achievement, would be increased, while time in school may decrease. The latter should be to the advantage of students but may cause problems for some parents as discussed below.

With the near infinite capacity of computers to catalog available curricular materials and to record pupil progress, and with the availability of electronic media to deliver prescribed educational stimuli to a child on call, learning experiences themselves should be more interesting and certainly varied beyond the present teacher, text, and test.

In short, the school should be restored as a place that is exciting for children to be in. With the rapid increase in demand for education a century ago, the nation was forced into a period of "mass education" which, given the then existing technology, and the societal goal of raising the literacy level, kept educational costs from rising as rapidly as they could have done had society attempted to extend the concept of individualized learning then present in the American Common School. "Mass education" was, and is, characterized by homogeneous grouping of children by age into grades, homogeneous grouping within grades by achievement, departmentalization, a fractured curriculum, and specialists who try to salvage the casualties of the system.

Initially, the mass school did have a sense of excitement about it because, despite its impersonal atmosphere, many new experiences awaited the child. Books were not then common in the home, especially books that would appeal to young children. Many children had their first exposure to recordings, motion pictures, slides, science labs, workshops, etc., in school. Today, most homes have a variety of books and magazines—even for the young. They also have records and record players; in many instances, there are highly sophisticated sound systems including recording and even broadcasting devices. Most homes have cameras, and an increasing number have movie cameras and projectors with sound attachments. Most homes are abundantly supplied with educational toys including microscopes, chemistry sets, and carpentry sets, with home workshops, and with facilities to carry on a variety of arts and crafts. Television has brought the whole world in "living color" to the modern child's family room or bedroom. The automobile and the airplane have taken him to more and more distant places than his grandparents had visited (or heard about) in a lifetime. There remains a portion of the school population, perhaps 25 percent (classified as "culturally deprived" in pedagogical terms), which does not readily have access to such advantages and still depends upon the schools for such stimulation. But for the other 75 percent, it is the *school* which appears "deprived," as it is compared in the mind of the child with the *real* world.

In a near-21st century world, the societal goal for education has changed. As the average level of literacy rises above the present secondary level of education, people tend to become both more analytical and more critical. While a *competency level of literacy* is still a necessary ingredient of the output demanded of education, an increasing percent of the human expectations relating to education is in the intelligent and literate *application of knowledge to human problems.* To be effective in this, the school must reflect the contemporary environment, not that of an earlier generation. Mass education, so called, is no longer adequate for a post-industrial, knowledge-based society.

Many adolescent children would also benefit from an early

introduction to gainful employment through new part-time job opportunities in the schools, in child care centers, or in the private sector under work/study arrangements.

"What's in it for parents?" The advantages to the child are also generally advantages to the parents. The only potentially significant disadvantage of the proposed system to parents is that their children, especially under the three-day model, would spend less time in school. The custodial role of contemporary schools is very important, especially for families where both parents are working. This in itself could defeat any attempt at modernizing the schools unless adequate provision is made for child-care. Such care could be accomplished with a portion of the savings in schooling costs now spent on child-care as opposed to time in learning. This could be done on school premises, or in other community facilities, using well-qualified supervisors (with older children acting as assistants, e.g., summer camp style). Since such centers could be technically part of the schooling function, they could make ideal locations for researching the affective and psychomotor parameters of learning. These areas receive little attention in conventional schools other than for "exceptional" (usually translated "problem") children. Child-care centers could be kept open longer than typical school hours to correspond to normal (even unusual) working hours. Centers specializing in child-care could also extend their services, perhaps at cost, to age groups younger than those served by the public schools.

As taxpayers, parents would also benefit financially from tax reductions and/or stabilization of school costs. A portion of this benefit would undoubtedly be passed on to their children.

"What's in it for the public/taxpayer?" The benefits to the public/taxpayer are not greatly different from the benefits to the student/parent, since the latter group makes up a substantial portion of the former. The benefit of greatest interest to the public/taxpayer at large, however, is the increased productivity of the educational system and the corresponding reduction or stabilization of public resources required by the educational establishment.

As noted earlier, whether measured in absolute terms or as a percent of the capacity of the economy to produce, American societal resources committed to education have reached an all-time high. This might still be defensible as public policy if projections of the traditional school age population pointed upward, or improvements of quality in education output could be readily shown, but neither of these justifications is valid.

While the numbers of persons in the 5-18 age group are declining, the opposite end of the age spectrum, over 65, which also makes a substantial demand for publicly supported services, is increasing. In addition, other demands on the public purse are growing, including: educational opportunities for those not presently served by public schools; welfare; medical assistance; and the rejuvenation of core cities.

Service industries, which include most public enterprises, now account for over half of the Gross National Product. As with education, these industries tend to be labor-intensive and technologically non-progressive (although there are important exceptions, such as the communications industry). If these industries continue to be non-progressive, they will seriously dampen the national growth potential. Each of the service industries needs to contemplate means for increasing its productivity as is contemplated here for education. Any increase could, and should, contribute to the general welfare.

What's in it for teachers and their professional organizations?" Stress has been placed upon the upgraded role of the teacher as a "new breed" of professional rather than the homogeneous role which is presently assigned to the great majority of educational personnel.

Some scholars have attempted to distinguish the professional from the non-professional. Vollmer and Mills (1966:34) in a survey of the literature cite William Goode,[5] who pointed out that

> a profession requires . . . (1) prolonged specialized training in a body of abstract knowledge, and (2) a collectivity or service

orientation in terms of professionally defined "needs" of the client, rather than what the client simply "wants."

Vollmer and Mills (1966:43-44) suggest the "basic elements" of professionalism fall

> into three categories: (1) acquisition of a specified technique supported by a body of theory; (2) development of a career supported by an association of colleagues; and (3) establishment of community recognition of professional status.

Perhaps the most complete definition cited by Vollmer and Mills (1966:vii) is that offered by Morris L. Cogan:[6]

> A profession is a vocation whose practice is founded upon an understanding of the theoretical structure of some department of learning or science, and upon the abilities accompanying such understanding. This understanding and these abilities are applied to the vital practical affairs of man. The practices of the profession are modified by knowledge of a generalized nature and by the accumulated wisdom and experience of mankind, which serve to correct the errors of specialism. The profession serving the vital needs of men, considers *its first ethical imperative* to be *altruistic service to the client.*

What "comes through" is the commitment to serving the needs of the client. This results in part from adequate training; but training alone is not enough. A delicate balance of training and empathy is essential for the "new" professional in education, and should be remunerated accordingly where demonstrated. How would such demonstration be evaluated? The sure answer will be in the attitudes of the final consumers of education, students and parents.

The "new" professional is a specialist not only in an area, or areas, of educational content, but also in procedural techniques. Training for the procedural techniques of diagnosis, prescription, motivation, facilitation, curriculum programming, and evaluation becomes fully as important as acquiring knowledge in a given subject area. Educational personnel who can be proficient in one or more content areas *and* in one or more kinds of procedural techniques will have longer periods of training (including internship experience), and will tend to command the highest level of remuneration in the learning centers proposed. The doctoral level (or equivalency) of educational achievement is undoubtedly implied for many professionals.

Paraprofessionals will also tend to specialize in both content and procedural techniques. In content, this may involve sub-areas of knowledge (e.g., arithmetic competency). In procedural techniques, a range of skills is probable, many of which are already developed in the growing number of teacher aides in the present system. Paraprofessionals are also educable within their rank. Most can, and will, improve their competency in both subject area and procedures. Some paraprofessionals will undoubtedly move on into the professional group as a result of both formal and on-the-job educational experience.

In observing the paraprofessional as used today, Leggatt (1969:182-183) points out that the teacher's role is affected by: (1) the provision of a "supplementary academic service for students"; (2) saving "the teacher from performing many subprofessional chores"; and (3) bringing about "a genuine restructuring of the teacher's role, a vertical rather than a horizontal . . . differentiation of work." All of these are implied to some degree in the proposed use of paraprofessionals in the designs discussed in this study, but restructuring the teacher's role is the most necessary. If factual information transmission is largely accomplished by nonhuman media, if supplementary drill and practice (i.e., "academic service"), and miscellaneous duties not directly related to the prime functions of the teacher are carried out by paraprofessionals, then both professional and paraprofessional roles will be clearly defined, specialization will become commonplace, and team interrelationships can be effective in creating and maintaining a learning environment for each student.

The obvious *caveat* pertains to morale and *esprit de corps.* Role definition and specialization are key components of a healthy working atmosphere. Upward mobility within rank (especially paraprofessional), and beyond rank, are also helpful. But the most important component is the inner attitude of the educator. Better controls than at present can and should be placed upon the entrance into the professional and paraprofessional roles of education of those individuals who, in the words of Silberman (1970), "don't like kids."

Specialization has been evolving in education for at least a century with the gradual creation of roles of principals (and vice-principals), librarians, guidance counselors, attendance officers, social workers, psychologists, nurse teachers, and subject specialists, including physical education, art, instrumental music, vocal music, and remedial teachers. Support personnel have also been added to the typical school staff, including custodians, secretaries, teacher aides, bus drivers, mechanics, dietitians, and lunchroom aides. The addition of these specialists has not been accompanied with a decline in the number of generalists, i.e., classroom teachers, as one might logically expect. Quite the contrary, while specialists have been added, the size of the typical class has declined. The result is that the average adult to pupil ratio is nearly double what it was 50 years ago.

As earlier chapters have shown, specialists *and* generalists are not needed in the numbers presently provided. Coordinated capital-intensive learning systems would permit substantial reductions in the numbers of generalists employed. Herein lies the greatest potential cost to teachers—one which eclipses the benefits associated with improved professional conditions.

This reduction in force and/or retraining can create substantial trauma for those involved and for their professional organizations. Movements of labor are essential if society is to improve its productivity through technological change, but it does *not* follow that it needs to be a financial burden to those concerned. Much of the *initial* saving from a capital-intensive mode would have to be used to offset any economic loss due to early retirement, or to cover costs of retraining and relocating younger educational personnel.

The classic case in modern labor history is a unique pact (signed in 1961 between the Pacific Maritime Association and the International Longshoremen's and Warehousemen's Union) known as the Mechanization and Modernization Agreement. It allowed shipowners to automate as necessary, and over a 5½ year period gave the Union $29 million for pensions and other purposes as its share of savings. In addition, a new approach to job security was developed (*Wall Street Journal,* November 20, 1964, p. 1).

Besides the welfare of its individual members, professional associations and/or unions will be concerned about their organizational futures, which depend upon membership and dues. If membership remains defined as has been typical to date, the potential membership would be smaller. This may happen in any event (though to a lesser extent) because of the decline in school age population, but salaries under traditional education can only be pushed so high, thus limiting income from dues assessments. Unions can counter this, and the movement has already begun, by including support personnel in their rank-and-file. Also, as indicated earlier, much of the new employment in the education industry is likely to be in private firms producing supporting hardware and software. Professional associations and unions can develop strategies to recruit membership in these areas. Finally, as noted, specialists tend to be more highly trained and therefore more highly paid. This will enable professionally-related organizations to levy higher membership dues, offsetting losses resulting from membership decline.

Implications for Policy

The "typical" school may not approach that which is described herein until approximately the year 2000. Even that date will not be realized unless immediate changes are made in public policy to facilitate transition. The first step is to appropriate sufficient funds at the federal and/or state levels to support the development of operating models. This needs to be followed by the development of a strategy for operationalizing as many capital-intensive schools as there are supplies of qualified professionals to staff them. At the same time, pre-service preparation programs for paraprofessionals and retraining programs for in-service teachers will need to be developed. Schools of education must also revise their curricula for professional training.

Most of the pieces for capital-intensive learning centers already exist, but not in one place, and no attempt has been made to organize them into a continuous learning system. In an article discussing the "Individually Guided Education" materials (IGE), itself a likely piece in the capital-intensive puzzle, B. Othanel Smith (1977) writes:

> Education, like other fields, tends to become saturated with pieces of information and materials which seem to bear little relation to one another. A significant breakthrough occurs when someone seizes upon a set of pieces, puts them together, adds a few pieces, and forms a new cluster of relationships that render teachers and other school personnel more effective.

Many of the major foundations and corporations, along with grants from the federal government, have facilitated the creation of *pieces* of the capital-intensive puzzle. Add to that what has been generated by alert researchers, curriculum specialists, and teachers, and most of the pieces (including supportive advances in educational philosophy and curricular theory) now exist. All that remains to be done is to mount an intensive effort to gather the pieces, put them together, and fill in the gaps. Such an effort is beyond the capacity of most school districts. Because the benefit of such developmental activities would be nationwide, it would seem that the National Institute of Education would be the appropriate funding source; but the benefit to most states is sufficient to justify their providing the developmental costs on their own. Developmental costs are estimated to total a relatively meager $5,000,000 over a five-year period, in 1977 dollars. This estimate does not include the operating costs of pilot models. The primary expense is for assembling a staff of curricular, media, psychological, sociological, and subject-matter evaluation specialists to design a *working plan* (as opposed to the "architectural sketches" which were presented in earlier chapters).

Design tasks include:

1. Develop a detailed "Calendar of Procedures" to be performed.

2. Inventory and catalog retrieval software and hardware now available for use in a capital-intensive, man-machine system of learning.

3. Assemble curriculum for a K-12 learning system (K-6 could be an initial model).

4. Write specifications for the necessary hardware, including a determination of the benefit-cost data relative to owning, or leasing, all or part.

5. Outline the diagnostic techniques for assessing individual student strengths and weaknesses in relation to learning activities K-12.

6. Prepare procedures for curriculum and learning activities prescriptions to meet individual student needs which have been diagnosed.

7. Arrange typical models of individual, small-group, and large-group scheduling of learning activities for the most efficient use of both human and nonhuman media in the learning process.

8. Determine and record the necessary evaluation and feedback instruments that will be used to maintain each student in continuous, individual, educational achievement through a secondary level of educational competence as that level is currently defined.

9. Make detailed job descriptions for each of the professional, paraprofessional, and student assistant categories of staff as previously outlined.

10. Design a program for evaluating the effectiveness of the pilot model.

Once a basic design is developed (a two- or three-year undertaking), it needs to be tested in, and adapted to, a variety of situations. To maximize the variety of settings, it again would make sense to have the coordination take place at the federal level. Implementing procedures include (not necessarily in this order):

1. Compile pilot-project budgets based upon each planning process, above, plus estimated administrative budget(s) for pilot-project(s) plus estimated budget(s) for lease of space for pilot-project(s).
2. Secure adequate funding for pilot models from federal and state governments, school districts, and/or foundations.
3. Establish liaison with pilot-project(s) funding agencies, including the development of the evaluation criteria required by such agencies.
4. Develop and activate (a) planning, development, and research component for pilot project(s), and (b) public information component.
5. Procure necessary hardware, software, space, transportation (if required), etc.
6. Set up an orientation program, and develop job application forms and interview questions for pilot-model staff(s).
7. Recruit and train staff for pilot project(s).
8. Formulate alternative student recruitment procedures for submission to pilot-project funding agencies (e.g., school districts, intermediate type districts, state education departments, etc.).
9. Recruit students, and orient them to the pilot-project(s), and secure pre-project baseline data.
10. Orient the parents of students to the pilot project(s).

As noted above, the savings resulting from capital-intensive education are likely to be the primary public appeal of the innovation initially; however, this may be surpassed in time by the appeal of the inherent beneficial qualities of the innovation itself. The primary forces working against the spread of the innovation may be teacher unions (although this opposition can be alleviated by previously suggested policies) and parental loyalty to tradition (inertia). The availability of appropriately trained personnel will also govern the rate at which dissemination may take place.

It is neither necessary nor desirable for an entire district to shift immediately to a capital-intensive mode of instruction; but at the school level, there is no middle ground. The philosophy, organization, staffing, and scheduling of the proposed innovation is not compatible with the "mass-school." Because of the perceived experimental nature of the schools, it would be ill-advised to require attendance—at least at first—within a given attendance area, as is typical practice today. Capital-intensive learning centers should be open to those preferring this mode of education from the entire district or region served by the sponsor, as special high schools have done for years in large cities, and as "magnet" schools have done more recently.

There is already a sizeable pool of teachers who are qualified and would welcome the opportunity to function in educational settings such as those envisioned. Scattered throughout the nation, there is a reading program here, a social studies program there, a science, or mathematics program, etc., designed in keeping with the proposed philosophy. Interestingly, capital-intensive individualized instruction is almost the rule rather than the exception in classes for exceptional children. Here the individual differences are so apparent that it is difficult to ignore them in prescribing instructional activities.

A district of 10,000 or more pupils should be able to operate one or two capital-intensive schools by drawing sympathetic professionals from existing staff. Smaller districts may have to cooperate at first, perhaps through an intermediate unit. State subsidy[7] of start-up costs would greatly facilitate the spread of the innovation until general public acceptance is established and its cost-saving potential is thoroughly documented.

Pre-service teacher preparation programs would have to be modified substantially and, to the extent possible, student teaching experiences should be shifted from conventional to pilot schools. The responsibilities of paraprofessionals would be upgraded to the point where increased formal training would be desirable. Such training would require the creation of new programs, probably at the junior college level (another employment opportunity for surplus educators). For persons already in service, retraining and reorientation programs would be necessary. These should be provided at no cost to the teacher by the district or intermediate unit.

Thus, state, federal, and/or foundation funds would be required to prime the pump by financing research and development costs, subsidizing early start-up costs, and financing the costs involved in establishing new pre-service programs for teachers and paraprofessionals. As understanding of, acceptance of, and demand for capital-intensive systems spread, districts and/or intermediate units would gradually expand the number of capital-intensive schools through local financing. Over a period of 20 years, capital-intensive schools could pervade the system, providing to society a more relevant educational process at substantially lower costs than projections for the contemporary system would indicate are possible.

Suggestions for Implementation

The learning systems envisioned in the preceding chapters assume an atmosphere of collaboration (or partnership) between educators, parents, and students. They all become "learners together" in assisting each individual student to become what that student can, and is willing to, become. Except under certain limited and special circumstances, age is irrelevant, just as it was in the American Common School ("Little Red Schoolhouse") of 100 years ago. Such a collaborative framework requires that a community (or school district) have *perception, preparation,* and *perseverance* in establishing the lines of communication necessary,

in order to replace the assumptions underlying traditional education with the new assumptions which make individualized,
capital-intensive learning possible. The hierarchical model of
yesterday must be metamorphosed into the collaborative model of
tomorrow.

Ryan (1976) has surveyed the research which related modern
organizational theory to the learning systems approach to education. She highlights the problem:

> ... there is much waste of talent, energy, and money because
> responsible agencies and organizations build walls around their
> own jurisdictions and prerogatives (Preface: xi).

She continues:

> It is a paradox of education that what is essentially a collabora-
> tive process—the process of learning and teaching—is increasingly
> fraught with differences and rivalries. People who should be
> working together are often at odds, and thus impair the learning
> which is their common objective (1976:1).

Most present proposals for reform tend to be similar to those tried
in various periods of the past. According to Ryan (1976:3-5),
these trusted remedies have been: revolution; change in the
balance of power; adversary action; advocacy; negotiation; and
collaboration. Of all of these methods, collaboration, though tried
the least, tends to succeed where the others either exacerbate the
problem(s), or fail to reach long run solution(s). Her case histories
(1976:7-27) indicate that where communities have determined to
try collaboration in solving educational problems:

> The prime characteristic common to all of these schools is that
> diverse groups of people worked together for a common objective
> (1976:17).

Perception. In every community there are generally individuals—parents, educators, and mature, discerning students—who sense that as the United States becomes more and more literate, organizations (business, education, government) must adapt to a greater sharing of the decision-making process, for, as Ryan puts it (1976:25), "human beings respond as positively to being involved in responsibility as they do negatively to being excluded from decision-making." If those in each community who perceive this prerequisite for improving education in their locality will ally themselves, and discuss their common concerns, the first step will have been taken.

Preparation. Two key steps are: (1) the establishment of effective fact-finding procedures; and (2) the development of certain basic skills in all of the people involved—skills which Ryan (1976:20) lists as:

> patience in hearing what a colleague *feels* in addition to what he seems to be saying; willingness to begin 'where people are' and patience to find out where that is; willingness to explore the issues raised; [and] learning how to be both lucid and honest in expressing one's views [italics added].

The preparation process will of necessity involve many hours of sharing views, analyzing facts, itemizing possible alternatives, and eventually obtaining a consensus on the most rational procedure, given all of the circumstances.

Perseverance. This undoubtedly overlaps and/or permeates both perception and preparation. Ryan writes (1976:27):

> As the experience of the identified partnership schools indicates, one does not successfully 'sell' change, or impose it. Change comes about by interaction, involving and affecting the individual or group acting as change agent as much as any others.

The result, however, is worth the effort since all parties to a collaborative (or partnership) approach benefit far more than they individually stand to benefit by any other alternative which has been tried. The key is to *listen* to each other, to *hear* each other, to *build confidence* in each other. Only when this has occurred can a commonly agreed upon philosophy of education lead to a commonly shared implementation. Surely, if education is what we say it is—to learn to think: broadly, but specifically; critically, but compassionately; tolerantly, but assuredly—then the proof that education has been acquired by those who profess to be educated will be in their ability to address the present problems of education in a collaborative spirit, recognizing that all that our civilization has achieved can be destroyed by our unwillingness to apply what we now know.

In Conclusion

The prime assumption of this book was stated at the outset: existing research already provides the data necessary to make a preliminary cost-comparison of traditional education versus a man-machine system. No sophisticated methodology has been employed; no far frontiers have been surveyed. There has only been a sincere attempt to envision (in the words of Milton Friedman) "something new in familiar material" (1953:43).

There is no mystique about this inquiry. Its assumptions and data are open. They should be challenged. If corrections which are needed are made, the decisions on future public policy may be less subject to the perpetuation of ideas which might impede giving the youth of this country the best opportunity to deal with the massive problems which their generation, like all other generations, must face.

If the conclusion of this research should prove sound, and the implementation practical, then it could happen that *both* students and teachers might enjoy learning—together.

The director of new media for a nationally known publisher stated to one of the authors, in a personal interview, October 1971, "Our organization has the capability to implement what you are proposing, but we do not want to be too far ahead of the market." *We*—parents, students, educators, *et al.*—*are* "the market." *Our* demand for relevant, technologically up-to-date education will elicit the private and public sector response which has helped our society solve past problems efficiently, and in the best interests of all concerned. May we recognize that this can be accomplished in the same spirit of partnership which has facilitated American development in the past.

Notes

1. This includes phasing out surplus personnel (see pp. 185-186).
2. This assumes national policies which do not adversely restrict growth in *real* aggregate demand.
3. As conditions change, these ratios can change in *either* direction. Should lower ratios be needed, the resources are available. The *caveat* is: only *change* which has been *demonstrated* (by learning theory) to be *necessary* should take place.
4. Organization for Economic Cooperation and Development.
5. See William Goode, "The Librarian: From Occupation to Profession?" *The Library Quarterly*, October 1961, *31*(4), 306-318.
6. See Morris L. Cogan, "Toward a Definition of Profession," *Harvard Educational Review*, Winter 1953, *23*, 33-50.
7. The authors are not referring to "grants" as that concept is now understood, but to the underwriting of carefully spelled-out *contractual agreements*.

BIBLIOGRAPHY

American Library Association. *Standards for School Library Programs.* Chicago: The Association, 1960.

Archer, L. Bruce. "Technological Innovation and Added-Value." In *Technological Innovation and the Economy.* Edited by Maurice Goldsmith. New York: John Wiley and Sons, 1970.

Arrow, Kenneth. *Social Choice and Individual Values,* 2nd ed. New York: John Wiley and Sons, 1963.

Ashby, Eric. "Machines, Understanding, and Learning: Reflections on Technology in Education," *The Graduate Journal,* 7(2), 1967. Quoted in The Carnegie Commission on Higher Education, *The Fourth Revolution: Instructional Technology in Higher Education.* New York: McGraw-Hill, 1972.

Atkinson, A.B. *The Economies of Inequality.* London: Oxford University Press, 1975.

Averch, Harvey, Stephen J. Carroll, Theodore S. Donaldson, Herbert J. Kiesling, and John Pincus. *How Effective Is Schooling: A Critical Review and Synthesis of Research Findings.* Santa Monica, California: The Rand Corporation, December 1971.

Barnet, Homer G. *Innovation, The Basis of Cultural Change.* New York: McGraw-Hill, 1953.

Baumol, William J. "Macroeconomies of Unbalanced Growth: The Anatomy of Urban Crisis." *American Economic Review,* 57(3), June 1967.

Baumol, William J. "Macroeconomies of Unbalanced Growth: Reply." *American Economic Review,* 62(1), March 1972.

Beck, Carlton, E., Normand R. Bernier, James B. MacDonald, and Thomas W. Walton. *Education for Relevance: The School and Social Change.* New York: Houghton-Mifflin, 1968.

Becker, Gary S. *Human Capital.* New York: National Bureau of Economic Research, Columbia University Press, 1964.

Bell, T.H. "Implications of the New Technologies for School and College Organization and Administration." In *To Improve Learning: An Evaluation of Educational Technology,* Vol. II. Edited by Sidney G. Tickton. New York: R.R. Bowker Company, 1971.

Bentham, Jeremy (1780). *An Introduction to the Principles of Morals and Legislation.* New York: Hafner, 1948.

Block, J.H., ed. *Mastery Learning: Theory and Practice.* New York: Holt, Rinehart, and Winston, 1971.

Bloom, Benjamin S. "Learning for Mastery." *Evaluation Comment,* 1(2), 1968.

Bloom, Benjamin S., ed. *Taxonomy of Educational Objectives: The Classification of Educational Goals, Handbook I: Cognitive Domain.* New York: David McKay Company, Inc., 1956.

Bloom, Benjamin S., J.T. Hastings, and G.F. Madaus. *Handbook of Formative and Summative Evaluation.* New York: McGraw-Hill, 1971.

Bolvin, John O. "The New Technology: Its Implications for Organizational and Administrative Change." In *To Improve Learning: An Evaluation of Educational Technology,* Vol. II. Edited by Sidney G. Tickton. New York: R.R. Bowker Company, 1971.

Bourne, Randolph S. *The Gary Schools.* Boston: Houghton-Mifflin, 1916.

Bowles, Samuel and Henry M. Levin. "The Determinants of

Scholastic Achievement—An Appraisal of Some Recent Evidence." *Journal of Human Resources*, 3(1), Winter 1968.

Buhler, Charlotte. "The Goal Structure of Human Life." *Journal of Humanistic Psychology*, 1(2), 1961, pp. 8-19.

Burkhead, Jesse. *Public School Finance: Economics and Politics.* Syracuse: Syracuse University Press, 1964.

Burkhead, Jesse *et al. Input and Output in Large-City High Schools.* Syracuse: Syracuse University Press, 1967.

Callahan, Raymond E. *Education and the Cult of Efficiency.* Chicago: University of Chicago Press, 1962.

Carnegie Commission on Higher Education. *The Fourth Revolution: Instructional Technology in Higher Education.* New York: McGraw-Hill, 1972.

Carter, Launor F. "The Challenge of Automation in Education." In *Programmed Learning and Computer-Based Instruction.* Edited by John E. Coulson. New York: John Wiley and Sons, Inc., 1962.

Center for Educational Research and Innovation. *Educational Technology: The Design and Implementation of Learning Systems.* Paris: Organization for Economic Cooperation and Development, 1971.

Center for Educational Research and Innovation. *Alternative Educational Futures in the United States and in Europe.* Paris: Organization for Economic Cooperation and Development, 1972.

Central Advisory Council for Education (England). *Children and Their Primary Schools,* (two volumes). London: Her Majesty's Stationery Office, 1967.

Chamberlain, Neil W. "Some Second Thoughts on the Concept of Human Capital." In *Human Capital Formation and Manpower Development.* Edited by Ronald A. Wystra. New York: The Free Press, 1971.

Chase, Clinton I. and H. Glenn Ludlow, eds. *Readings in Educational and Psychological Measurement.* Boston: Houghton Mifflin Company, 1966.

Christenson, P.E. "Work Sampling: A Stroboscopic View of Teaching." *Educational Administration and Supervision.* April 1956, pp. 230-243. Quoted in George Sullivan. *The Image of the Effective Teacher,* p. 23. New York: The Central School Study, Teachers College, Columbia University, 1962.

Cogan, Morris L. "Toward a Definition of Profession." *Harvard Educational Review,* 23, Winter 1953, pp. 33-50.

Cohn, Elchanan, assisted by Stephen D. Millman. *Economics of State Aid to Education.* Lexington, Massachusetts: Lexington Books (D.C. Heath and Company), 1974.

Coleman, James S. *et al. Equality of Educational Opportunity.* Washington, D.C.: Government Printing Office, 1966.

Coleman, James S. "Equality of Educational Opportunity: Reply to Bowles and Levin." *Journal of Human Resources,* 3(2), Spring 1968.

Combs, Arthur W. *Educational Accountability: Beyond Behavioral Objectives.* Washington, D.C.: Association for Supervision and Curriculum Development, 1972.

Committee for Economic Development. *Innovation in Education: New Directions for the American School.* New York: The Committee, July 1968.

Conant, Eaton H. *Teacher and Paraprofessional Work Productivity.* Lexington, Massachusetts: D.C. Heath and Company, 1973.

Conant, James B. *The American High School Today.* New York: McGraw-Hill, 1959.

Coombs, Philip H. *The World Educational Crisis: A Systems Analysis.* New York: Oxford University Press, 1968.

Curriculum Product Review, February 1974.

Dahl, R.A. and C.E. Lindblom. *Politics, Economics, and Welfare.* New York: Harper and Bros., 1953.

Davis, Robert H., Lawrence T. Alexander, and Stephen L. Yelon. *Learning System Design: An Approach to the Improvement of Instruction.* New York: McGraw-Hill, 1974.

Denemark, George W. "The Teacher and His Staff." *National Education Association Journal,* December 1966.

Denison, Edward F. *The Sources of Economic Growth in the United States and the Alternatives Before Us,* Supplementary Paper No. 13. New York: Committee for Economic Development, 1962.

Denison, Edward F. *Accounting for U.S. Economic Growth, 1929-69.* Washington, D.C.: Brookings Institution, 1972.

Dewey, John (1929). *The Quest for Certainty: A Study of the Relation of Knowledge and Action.* New York: Capricorn Books, 1960.

Dewey, John (1938). *Experience and Education.* New York: Collier Books, Crowell-Collier Publishing Company, 1963.

Digest of Educational Statistics, 1975 Edition. Washington, D.C.: U.S. Government Printing Office, 1976.

Dunn, Rita Stafford. "Individualizing Instruction—Teaming Teachers and Media Specialists to Meet Individual Student Needs." *Audiovisual Instruction,* 16(5), May 1971.

Dunn, Rita Stafford and Kenneth Dunn. "Practical Questions Teachers Ask About Individualizing Instruction—and Some Answers." *Audiovisual Instruction,* 17(1), January 1972.

Ebel, Robert L. "The School Consequences of Educational Testing." *School and Society,* November 14, 1964. In *Readings in Educational and Psychological Measurements.* Edited by Clinton I. Chase and H. Glenn Ludlow. Boston: Houghton Mifflin Company, 1966.

Eckstein, Otto. *Public Finance,* 2nd ed. Englewood Cliffs, New Jersey: Prentice-Hall, Inc., 1967.

Economic Report of the President, 1972. Washington, D.C.: Superintendent of Documents, 1972.

Edding, Friederick. "Educational Resources and Productivity." In *Essays on World Education: The Crisis of Supply and Demand.* Edited by George Z.F. Bereday. New York: Oxford University Press, 1969.

Education USA, "Individualization in Schools: The Challenge and the Options." Washington, D.C.: National School Public Relations Association, 1971.

Erickson, Carlton W.H. *Administering Instructional Media Programs.* New York: The Macmillan Company, 1968, Fourth Printing, 1970.

Erickson, Erik H. *Childhood and Society,* 2nd ed. New York: W.W. Norton and Company, Inc., 1963.

Erickson, Erik H. *Identity, Youth, and Crisis.* New York: W.W. Norton and Company, Inc., 1968.

Finley, Robert M. "Changes Required in Patterns of School Organization, Management, Staffing, Facilities, and Finance for Technology to Effectively Improve Instruction." In *To Improve Learning: An Evaluation of Educational Technology,* Vol. II. Edited by Sidney G. Tickton. New York: R.R. Bowker Company, 1971.

Foley, Cornelius J. and Mark Gelula. *Financing Our Schools, 1972.* Williamsville, New York: Western New York School Development Council, March 1972.

"Four-Day Week SAD, Maine." *Saturday Review Education Supplement,* 1(2), February 1973, p. 61.

Friedman, Milton. *Essays in Positive Economics.* Chicago: University of Chicago Press, 1953.

Gagne, Robert M. *The Conditions of Learning,* 2nd ed. New York: Holt, Rinehart, and Winston, Inc., 1970.

Garner, William T. " 'Discussion,' on papers by John Hause and Eric Hanushek." *American Economic Review,* 61(2), May 1971.

Gartner, Alan. *Paraprofessionals and Their Performance: A Survey of Education, Health, and Social Service Programs.* New York: Praeger Publishers, 1971.

Gartner, Alan, Mary Conway Kohler, and Frank Riessman. *Children Teach Children: Learning by Teaching.* New York: Harper and Row, 1971.

Gentile, J. Ronald, Thomas W. Frazier, and Mary C. Morris. *Instructional Applications of Behavior Principles.* Monterey, California: Brooks/Cole Publishing Company, 1973.

Gibbons, Maurice. *Individualized Instruction: A Descriptive Analysis.* New York: Teachers College Press, Columbia University, 1971.

Gibson, R. Oliver and Paul Lafornara. "Collective Legitimacy and Organizational Attachment: A Longitudinal Case Study of School Personnel Absences." Paper presented at American Educational Research Association, Chicago, April 4, 1972.

Ginsburg, Herbert. *The Myth of the Deprived Child: Poor Children's Intellect and Education.* Englewood Cliffs, New Jersey: Prentice-Hall, Inc., 1972.

Gintis, Herbert J. "Education, Technology, and the Characteristics of Worker Productivity." *American Economic Review,* 61(2), May 1971, pp. 266-279.

Glaser, Robert. *Teaching Machines and Programmed Learning, II: Data and Directions.* Washington, D.C.: Department of Audio-visual Instruction, National Education Association of the United States, 1965.

Goldberg, M.H., R.L. Dawson, and R.S. Barrett. "Comparison of Programmed and Conventional Instruction Methods." *Journal of Applied Psychology,* 48, 1944, pp. 110-114.

Goldman, Thomas A., ed. *Cost-Effectiveness Analysis: New Approaches in Decision-Making.* New York: Frederick A. Praeger, 1967.

Goode, William. "The Librarian: From Occupation to Profession?" *The Library Quarterly,* 31(4), October 1961, pp. 306-318.

Gordon, George N. *Educational Television.* New York: The Library of Education, Center for Applied Research in Education, Inc., 1968.

Grant, W. Vance and George Lind. *Digest of Educational Statistics, 1975 Edition.* Washington, D.C.: U.S. Government Printing Office, 1976.

Guthrie, James W. "What the Coleman Reanalysis Didn't Tell Us." *Saturday Review,* 55(3), July 22, 1972, p. 45.

Guthrie, James W. "Alternative Concepts of School Efficiency." Unpublished paper delivered at the New York State Education Department Conference on School Efficiency, Albany, New York, June 9, 1977.

Hallak, Jacques. *The Analysis of Educational Costs and Expenditure,* Fundamentals of Educational Planning, Booklet No. 10. Paris: UNESCO International Institute for Educational Planning, 1969.

Hansen, W. Lee, ed. *Education, Income, and Human Capital.* New York: National Bureau of Economic Research, 1970.

Hanushek, Eric. "The Production of Education, Teacher Quality, and Efficiency." In *Do Teachers Make a Difference?* U.S. Department of Health, Education, and Welfare, Office of Education. Washington, D.C.: U.S. Government Printing Office, 1970.

Hanushek, Eric. "Teacher Characteristics and Gains in Student Achievement: Estimation Using Micro Data." *American Economic Review,* 61(2), May 1971, pp. 280-288.

Harrington, Michael. *The Other America.* New York: Macmillan Company, 1962.

Havighurst, Robert J. *Developmental Tasks and Education,* 3rd ed. New York: David McKay Company, Inc., 1972.

Hempel, Marvin W. "Accountability and Technology: A Change of Emphasis in Business Education." *Audiovisual Instruction,* 16(5), May 1971.

Hermansen, Kenneth L. and James R. Gove. *The Year-Round School.* Hamden, Connecticut: Linnet Books, 1971.

Hicks, J.R. *Value and Capital, An Enquiry into Some Fundamental Principles of Economic Theory.* Oxford: Clarendon Press, 1939.

Hinrichs, Harley H. and G.M. Taylor. *Program-Budgeting and Benefit-Cost Analysis.* Pacific Palisades, California: Goodyear Publishing Company, Inc., 1969.

Hughes, John L., ed. *Programmed Learning: A Critical Evaluation.* Chicago: Education Methods, Inc. (Subsidiary of Aldine Publishing Company), 1963.

Hughes, John L. and W.J. McNamara. "A Comparative Study of Programmed and Conventional Instruction in Industry." *Journal of Applied Psychology,* 1961, pp. 225-231.

Hughes, Marie. "Development of the Means for the Assessment of the Quality of Teaching in Elementary Schools, a Research Report." Salt Lake City: The University of Utah, 1959. Quoted in George Sullivan. *The Image of the Effective Teacher,* pp. 59-74. New York: The Central School Study, Teachers College, Columbia University, 1962.

Husen, Torsten. "Does More Time in School Make a Difference?" *Saturday Review,* 55(18), April 29, 1972, pp. 32-35.

Huxley, Aldous. *Brave New World.* London: Chatto and Windus, 1932.

Igoe, Joseph. "The Development of Mathematical Models for the Allocation of School Funds in Relation to School Quality." Ed.D. dissertation, State University of New York at Buffalo, 1968.

James, H. Thomas and Henry M. Levin. "Financing Community Schools." *Community Control of Schools.* Henry M. Levin, ed. Washington, D.C.: The Brookings Institution, 1970.

Jamison, Dean, Patrick Suppes, and Stuart Wells. "The Effectiveness of Alternative Instructional Media: A Survey." *Review of Educational Research,* 44(1), 1974.

Jencks, Christopher. "Is the Public School Obsolete?" *The Public Interest,* 2, Winter 1966, pp. 18-27.

Jencks, Christopher *et al. Inequality: A Reassessment of the Effect of Family and Schooling in America.* New York: Basic Books, 1972.

Jevons, William S. (1882). *The State in Relation to Labour.* Quoted in Edmund Whittaker. *Schools and Streams of Economic Thought.* Chicago: Rand McNally, 1960, p. 272.

Katzman, Martin T. "Distribution and Production in a Big City Elementary School System." *Yale Economic Essays,* 8(1), Spring 1968.

Katzman, Martin T. *The Political Economy of the Urban Schools.* Cambridge, Massachusetts: Harvard University Press, 1971.

Kiesling, Herbert J. *High School Size and Cost Factors.* Final Report for the U.S. Office of Education, Bureau of Research, Project No. 6-1590, March 1968.

Kiesling, Herbert J. "On the Economic Analysis of Educational Technology." In *To Improve Learning: An Evaluation of Educational Technology,* Vol. II. Edited by Sidney G. Tickton. New York: R.R. Bowker Company, 1971.

Kiesling, Herbert J. *Multivariate Analysis of Schools and Educational Policy,* P4595. Santa Monica, California: The Rand Corporation, 1971.

Kindleberger, Charles P. *Economic Development,* 2nd ed. New York: McGraw-Hill, 1965.

Kliebard, Herbert M. "Bureaucracy and Curriculum Theory." In *Freedom, Bureaucracy, and Schooling, 1971 Yearbook,* pp. 74-93. Edited by Vernon Haubrich. Washington, D.C.: Association for Supervision and Curriculum Development, 1971. Reprinted in *Curriculum Theorizing: The Reconceptualists.* Edited by William Pinar. Berkeley, California: McCutchan Publishing Corp., 1975, pp. 51-69.

Koerner, James D. *The Miseducation of American Teachers.* Boston: Houghton-Mifflin, 1963.

Kozol, Jonathan. *Death at an Early Age.* Boston: Houghton-Mifflin, 1967.

Krathwohl, David R., B.S. Bloom, and B.B. Masia. *Taxonomy of Educational Objectives: The Classification of Educational Goals, Handbook II: Affective Domain.* New York: David McKay Company, Inc., 1964.

Kuznets, Simon. *Modern Economic Growth: Rate, Structure, and Spread.* New Haven: Yale University Press, 1966.

Leggatt, Timothy. "The Use of Nonprofessionals in Large-City Systems." In *Innovation in Mass Education.* Edited by David Street. New York: John Wiley and Sons, 1969.

Leonard, George B. *Education and Ecstasy.* New York: Delacorte Press, 1968.

Levin, Henry M. "Cost-Effectiveness Analysis and Educational Policy-Profusion, Confusion, Promise." Research and Development Memorandum No. 41. Stanford, California: School of Education, Stanford University, December 1968.

Levin, Henry M. "A Cost-Effectiveness Analysis of Teacher Selection." *The Journal of Human Resources,* 5(1), Winter 1970.

Levin, Henry M. "A New Model of School Effectiveness." *Do Teachers Make a Difference?* Washington, D.C.: Office of Education, 1970.

Levine, Donald M. "Educational Policy After Inequality." *Teachers College Record,* 75(2), 1972.

Lineberry, William P. *New Trends in the Schools.* New York: The H.W. Wilson Company, 1967.

Lippitt, Peggy. *Students Teach Students.* Bloomington, Indiana: The Phi Delta Kappa Educational Foundation, 1975.

Little, I.M.D. *A Critique of Welfare Economics,* 1st ed. Oxford: Oxford University Press, 1957.

Loughary, John W. *et al. Man-Machine Systems in Education.* New York: Harper and Row, 1966.

Lumsdaine, A.A. and R. Glaser, eds. *Teaching Machines and Programmed Learning: A Source Book.* Washington, D.C.: National Education Association, 1960.

Luskin, Bernard J. *et al. Everything You Always Wanted to Know About CAI But Were Afraid to Ask.* Huntington Beach, California: Computer Uses in Education, 1972.

Mansfield, Edwin. *Technological Change,* 2nd ed. New York: W.W. Norton and Company, Inc., 1971.

Martin, John H. and Charles H. Harrison. *Free to Learn: Unlocking and Ungrading American Education.* Englewood Cliffs, New Jersey: Prentice-Hall, Inc., 1972.

May, Rollo. *Man's Search for Himself.* New York: The New American Library, Inc., 1967.

Mayer, Martin. *The Schools.* New York: Harper and Row, 1961.

Mayeske, George W. *et al. A Study of Our Nation's Schools.* Washington, D.C.: U.S. Government Printing Office, 1972.

McConnell, Campbell R. *Economics: Principles, Problems, and Policies, Sixth Edition.* New York: McGraw-Hill Book Company, 1975.

McCusker, Henry F., Jr. and Philip H. Sorensen. "The Economics of Education." In *The New Media and Education: Their Impact on Society.* Edited by Peter H. Rossi and Bruce J. Biddle. Chicago: Aldine Publishing Company, 1966: reprint ed., Doubleday and Company, Inc., Anchor Books Edition, 1967.

McKenna, Bernard H. and James B. Pugh, Jr. "Performance of Pupils and Teachers in Small Classes Compared to Large." *IAR-Research Bulletin,* 4(2), February 1964, pp. 1-4.

McMullen, David W. "Generating Concepts by Computer." Paper presented at Fourth Annual Invitational Interdisciplinary Meeting on Structural Learning, Philadelphia, 1973.

McNeil, J.D. "Programmed Instruction Versus Usual Classroom Procedures in Teaching Boys to Read." *American Educational Research Journal,* (1) 1964, pp. 113-119.

Mill, John Stuart (1861). *Utilitarianism, Liberty, and Representative Government,* Everyman's Library Edition, New York and London, 1914.

Morrison, Henry C. *The Curriculum of the Common School.* Chicago: University of Chicago Press, 1940.

Moynihan, Daniel S. *et al. On Equality of Educational Opportunity.* New York: Random House, 1972.

Murphy, Judith and Ronald Gross. *Learning by Television.* New York: Fund for the Advancement of Education, 1966.

Myint, Hla. *Theories of Welfare Economics.* Cambridge, Massachusetts: Harvard University Press, 1948.

National Audio-Visual Association, Inc. *The Audio-Visual Equipment Directory,* 1977-78 Edition. Fairfax, Virginia: The Association, 1977.

Nephew, Charles T. "Guides for the Allocation of School District Financial Resources." Ed.D. dissertation, State University of New York at Buffalo, 1969.

Newsweek, August 13, 1973.

Nikolai, Irvin. "Differentiated Personnel: A Rationale." In *Educational Manpower.* Edited by James L. Olivero and Edward G. Buffie. Bloomington, Indiana: Indiana University Press, 1970.

O'Donoghue, Martin. *Economic Dimensions in Education.* Chicago: Aldine-Atherton, 1971.

Oettinger, Anthony G. and Sema Marks. *Run, Computer, Run: The Mythology of Educational Innovation.* Cambridge, Massachusetts: Harvard University Press, 1969.

Ogburn, William Fielding (1922). *Social Change.* Gloucester, Massachusetts: reprint, Peter Smith, 1964.

Pearl, Arthur. "An Address at the Planning Conference on New Careers," Kansas City, Missouri, 1967. In *Paraprofessionals and Their Performance: A Survey of Education, Health, and Social Service Programs,* pp. 19 and 34. Edited by Alan Gartner. New York: Praeger Publishers, 1971.

Peterson, Gary T. "Salaries of Doctoral Instructional Media/Technology Graduates, 1968-70." *Audiovisual Instruction,* 17(7), September 1972, pp. 47-49.

Piaget, Jean. *The Child and Reality.* New York: The Viking Press, Inc., 1973.

Pigou, Arthur C. (1920). *The Economics of Welfare,* 4th ed. New York: St. Martin's Press, 1960.

Postlethwait, S.N., J. Novak, and H.T. Murray, Jr. *The Audio-Tutorial Approach to Learning,* 2nd ed. Minneapolis, Minnesota: Burgess Publishing Company, 1969.

Potter, Robert E. *The Stream of American Education.* New York: American Book Company, 1967.

Rawls, James R., Oliver Perry, and Edwin O. Timmons. "A Comparative Study of Conventional Instruction and Individual Programmed Instruction in the College Classroom." In *Educational Research: Readings in Focus,* pp. 388-394. Irwin J. Lehmann and William A. Mehrens. New York: Holt, Rinehart, and Winston, Inc., 1971.

Reder, Melvin W. *Studies in the Theory of Welfare Economics.* Oxford: Oxford University Press, 1947.

Richmond, George. "An Alternative to the Deschooled Society." *Saturday Review,* 55(26), June 24, 1972, pp. 44-45.

Robbins, Lionel. *An Essay on the Nature and Significance of*

Economic Science. London: Macmillan & Company, Ltd., 1946.

Roe, A. "Automated Teaching Methods Using Linear Programs." *Journal of Applied Psychology,* 46, 1962, pp. 198-201.

Rossi, Peter H. and Bruce J. Biddle, eds. *The New Media and Education: Their Impact on Society.* Chicago: Aldine Publishing Company, 1966.

Rott, Marilyn Hopkins *et al. Financing Our Schools, 1976.* Lancaster, New York: Board of Cooperative Educational Services, First Supervisory District of Erie County, 1976.

Rubin, Louis. *The Future of Education: Perspectives on Tomorrow's Schooling.* Boston: Allyn and Bacon, Inc., 1975.

Ryan, Charlotte P. *The Open Partnership: Equality in Running the Schools.* New York: McGraw-Hill, 1976.

Saettler, Paul. *A History of Instructional Technology.* New York: McGraw-Hill Book Company, 1968.

Samuelson, Paul A. *Economics: An Introductory Analysis,* Tenth Edition. New York: McGraw-Hill Book Company, 1976.

Schaefer, William T. (Chicago: Univac Division of Sperry Rand Corporation.) Personal letter to Edward J. Willett, December 20, 1972.

"School Taxes Up 17% in Year, Levitt Reports." *Buffalo Evening News,* October 26, 1972.

Schultz, Theodore W. "Investment in Human Capital." *American Economic Review,* 51(1), March 1961.

Schultz, Theodore W. *The Economic Value of Education.* New York: Columbia University Press, 1963.

Schultz, Theodore W. "The Human Capital Approach to Education." In *Economic Factors Affecting the Financing of Education,* Vol. 2. Edited by R.L. Johns *et al.* Gainesville, Florida: National Educational Finance Project, 1970.

Shapiro, Eli and William L. White, eds. *Capital for Productivity and Jobs.* Englewood Cliffs, New Jersey: Prentice-Hall, Inc., 1977.

Sidgwick, Henry. *The Principles of Political Economy,* 3rd ed. London: 1901.

Silberman, Charles E. "Investment in Human Capital." *American Economic Review,* 51(1), March 1962.

Silberman, Charles E. *Crisis in the Classroom.* New York: Random House, 1970.

Silberman, Harry F. "Characteristics of Some Recent Studies of Instructional Methods." In *Programmed Learning and Computer-Based Instruction.* Edited by John E. Coulson. New York: John Wiley and Sons, Inc., 1962.

Simon, Kenneth A. and W. Vance Grant. *Digest of Educational Statistics, 1970 Edition.* Washington, D.C.: U.S. Government Printing Office, September 1970.

Skinner, B.F. *The Technology of Teaching.* New York: Appleton-Century-Crofts, 1968.

Smith, Adam. *An Inquiry into the Nature and Causes of the Wealth of Nations,* The Harvard Classics, Vol. 10. New York: P.F. Collier and Son, 1909.

Smith, B. Othanel. "A Concept of Teaching." *Teachers College Record,* 61, 1960.

Smith, B. Othanel. "IGE and Teacher Education." An unpublished paper circulated by The Wisconsin Research and Development Center for Cognitive Learning, Madison, Wisconsin, 1977.

State of New York, Department of Audit and Control. "Uniform System of Accounts for School Districts—Double Entry Basis." Albany: The Department, 1965.

Stoddard, Alexander J. *Schools for Tomorrow.* New York: Fund for the Advancement of Education, 1957.

Stodolsky, Susan S. and Gerald Lesser. "Learning Patterns in the Disadvantaged." *Harvard Educational Review,* 37(4), 1967, pp. 546-593.

Stolurow, Lawrence M. "Model the Master or Master the Teaching Model." In J.D. Krumboltz (Ed.), *Learning and the Educational Process.* Chicago: Rand McNally and Co., 1965.

Stolurow, Lawrence M. "Programmed Instruction and Teaching Machines." *The New Media and Education: Their Impact on Society.* Edited by Peter H. Rossi and Bruce J. Biddle. Garden

City, New York: Doubleday and Company, Inc., Anchor Books Edition, 1967.

Stone, I.F. Quoted in *The Wall Street Journal*, March 4, 1977, p. 10.

Street, David, ed. *Innovation in Mass Education*. New York: John Wiley and Sons, 1969.

Sullivan, George. *The Image of the Effective Teacher*. New York: The Central School Study, Teachers College, Columbia University, 1962.

Swanson, Austin D. *Effective Administrative Strategy*. New York: Institute of Administrative Research, Teachers College, Columbia University, 1961.

Swanson, Austin D. *The Effect of School District Size on School Costs*. Buffalo: The Western New York School Study Council, 1966.

Swanson, Austin D. "Administrative Accountability Through Cost-Effectiveness Analysis: A Proposal." In *Emerging Patterns of Administrative Accountability*. Edited by Lesley H. Browder, Jr. Berkeley, California: McCutchan Publishing Company, 1971.

Swanson, Austin D. *et al*. *A Study of the Benefits and the Effectiveness of Occupational Programs*. Buffalo, New York: The Western New York Educational Service Council. State University of New York, 1976.

Swanson, Austin D. "Equality, Integration, and Metropolitanism: New Public School Compromise," *Educational Administration Quarterly*, 13(1), 1977.

Swanson, Austin D. *et al*. "A Study of the Costs, Benefits, and Effectiveness of Occupational Education." An unpublished paper read at the 1976 Annual Meeting of the American Educational Research Association, San Francisco, California, March 1976.

Swanson, Austin D. and Edward J. Willett. "Modernizing the Little Red Schoolhouse." An unpublished paper presented to the Western New York School Boards Institute, State University of New York at Buffalo, 1974.

Swanson, Austin D. and Edward J. Willett. "A Pilot Model of Capital-Intensive Education to Promote Individualized Instruction and the Stabilization of Educational Costs." Proposal submitted to the National Science Foundation by The Research Foundation of State University of New York in behalf of The State University of New York at Buffalo, 1975.

Swanson, Austin D. and Edward J. Willett. "Updating the Little Red Schoolhouse: Toward Developing a Pilot Model of Capital-Intensive Education to Promote Individualized Instruction and Stabilize Educational Costs." *Educational Technology*, 17(1), January 1977, pp. 27-33.

Thomas, J. Alan. *Efficiency in Education: A Study of the Relationship Between Selected Inputs and Mean Test Scores in a Sample of Senior High Schools.* Ph.D. dissertation, Stanford University, School of Education, 1962.

Tickton, Sidney G., ed. *To Improve Learning: An Evaluation of Educational Technology,* Vol. I and II. New York: R.R. Bowker Company, 1970, and 1971, respectively.

Toffler, Alvin. *Future Shock,* Bantam Edition. New York: Bantam Books, Inc., 1971.

Tyack, David B. *The One Best System: A History of American Urban Education.* Cambridge, Massachusetts: Harvard University Press, 1974.

Tyler, Ralph W. "General Statement on Evaluation." *The Journal of Educational Research,* 35, March 1942, pp. 492-501. In *Readings in Educational and Psychological Measurement.* Edited by Clinton I. Chase and H. Glenn Ludlow. Boston: Houghton Mifflin Company, 1966.

U.S. Department of Health, Education, and Welfare, Office of Education. *The Common Core of State Educational Information,* State Educational Records and Reports Series: Handbook I, Bulletin, 1953, No. 8. Washington, D.C.: U.S. Government Printing Office, 1953.

U.S. Department of Health, Education, and Welfare, Office of Education. *Financial Accounting for Local and State School*

Systems—Standard Receipt and Expenditure Accounts: Handbook II, Bulletin, 1957, No. 4. Washington, D.C.: U.S. Government Printing Office, 1957.

U.S. Department of Labor. *Manpower Report of the President, 1972.* Washington, D.C.: U.S. Government Printing Office, March 1972.

"U.S. Schools to Spend a Record $90.5 Billion." *Buffalo Evening News*, September 15, 1972.

Usdan, Michael E. *The Political Power of Education in New York State.* New York: Institute of Administrative Research, Teachers College, Columbia University, 1963.

Usdan, Michael D., David W. Minar, and Emanuel Hurwitz, Jr. *Education and State Politics.* New York: Teachers College Press, Columbia University, 1969.

Uttal, William R. "On Conversational Interaction." *Programmed Learning and Computer-Based Instruction.* New York: John Wiley and Sons, Inc., 1962.

Vaizey, John. *The Economics of Education.* London: Faber and Faber, 1962.

Vaizey, John. *Education in the Modern World.* New York: McGraw-Hill, 1967.

Vincent, William S. "Further Clarification of the Class Size Question." *IAR-Research Bulletin*, 9(1), November 1968.

Vollmer, Howard M. and Donald L. Mills, eds. *Professionalization.* Englewood Cliffs, New Jersey: Prentice-Hall, 1966.

Von Bohm-Bawerk, Eugene. *The Positive Theory of Capital.* London: MacMillan and Company, 1891 (Published in German in 1889; translated by W. Smart).

Washburne, Carleton W., Mabel Vogel, and William S. Gray. *A Survey of the Winnetka Public Schools.* Bloomington, Illinois: Public School Publishing Company, 1926.

Weintraub, Sidney. *Intermediate Price Theory.* Philadelphia: Chilton Books, 1964.

Welch, Finis. "Measurement of the Quality of Schooling." *American Economic Review*, 56(2), May 1966.

Welsh, P., J.A. Antionetti, and P.W. Thayer. "An Industry-Wide Study of Programmed Instruction." *Journal of Applied Psychology*, 1965, 49, pp. 61-73.
White, Peter T. "Behold the Computer Revolution." *National Geographic*, 138(5), November 1970.
Whitehead, Alfred N. (1929). *The Aims of Education.* New York: The New American Library of World Literature, Inc., 1949.
Whittaker, Edmund. *Schools and Streams of Economic Thought.* Chicago: Rand McNally and Company, 1960.
Willett, Edward J. "A Macro-Approach to Education Production Functions." Paper presented at the New York State Economic Association, Rensselaer Polytechnic Institute, Troy, New York, April 17, 1971.
Willett, Edward J. "Designs for Structuring Capital-Intensive (Rather than Labor-Intensive) Education Production Functions for the Promotion of Individualized Learning Below College Level." Ed.D. dissertation, State University of New York at Buffalo, 1973.
Willey, Lawrence V., Jr. "Computers and Instructional Productivity." Report to International Business Machines Corporation, Data Processing Division, Bethesda, Maryland, May 1, 1975.
Woodson, Marshall S. "Effect of Class Size as Measured by an Achievement Test Criterion." *IAR-Research Bulletin*, 8(2), February 1968, pp. 1-6.

APPENDIX

COST ESTIMATES FOR MEDIA EQUIPMENT UNITS FOR AN 800-1200 STUDENT LEARNING CENTER[1]

Kinds of Media Equipment	Units Needed E^2	W/S^3	Unit Cost (Erickson) 1968 Dollars	Total Cost (Erickson) 1968 Dollars	1977-78 Cost Per Unit[4]	Total Cost in 1977 Dollars
For Learning-Center-wide use:						
1. Light Control System	92	10	$300	$27,600	$400	$4,000
2. Electrical Outlets	184	40	30	5,520	50	2,000
3. Projection Screens	92	10	60	5,520	75	750
4. Projection Stands	92	10	35	3,220	65	650
5. Motion Picture Projectors (Standard Type)	46	10	600	27,600	883	8,830
6. Ditto 8 mm Cartridge Type	20	10	90	1,800	219	2,190
7. Filmstrip/Slide Projectors	60	10	100	6,000	115	1,150
8. Ditto-Remote Control - 2 x 2	30	10	120	3,600	208	2,080
9. Tachistoscopic Projectors (35 mm) (continued)	30	10	250	7,500	265	2,650

[1]Based on Erickson, Carlton W.H., *Administering Instructional Media Programs* (New York: Macmillan Company, 1968, 1970), pp. 548-549.

[2]Erickson, for a 1600-student middle school, 92 Teaching Stations.

[3]Willett/Swanson for an 800-1200-student learning center, K-12, 10 Learning Areas.

[4]Except for items 1 and 2, which are estimated, prices are from *The Audio-Visual Equipment Directory*, 1977-78 Edition (National Audio-Visual Association, Inc., Fairfax, VA 22030), and are for the lowest priced equipment listed which will accomplish the instructional purpose required. Figures are rounded.

APPENDIX A (continued)

Kinds of Media Equipment	Units Needed E	Units Needed W/S	Unit Cost (Erickson) 1968 Dollars	Total Cost (Erickson) 1968 Dollars	1977-78 Dollar Cost Per Unit	Total Cost in 1977 Dollars
10. Slide Projectors (3¼ x 4)	15	10	$150	$ 2,250	$ 464	$ 4,640
11. Overhead Projectors (Heavy Duty)	50	10	400	20,000	156	1,560
12. Ditto-Lightweight	42	None	160	6,720	None	None
13. Opaque Projectors	5	10	350	1,750	289	2,890
14. Tape Recorders—Manual Control Model	50	10	200	10,000	260	2,600
15. Tape Recorders—Cassette	None	100	None	None	65	6,500
16. Portable, 10-Station Tape Listening Units with Plug-in Jacks and Headsets	15	None (replaced by cassette equipment, above)	450	6,750	None	None
17. Record Players with Plug-in Boxes and Headsets	20	20	200	4,000	225	4,500
18. Portable Public Address Systems	3	2	250	750	305	610
19. Microform Projectors and Readers	not listed	10	not listed	----	600	6,000
Sub-Totals				$140,580		$ 53,600
For Learning-Area Use:						
20. Electronically Equipped Carrels (ITV, Audio, etc.) for Individualized Study in each Area	30	200[1]	650	19,500	1,265	253,000
Sub-Totals				$160,080		$306,600
(continued)						

[1] See next page.

228

APPENDIX A (continued)

Kinds of Media Equipment	Units Needed E	Units Needed W/S	Unit Cost (Erickson) 1968 Dollars	Total Cost (Erickson) 1968 Dollars	1977-78 Dollar Cost Per Unit	Total Cost in 1977 Dollars
20-A. Carrels for Microform Reading (now incl. in Item 20)	30	None	$ 400	$ 12,000	None	None
(Sub-total)				172,080		306,600
20-B. Reserve Fund						3,101
For Auditorium Use:						
21. Motion Picture Projector (Auditorium Model)	2	2	1,500	3,000	$1,031	$ 2,062
22. Overhead Projector (Heavy-duty Model)	1	1	600	600	675	675
23. Slide Projector (Auditorium Model, Combination 3¼ x 4 and 2 x 2 Slides)	2	2	400	800	182	364
24. Motorized, Auditorium Projection Screen	1		600	600	646	646
25. Tape Recorder (Matched to Sound System)	1		1,500	1,500	1,810	1,810
Sub-Totals				$ 6,500		$ 8,658
TOTALS				$178,580[2]		$315,258[2]

---

[1] (continued from preceding page) Number of Carrels per Learning Area as determined by multimedia mix requirements. Assuming one hour per day per student, one Carrel serves six students, two hundred Carrels, 1200. The American Association of School Librarians recommends seating capacity for at least 10 percent of the student body. See *Standards for School Library Programs* (Chicago: American Library Association, 1960), pp. 25-26.

[2] The difference between the two totals is not wholly due to inflation, but also involves modified equipment, and *relatively* lower 1977 prices for many items because of increased production economies, etc. What is significant is that the capital equipment for technologically up-to-date schooling is *much less expensive* when compared with present-day labor costs.

APPENDIX B

COST ESTIMATES FOR MEDIA *PREPARATION* EQUIPMENT FOR AN 800-1200 STUDENT LEARNING CENTER[1]

Kind of Equipment	Units Needed E[2] W/S[3]	Unit Cost (Erickson) 1968 Dollars	Total Cost (Erickson) 1968 Dollars	1977 Dollar Cost Per Unit	Total Cost in 1977 Dollars
1. Still Picture Cameras, Single Lens Reflex Model, with Copy Stands and Attached Lights, Exposure Meter, Close-up Lenses, Adaptor Rings, and Blue Filter	3	$280	$840	$ 350	$1,050
2. Still Picture Cameras and Light Meter with Carrying Case for Class Projects	2	150	300	175	350
3. Slide Duplicating Unit (such as Heiland Repronar, with Accessories)	1	360	360	500	500
4. Motion Picture Camera with Turret and Three Lenses, or Zoom Lens, and Carrying Case for Clip Production, Heavy-Duty Tripod, and Several Lights	1	850	850	1,000	1,000
5. Still Picture Cameras, Polaroid, Copying Stand, Lights	1	250	250	350	350
6. Still Picture Camera, Polaroid, MP-3 Model, Reflex Unit, Stand and Lights, Special Lens for 2 x 2" Slides	1	800	800	1,000	1,000
(continued) Sub-Totals			3,400		4,250

[1] Based on Erickson, *op. cit.*, p. 548. Updated by Professor Arnold W. Cook, Coordinator of Instructional Media, Houghton College, Houghton, NY.
[2] Erickson for 1600-student school.
[3] Willett/Swanson for an 800-1200-student learning center.

APPENDIX B (continued)

Kind of Equipment	Units Needed E	Units Needed W/S	Unit Cost (Erickson) 1968 Dollars	Total Cost (Erickson) 1968 Dollars	1977 Dollar Cost Per Unit	Total Cost in 1977 Dollars
7. Dry-Process Copier, Single-Sheet Model	4		$ 400	$1,600	Substitute one modern copier: Xerox, IBM, SCM, etc.	$15,000
8. Dry-Process Copier for using Intermediate Sheets for use with books and booklets	2		380	760	350	700
9. Diazo-Coated Transparency-Making Equipment, including Exposing and Developing Units	2	2	300	600		700
10. Dry Press for Mounting Pictures and Laminating	2	2	300	600	350	700
11. Primer-Size Type Typewriter	1	1	250	250	350	350
12. Paper Cutters (24" and 15")	2	2	40	80	50	100
13. Motorized Spirit Duplicator	2	2	370	740	495	990
14. Tape Recorders (for High Fidelity Programs) Portable	2	2	600	1,200	450	900
15. Transparency Maker/document laminator	0	2	- - -	- - -	400	800
TOTAL			$9,230[1]			$23,790[1]

[1]The major difference between the two totals is the substitution of a *modern* dry process copier (see Items 7 and 8, above).

APPENDIX C
COST ESTIMATES FOR INSTRUCTIONAL TELEVISION PRODUCTION AND SYSTEMS UTILIZATION
FOR AN 800-1200 STUDENT LEARNING CENTER[1]

Kinds of Equipment	Units Needed E[1]	Units Needed W/S	Unit Cost (Erickson) 1968 Dollars	Total Cost (Erickson) 1968 Dollars	1977 Dollar Cost Per Unit[4]	Total Cost in 1977 Dollars
1. TV Studio Package incl. 2 Vidicon Cameras, 2 Video Tape Recorders w. Electronic Ed., Lights, Console Multiplexer, Monitors	1	1		$ 25,000	$50,000	$ 50,000
2. Mobile TV Recorder-Playback Unit for Classroom Use	2	2	$6,000	12,000	Not needed due to additional electronically equipped carrels (see Appendix A)	
3. Coaxial-Cable ITV Dist. System	1	1	4,600	4,600	10,000	10,000
4. TV Receiver w. Mobile stand or Cradle mount per Teaching Station	92	10	200	18,400	900	9,000
5. Electronic Learning Lab, 30 position Dial-Retrieval for Audio Programs, Recording and Comparison Operations	1	1	600 (per booth)	18,000	1,000	30,000
6. Elec. Learning Lab. w. Audio Tape, Programmed Projections	0[2]	1	650 (per booth)	26,000		Not needed
7. Auto. Multimedia System in Auditorium w. Group-Response Units at 300 seats for Film, Slide, Tape, TV. (Wired for computer installation)	1	1[3]		28,000	40,000	40,000
TOTALS				$132,000		$139,000

[1]Based on Erickson, op. cit., p. 549—1600 students, 92 teaching stations, adapted to 800-1200 students, 10 learning areas.
[2]Not needed in view of the 200 electronically equipped carrels listed in Appendix A.
[3]Erickson provides for 3/16 of 1600 students. Willett/Swanson provide for 4/16 of 1200 students.
[4]Estimated based on The Audio-Visual Equipment Directory, 1977-78 Edition.

232

APPENDIX D
COST ESTIMATES FOR PURCHASE OF MEDIA MATERIALS FOR AN 800-1200 STUDENT LEARNING CENTER[1]

MEDIA SUBJECTS	Units Needed E[2]	Units Needed W/S[3]	Unit Cost (Erickson) 1968 Dollars	Total Cost (Erickson) 1968 Dollars	1977 Dollar Cost Per Unit[5]	Total Cost in 1977 Dollars
Commercial Media Materials (General Use) (not including Science Apparatus and Maps for Social Science)[4]						
1. Filmstrips	2,000	1,000	$ 5	$10,000	$ 6	$ 6,000
2. Audio-Program Tapes and Records	550	300	3	1,650	4	1,200
3. Slide Sets	200	200	5	1,000	6	1,200
4. Study Print Sets	200	100	4	800	5	500
5. Globes (Floor and Desk)	40	20	50	2,000	60	1,200
6. Transparencies	500	300	4	2,000	5	1,500
Sub-Totals (continued)				$17,450		$11,600

---

[1] Based on Erickson, *op. cit.*, pp. 550-551. Erickson stresses that his estimates (1) do not include materials distributed from a district central storage (Willett/Swanson provide separately for this), but (2) encompass "advanced operational programs that provide a flow of media to meet significant and basic instructional needs."

[2] Erickson

[3] Willett/Swanson depend on District Media Service to supplement on a sharing basis. See Appendix K.

[4] Willett/Swanson provide for this, plus music and physical education equipment in Appendix E.

[5] Estimated

APPENDIX D (continued)

MEDIA SUBJECTS	Units Needed E[1]	W/S[2]	Unit Cost (Erickson) 1968 Dollars	Total Cost (Erickson) 1968 Dollars	1977 Dollar Cost Per Unit[3]	Total Cost (Willett) 1977 Dollars
Commercial Media Packages (Instructional System Use)						
1. Video-Tape Sets (1", half-hour) 4	50	30	$600	$30,000	$720	$21,600
2. 8mm Catridge Film Sets (10 Films each)	50	50	80	4,000	100	5,000
3. Audio-Program Tape Sets (20 Tapes each)	50	50	60	3,000	75	3,750
4. Slide Sets (30 Slides each)	100	60	15	1,500	20	1,200
5. Filmstrip Sets, Silent (4 Filmstrips each)	100	60	12	1,200	15	900
6. Filmstrip Sets, Sound (4 Filmstrips each)	100	60	20	2,000	25	1,500
Sub-Totals				$41,700		$33,950
TOTALS				$59,150		$45,550

[1]Erickson
[2]Willett/Swanson
[3]Estimated

COST ESTIMATES OF CAPITAL OUTLAY[1] FOR ART, MUSIC, PHYSICAL EDUCATION, AND
SCIENCE EQUIPMENT FOR 800-1200 STUDENT LEARNING CENTER[2]

Area	Estimated Initial Outlay	Per Student (÷ 800)	Amortized – 5 Yrs.–Per Yr.	Per Student Per Year
Art	$ 8,000	$10	$ 8,000 ÷ 5 = $ 1,600	$ 2
Music	8,000	10	8,000 ÷ 5 = 1,600	2
Physical Education	24,000	30	24,000 ÷ 5 = 4,800	6
Science	32,000	40	32,000 ÷ 5 = 6,400	8
TOTALS	$72,000	$90	$72,000 ÷ 5 = 14,400 ÷ 800 =	$18

NOTE: The reader should remember that if the estimates above seem low, a 25 percent increase would only
increase the per student cost by $4.50 per student for five years

[1]These figures are arbitrary estimates, because the amounts spent on *initial* outlay vary. A typical
1000-student school in Western New York spends about $60 to $90 per student per year on "Teaching
Materials and Textbooks." The total per student which we use, above, is 90.
[2]See Appendix I for integration of *this* capital outlay with the capital outlay for new nonhuman media.

COST ESTIMATES OF ANNUAL OUTLAY FOR SUPPLIES AND REPLACEMENT
OF EQUIPMENT FOR PRINT-MEDIUM, ART, MUSIC, PHYSICAL EDUCATION
AND SOCIAL SCIENCE[1]

Item	Total Per Year	(÷ by 800) =	Per Student Per Year
Print-Medium (i.e. textbooks)[2]	$38,400		$48
Miscellaneous Instructional Material[3]	2,400		3
Sub-Total			$51
Replacement of Equipment (See Appendix E−1)			
$72,000 (11%)[4]	7,920		10
TOTAL	$48,720		$61

[1]These items are *not* included in Erickson's estimates.
[2]This is a median figure for Western New York schools, 1974-75, and assumes 800 students are enrolled. It is derived by subtracting "non-text. teachers materials" from "textbooks and teaching aids." See Rott, *et al.*, 1976, pp. 18-29.
[3]The figure is an arbitrary one.
[4]Assumes 3% per year for damage and 8% per year normal wear.

APPENDIX F
COST ESTIMATES FOR *ANNUAL REPLACEMENT* OF MEDIA EQUIPMENT AND MATERIALS FOR AN 800-1200 STUDENT LEARNING CENTER[1]

Total Value of Media Items Learning Center Inventory	Replacement for Accidental Damage	Outlay Due to: Normal Wear	Revision	Total Percent	Total Annual Cost
1. Media Materials: All-Center Use (Appendix D) $11,600	$ 232 (2%)	$ 928 (8%)	$ 580 (5%)	15	$ 1,740
2. Media Materials: Instructional Systems Use (Appendix D) $33,950	679 (2%)	2,716 (8%)	1,698 (5%)	15	5,093
3. Media Equipment: All-Center Use (Appendix A) $53,600	536 (1%)	6,432 (12%)		13	6,968
4. Media Equipment: Auditorium Use (Appendix A) $8,658	87 (1%)	1,039 (12%)		13	1,126
5. Media Equipment: Learning Area Use (Appendix A) $253,000	7,590 (3%)[2]	25,300 (10%)[3]		13	32,890
6. Media Equipment: Media Preparation (Appendix B) $23,790	238 (1%)	2,855 (12%)		13	3,093
7. Media Equipment: ITV Learning Systems Service (Appendix C) $139,000	1,390 (1%)	6,950 (5%)[4]		6	8,340
TOTALS	$10,752	$46,220	$2,278		$59,250

[1] Based on Erickson, *op. cit.*, p. 553.
[2] This is an increase of 2% over Erickson. It assumes greater rate of use.
[3] This is an increase of 7% over Erickson. It assumes shorter technological adequacy. In the Erickson calculations this corresponds to School Library installations (pp. 549 and 554).
[4] This is an increase of 2% over Erickson. It assumes greater rate of use.

237

COST ESTIMATES OF ANNUAL OUTLAY FOR MEDIA DESIGN AND
PREPARATION *SUPPLIES* FOR AN 800-1200 STUDENT LEARNING CENTER[1]

Item	Annual Estimated Cost
Photographic Film and Supplies for Color Slides	$ 800
Polaroid Film and Supplies for Polaroid-Type Slides	400
Transparency Supplies and Diazo	1,300
Spirit Reflex Masters	200
Motion Picture Film Stock	300
Heavy Paper Stock for Media-Preparation Uses (not Spirit or Mimeo)	400
Dry-Mount Press Supplies	300
Lettering Supplies for Media Uses	700
Pressure-Sensitive Tapes	400
Magnetic Recording Tape: Audio	500
Magnetic Recording Tape: Video (based on 20 hrs. of one-inch)	1,000
Erickson Total	$6,300
Less 25%[2]	1,575
Sub-Total	$4,725
Plus 30% Inflation	1,418
Willett/Swanson Total	$6,143

[1]Based on Erickson, op. cit., p. 554.
[2]Erickson 1968 figures are based on 1600 pupils. Willett/Swanson adjust to 800-1200 students by reducing supply costs 25%, then adding 30% price inflator to simulate 1977 dollars.

238

COST OF ESTIMATED *ANNUAL OUTLAY* FOR MISCELLANEOUS AUDIOVISUAL
MEDIA SERVICE ITEMS FOR AN 800-1200 STUDENT LEARNING CENTER[1]

Item	*Annual Estimated Cost*
Repair Supplies (Tubes, Transistors, Lamps, Belts, Connectors, Leader Film, Cleaning Fluids, Film Cement, Splicing Tape, Containers, Boxes, Reels, Wire and Cable)	$2,600
Spare Parts (Gears, Claws, Lenses, Parts)	1,000
Office Supplies	300
Mimeo and Spirit Duplication Paper Stock	3,000
Printing of Business Forms	600
Travel Funds for Media Staff	200
Erickson Total	$7,700
Less 25%[2]	1,925
Sub-Total	$5,775
Plus 30% Inflation	1,733
Willett/Swanson Total	$7,508

[1]Based on Erickson, *op. cit.,* p. 555.
[2]Erickson figures are based on 1600 pupils. Willett/Swanson adjust to 800 to 1200 students, by reducing supply costs 25%, then adding 30% price inflator to simulate 1977 dollars.

APPENDIX I
Five-Day Design (Transitional)
SUMMARY OF ESTIMATED COSTS FOR NONHUMAN MEDIA AND MEDIA SERVICES
(EXCLUDING DISTRICT SERVICES) FOR AN 800-1200 STUDENT LEARNING CENTER[1]—Stated in 1977 Dollars

Category	Capital Outlay — Total Outlay W/S[2]	Capital Outlay — Per Student Per Year W/S	Total Outlay W/S	Annual Outlay — Per Student Per Year[10] W/S 800	1000	1200
1. *Equipment and Facilities:*[3]						
All-Center Use	$ 53,600 ÷ 800 =	$ 67				
Learning Area Use	253,000 ÷ 800 =	316				
Auditorium Use	8,658 ÷ 800 =	11				
Fixed Items (ITV, etc.)[4]	139,000 ÷ 800 =	173				
	Sub-total	567				
2. *Media Preparation:*						
Equipment[5]	23,790	30				
Supplies[6]	"		$ 6,413	$ 8.02	$ 6.41	$ 5.34
3. *Media Materials:*[7]						
General Use	11,600	15				
Instructional Systems Use	33,950	43				
4. *Replacement of Equipment and Materials*[8]			59,250	74.06	59.25	49.37
5. *Miscellaneous:*						
Spare Parts, etc.[9]			7,508	9.38	7.50	6.26
Sub-Totals	$523,598 "	$65[10]	$73,171	$91.46	$73.16	$60.97[10]

(continued)

[1]Based on Erickson, *op. cit.*, p. 557.
[2]Willett/Swanson. To keep the estimates conservative, capital outlay totals have been divided by 800 students. Figures are rounded.

[3]Appendix A	[5]Appendix B	[7]Appendix D	[9]Appendix H
[4]Appendix C	[6]Appendix G	[8]Appendix F	[10]Figures have been rounded

APPENDIX I (continued)

Category	Capital Outlay Total Outlay W/S	Per Student Per Year W/S	Total Outlay W/S	Annual Outlay Per Student Per Year W/S 800	1000	1200
			Forwarded	$ 91	$ 73	$ 61
Addition for:[1]						
1. Art, Music, Physical Education and Science Equipment	$ 72,000 ÷ 800 =	$ 90				
2. Replacement of Equipment			(See Appendix E–2 for Calculation)	10	10	10
Sub-Totals				$101	$ 83	$ 71
Addition for:[2]						
Print Medium and Miscella-neous Instructional Material			(See Appendix E–2)	51	51	51
TOTALS	$595,598	$745		$152	$134	$122

[1] Appendix E–1
[2] Appendix E–2

COST ESTIMATES OF ANNUAL OUTLAY FOR AUDIOVISUAL MEDIA SPECIALIST STAFF AT DISTRICT LEVEL (To serve Districts of 12,000 to 24,000 students)[1]

Quantity	Position or Service	Salaries 1974-75 Levels	Fringe Benefits	Total Outlay 1974-75	Per Student Per Year (High to Low)
1	District Coordinator—12 months	$24,000[2]	$6,000	$ 30,000	
2	Full-time professional assistant—12 months[3]	16,000	4,000	40,000	
2	Graphic Technicians—12 months[4]	12,000	3,000	30,000	
2	Electronics Technicians—12 months[4]	12,000	3,000	30,000	
2	Secretaries—12 months[4]	8,000	2,000	20,000	
500 hours	Outside Technical and Consulting service @ $10/hr.	------	------	5,000	
	TOTALS			$155,000	$13 $10 $7[5]

[1]Partially based on Erickson, *op. cit.*, p. 554.
[2]Based on Peterson, Gary T. "Salaries of Doctoral Instructional Media/Technology Graduates, 1968-70," *Audiovisual Instruction*, 17(7), Sept. 1972, pp. 47-49, adjusted to 1974-75 estimated levels.
[3]A teacher, for programming and in-service education work.
[4]Based on Erickson, *op. cit.*, p. 554, plus inflation factor.
[5]Figures are rounded, and slightly inflated for the median and low estimates of $10 and $7, respectively. The total of $155,000 has been divided by 12,000 students to obtain the high figure of $13, and by 24,000 students to obtain the low figure of $7.

Five-Day Design (Transitional)
COST ESTIMATES OF *ANNUAL OUTLAY FOR EQUIPMENT AND SUPPLIES* FOR
THE DESIGN AND PREPARATION OF AUDIOVISUAL MEDIA BY DISTRICT STAFF
(12,000 to 24,000 Students)

Total Annual Replacement Cost	*Extra Use Factor*[1]	*New Total*	*Per Student Per Year*		
			12,000	*18,000*	*24,000*
From Appendix F	EQUIPMENT[2]				
$3,093	100%	$ 6,186			
From Appendix G	SUPPLIES				
$6,143	100%	$12,286			
TOTALS		$18,472	$1.54	$1.03	$.77

---

[1] Learning Center figure is doubled as an arbitrary assumption.
[2] Total cost of *initial outlay* for equipment (from Appendix B) is $20,320. If amortized over five years (no interest included) this would only increase per student per year cost by $2 for five years based on a minimum of 12,000 students.

243

Five-Day Design (Transitional)

COST ESTIMATES OF SALARIES OF PROFESSIONAL STAFF FOR AN 800-STUDENT
LEARNING CENTER (Not Including Fringe Benefits)[1]
1974-75 Dollars

From Table 8.2

		Total Annual Remuneration			÷	800 Students = Per Student Per Year Cost[4]		
Position	*Number*	*High*	*Median*	*Low*		*High*	*Median*	*Low*
Administrator	1	$ 40,000	$ 34,000	$ 28,000		$ 50	$ 43	$ 35
Teacher-Senior[2]	1	34,000	28,000	22,000		43	35	28
Teachers[3]	6	120,000	105,000	90,000		150	131	113
Special Service	4	80,000	70,000	60,000		100	88	75
TOTALS	12	$274,000	$237,000	$200,000		$343	$297	$251

[1]Fringe benefits included under District costs.
[2]Based on Elementary School Principal's salary scale in Western New York, 1974-75.
[3]Teacher and Special Service salaries are estimated as: High—$20,000; Median—$17,500; Low—$15,000.
[4]Figures are rounded, and may not total.

APPENDIX L-2

Five-Day Design (Transitional)

COST ESTIMATES OF SALARIES OF PROFESSIONAL STAFF FOR A 1000-STUDENT
LEARNING CENTER (Not Including Fringe Benefits)[1]

1974-75 Dollars

From Table 8.2

Position	Number	Total Annual Remuneration			÷ 1000 Students = Per Student Per Year Cost[4]		
		High	Median	Low	High	Median	Low
Administrator	1	$ 40,000	$ 34,000	$ 28,000	$ 40	$ 34	$ 28
Teacher-Senior[2]	1	34,000	28,000	22,000	34	28	22
Teachers[3]	6	120,000	105,000	90,000	120	105	90
Special Service	4	80,000	70,000	60,000	80	70	60
TOTALS	12	$274,000	$237,000	$200,000	$274	$237	$200

[1] Fringe benefits included under District costs.
[2] Based on Elementary School Principal's salary scale in Western New York, 1974-75.
[3] Teacher and Special Service Salaries are estimated as: High—$20,000; Median—$17,500; Low—$15,000.
[4] Figures are rounded, and may not total.

Five-Day Design (Transitional)
COST ESTIMATES OF SALARIES OF PROFESSIONAL STAFF FOR A 1200-STUDENT LEARNING CENTER (Not Including Fringe Benefits)[1]
1974-75 Dollars

From Table 8.2

Position	Number	Total Annual Remuneration			1200 Students = Per Student Per Year Cost[4]		
		High	Median	Low	High	Median	Low
Administrator	1	$ 40,000	$ 34,000	$ 28,000	$ 34	$ 28	$ 24
Teacher-Senior[2]	1	34,000	28,000	22,000	28	24	18
Teachers[3]	6	120,000	105,000	90,000	100	88	75
Special Service	4	80,000	70,000	60,000	67	58	50
TOTALS	12	$274,000	$237,000	$200,000	$229	$198	$167

[1] Fringe benefits included under District costs.
[2] Based on Elementary School Principal's salary scale in Western New York, 1974-75.
[3] Teacher and Special Service salaries are estimated as: High—$20,000; Median—$17,500; Low—$15,000.
[4] Figures are rounded, and may not total.

Five-Day Design (Transitional)

COST ESTIMATES OF SALARIES OF PARAPROFESSIONAL STAFF FOR AN 800-STUDENT LEARNING CENTER

(Not Including Fringe Benefits)[1]

1974-75 Dollars

From Table 8.3

Position	Number	Total Annual Remuneration			÷ 800 =	Per Student Per Year Cost[4]		
		High	Median	Low		High	Median	Low
Assistant to:[2]								
Administrator	2	$ 16,000	$ 14,000	$ 12,000		$ 20	$ 17	$ 15
Teacher-Senior	1	8,000	7,000	6,000		10	9	8
Technical Supervisor	1	8,000	7,000	6,000		10	9	8
Special Service (Art, etc.)	2	16,000	14,000	12,000		20	17	15
Business/Personnel Manager	1	22,000	18,500	15,000		27	23	19
Monitors[3]	7	44,800	39,200	33,600		56	49	42
Health Officer	1	14,000	12,000	10,000		18	15	13
Social Service Case Worker	2	28,000	24,000	20,000		35	30	25
Technical Supervisor	1	22,000	18,500	15,000		28	23	18
TOTALS	18	$178,800	$154,200	$129,600		$224	$193	$162

[1]Fringe benefits included under District costs.
[2]Based on a range of $4.00 to $3.00 per hour for 50 (40-hour) weeks.
[3]Based on a range of $4.00 to $3.00 per hour for 40 (40-hour) weeks.
[4]Figures are rounded, and may not total.

APPENDIX M–2
Five-Day Design (Transitional)
COST ESTIMATES OF SALARIES OF PARAPROFESSIONAL STAFF FOR A 1000-STUDENT LEARNING CENTER
(Not Including Fringe Benefits)[1]
1974-75 Dollars

From Table 8.3

Position	Number	Total Annual Remuneration			÷ 1000 = Per Student Per Year Cost[4]		
		High	Median	Low	High	Median	Low
Assistant to:[2]							
Administrator	2	$ 16,000	$ 14,000	$ 12,000	$ 16	$ 14	$ 12
Teacher-Senior	1	8,000	7,000	6,000	8	7	6
Technical Supervisor	1	8,000	7,000	6,000	8	7	6
Special Service (Art, etc.)	2	16,000	14,000	12,000	16	14	12
Business/Personnel Manager	1	22,000	18,500	15,000	22	19	15
Monitors[3]	7	44,800	39,200	33,600	45	39	34
Health Officer	1	14,000	12,000	10,000	14	12	10
Social Service Case Worker	2	28,000 1	24,000	20,000	28	24	20
Technical Supervisor	1	22,000	18,500	15,000	22	18	15
TOTALS	18	$178,800	$154,200	$129,600	$179	$154	$130

[1] Fringe benefits included under District costs.
[2] Based on a range of $4.00 to $3.00 per hour for 50 (40-hour) weeks.
[3] Based on a range of $4.00 to $3.00 per hour for 40 (40-hour) weeks.
[4] Figures are rounded, and may not total.

APPENDIX M-3
Five-Day Design (Transitional)
COST ESTIMATES OF SALARIES OF PARAPROFESSIONAL STAFF FOR A 1200-STUDENT LEARNING CENTER
(Not Including Fringe Benefits)[1]
1974-75 Dollars

From Table 8.3

Position	Number	Total Annual Remuneration			÷ 1200 = Per Student Per Year Cost[4]		
		High	Median	Low	High	Median	Low
Assistant to:[2]							
Administrator	2	$ 16,000	$ 14,000	$ 12,000	$ 13	$ 12	$ 10
Teacher-Senior	1	8,000	7,000	6,000	7	6	5
Technical Supervisor	1	8,000	7,000	6,000	7	6	5
Special Service (Art, etc.)	2	16,000	14,000	12,000	13	12	10
Business/Personnel Manager	1	22,000	18,500	15,000	18	15	13
Monitors[3]	7	44,800	39,200	33,600	37	33	28
Health Officer	1	14,000	12,000	10,000	12	10	8
Social Service Case Worker	2	28,000	24,000	20,000	23	20	17
Technical Supervisor	1	22,000	18,500	15,000	18	15	12
TOTALS	18	$178,800	$154,200	$129,600	$149	$129	$108

[1] Fringe benefits included under District costs.
[2] Based on a range of $4.00 to $3.00 per hour for 50 (40-hour) weeks.
[3] Based on a range of $4.00 to $3.00 per hour for 40 (40-hour) weeks.
[4] Figures are rounded, and may not total.

Five-Day Design (Transitional)
COST ESTIMATES OF WAGES FOR STUDENT ASSISTANTS
1974-75 Dollars

From Table 8.3

Position	Number	Total Annual[2] Remuneration $\div 800$ =	Per Student[3] Per Year Cost
Assistant to:[1]			
Administrator	1	$ 1,700	$ 2
Teacher-Senior	1	1,700	2
Teacher-Specialist	15	25,500	32
Technical Supervisor	3	5,100	6
Special Service	2	3,400	4
TOTALS	22	$37,400	$47

NOTE 1: If student population rose from 800 to 1000, and 10 student assistants were added =	10 @ $1700	=	$17,000	$\div 1000$ =		$17
LESS: Saving	(37,400 ÷ 1000)	=	$37 subtracted from $47 =			- $10
NET additional						$ 7

NOTE 2: If student population rose from 800 to 1200, and 20 student assistants were added =	20 @ $1700	=	$34,000	$\div 1200$ =		$28
LESS: Saving	(37,400 ÷ 1200)	=	$31 subtracted from $47 =			- $16
NET additional						$12

[1]Based on a minimum wage of $2.50 per hour for a maximum of 16 hours per week for 40 weeks.

[2]Example of calculation: 16 hours per week x $2.50 per hour = $40 per week; $40 per week x 40 weeks = $1600 per year; $1600 per year plus Liability Insurance ($100) = $1700 per year.

[3]Figures are rounded, and may not total.

APPENDIX O
Five-Day Design (Transitional)
COST ESTIMATES OF FRINGE BENEFITS FOR PROFESSIONAL AND PARAPROFESSIONAL STAFF
(Except District Staff)[1]
1974-75 Dollars

From Appendix L–1 or L–2 or L–3

Personnel	Total Annual Remuneration	Total Annual Fringe Benefits	Fringe Benefits Per Student Per Year[2]		
			800	1000	1200
1. Professional					
Instructional Staff					
High	$274,000	$82,200 (30%)	$103	$82	$69
Median	237,000	71,100 (30%)	89	71	59
Low	200,000	60,000 (30%)	75	60	50

TOTALS (Item 1 plus Item 2)

	High	Median	Low
800 students	170	136	114
1000 students	147	117	98
1200 students	124	99	82

From Appendix M–1 or M–2 or M–3

Personnel	Total Annual Remuneration	Total Annual Fringe Benefits	Fringe Benefits Per Student Per Year		
			800	1000	1200
2. Paraprofessional					
Instructional Staff					
High	$178,800	$53,640 (30%)	$ 67	$54	$45
Median	154,200	46,260 (30%)	58	46	39
Low	129,600	38,880 (30%)	49	39	32

[1]This is Instructional Staff only; thus, District Administrative Staff is omitted; however, fringe benefits for District Media Specialist Staff are included in calculations in Appendix J, since this personnel is supplemental to the instructional staff of each learning center.
[2]Figures are rounded, and yield totals per student per year which are considered adequate for foreseeable levels of employee bargaining.

CALCULATION OF PER STUDENT PER YEAR COST FOR *NONHUMAN MEDIA* (except CAI): BASED ON 10 PERCENT BLOCKS OF INSTRUCTIONAL TIME[1]

Kiesling "Strategy 12"[2]
"Departmental organization: heavy use of ITV, Film, and Programmed Instruction, Groups of 100 pupils; single teacher otherwise."

Nonhuman Media	Percent of Instructional Time Used	Rate for First 10% of Time−$	Total per Media for "Strategy 12"	If % of In-structional Time were doubled[4]
TV	8.3	$20	$16.60	$ 25.90[5]
Film	5.0	30	15.00	30.00
Teaching Machine[3]	8.3	60	49.80	99.60
	Total for Capital Input (*without CAI*)		$81.40	$155.50

	High	Median	Low
Total as a Spectrum[6]	$156	$119	$82

---

[1]See Kiesling (1971:989).
[2]See Kiesling (1971:996).
[3]Programmed Instruction.
[4]For TV, rate for second 10 percent of instructional time drops to $10. There is no change in rate for Films, Teaching Machines, or Computer Assisted Instruction.
[5]Because of economies in additional instructional time by TV, the doubling of instructional time would *not* double the cost.
[6]Figures are rounded. It is quite probable that these are too high in relation to 1977 equipment costs, given various changes in technology since 1970.

APPENDIX Q
CALCULATION OF PER STUDENT PER YEAR COST OF *COMPUTER-ASSISTED INSTRUCTION*: BASED ON 10 PERCENT BLOCKS OF INSTRUCTIONAL TIME

Research Base	If Percent of Instructional Time Used Is:[1]	Rate for First 10% of Time	Total for CAI	If Percent of Instructional Time were Doubled
Kiesling	8.3	$200.00	$166.00	$332.00
Univac				
(Actual)	3.3 @ $2.50/hr.	270.00	90.00	180.00
(Estimated)	8.3 @ $2.50/hr.	270.00	225.00	450.00
(Estimated)	8.3 @ $2.00/hr.	216.00	180.00	360.00
Urbana[2]				
(Estimated)	8.3 @ $ .50/hr.	54.00	45.00	90.00
(Estimated)	8.3 @ $ .35/hr.	37.80	31.50	63.00

Estimated Cost of CAI as a Spectrum[3]

	High	Median	Low
8.3% Instructional Time	$225.00	$129.00	$ 32.00
16.6% Instructional Time	450.00	257.00	63.00

---

[1] Assumes 1080 hours possible instructional time in a 36-week school year: 10 percent = 108 hours; 8.3 percent = 90 hours; 3.3 percent = 36 hours.

[2] By 1974.

[3] Figures are rounded.

253

1974-75 PER STUDENT PER YEAR COSTS FOR INSTRUCTIONAL SERVICES[1]—
TRADITIONAL (PLUS AUDIOVISUAL)—In Western New York[2]

Input	Third Quartile WADA	Median WADA	First Quartile WADA[3]
Instructional Services (Regular Day School):[4]	991	932	867

Curriculum Development and Supervision	NOTE: For comparison, the 1975-76
Supervision—Regular School	Cost *Estimates* of the above In-
Research, Planning and Evaluation	structional Services were:
Inservice Training	1,114; 1,050; and 976. The 1975-76
Teaching—Regular School	Estimates for 90 percent of
Instructional Media	Employee Benefits (as below) were:
Pupil Personnel Services and Pupil Activities	260, 239, and 223, for 1975-76
Pupils with Special Educational Needs	totals of 1374, 1289, and 1199.

Input	Third Quartile WADA	Median WADA	First Quartile WADA
Fringe Benefits (pertaining to Instructional services only)[5]	223	205	188
Totals[6]	1214	1137	1055

[1] Included in this category are all of the services also envisioned in the Willett-Swanson capital-intensive models.

[2] Source: Rott *et al.*, 1976: 1, 41, 83, 84.

[3] WADA stands for "Weighted Average Daily Attendance" which is defined as "Sum of average daily attendance with each category weighted as follows: ½K, .50; K-6, 1.00; 7-12, 1.25."

[4] Note specifically that this includes Instructional Media.

[5] These are estimated as 90 percent of all Employee Benefits.

[6] Of these totals, teacher salaries (plus fringe benefits were: 578 + 188 = 766 (72.6%); 621 + 205 = 826 (72.6%); and 663 + 223 = 886 (73%).

APPENDIX S-1
Three-Day Design (Future)
COST ESTIMATES OF SALARIES OF PROFESSIONAL STAFF FOR AN 800-STUDENT LEARNING CENTER ACCOMMODATING 1600 STUDENTS DURING A FIVE-DAY WEEK[1] (Not including Fringe Benefits)[2]
1974-75 Dollars

From Table 9.1

Position	Number	Total Annual Remuneration			÷ 1600 Students = Per Student Per Year Cost[4]		
		High	*Median*	*Low*	*High*	*Median*	*Low*
Administrator	1	$ 40,000	$ 34,000	$ 28,000	$ 25	$ 21	$ 17
Teacher-Senior	1	34,000	28,000	22,000	21	18	14
Teacher-Specialist[3]	10	200,000	175,000	150,000	125	109	94
Special Service—Co-ordinator	1	24,000	21,000	18,000	15	13	11
Special Service[3]—Specialist	3	60,000	52,500	45,000	38	33	28
TOTALS	16	$358,000	$310,500	$263,000	$224	$194	$164

[1] Each student has four half-days of instruction plus an all-school six-hour Activity Day for Co-curricular and Extra-curricular scheduling.
[2] Fringe benefits included under District costs.
[3] Teacher and Special Service salaries are estimated as: High—$20,000; Median—$17,500; Low—$15,000.
[4] Figures are rounded, and may not total.

Three-Day Design (Future)

COST ESTIMATES OF SALARIES OF PROFESSIONAL STAFF FOR A 1000-STUDENT LEARNING CENTER ACCOMMODATING 2000 STUDENTS DURING A FIVE-DAY WEEK[1] (Not including Fringe Benefits)[2]

1974-75 Dollars

From Table 9.1

Position	Number	Total Annual Remuneration			÷ 2000 Students = Per Student Per Year Cost[4]		
		High	*Median*	*Low*	*High*	*Median*	*Low*
Administrator	1	$ 40,000	$ 34,000	$ 28,000	$ 20	$ 17	$ 14
Teacher-Senior	1	34,000	28,000	22,000	17	14	11
Teacher-Specialist[3]	12	240,000	210,000	180,000	120	105	90
Special Service—Co-ordinator	1	24,000	21,000	18,000	12	11	9
Special Service—Specialist[3]	3	60,000	52,500	45,000	30	26	22
TOTALS	18	$398,000	$345,500	$293,000	199	173	146

[1] Each student has four half-days of instruction plus an all-school six-hour Activity Day for Co-curricular and Extra-curricular scheduling.
[2] Fringe benefits included under District costs.
[3] Teacher and Special Service salaries are estimated as: High—$20,000; Median—$17,500; Low—$15,000.
[4] Figures are rounded, and may not total.

Three-Day Design (Future)
COST ESTIMATES OF SALARIES OF PROFESSIONAL STAFF FOR A 1200-STUDENT LEARNING CENTER
ACCOMMODATING 2400 STUDENTS DURING A FIVE-DAY WEEK[1] (Not Including Fringe Benefits)[2]
1974-75 Dollars

From Table 9.1

Position	Number	Total Annual Remuneration			÷ 2400 Students = Per Student Per Year Cost[4]		
		High	*Median*	*Low*	*High*	*Median*	*Low*
Administrator	1	$ 40,000	$ 34,000	$ 28,000	$ 17	$ 14	$ 12
Teacher-Senior	1	34,000	28,000	22,000	14	12	9
Teacher-Specialist[3]	14	280,000	245,000	210,000	117	102	87
Special Service—Co-ordinator	1	24,000	21,000	18,000	10	9	8
Special Service—Specialist[3]	3	60,000	52,500	45,000	25	22	19
TOTALS	20	$438,000	$380,500	$323,000	$183	$159	$135

[1] Each student has four half-days of instruction plus an all-school six-hour Activity Day for Co-curricular and Extra-curricular scheduling.
[2] Fringe benefits included under District costs.
[3] Teacher and Special Service salaries are estimated as: High—$20,000; Median—$17,500; Low—$15,000.
[4] Figures are rounded and may not total.

Three-Day Design (Future)
COST ESTIMATES OF SALARIES OF PARAPROFESSIONAL STAFF FOR AN 800-STUDENT LEARNING
CENTER ACCOMMODATING 1600 STUDENTS DURING A FIVE-DAY WEEK[1] (not including Fringe Benefits)[2]
1974-75 Dollars

From Table 9.2

Position	Number	Total Annual Remuneration			÷ 1600 Students = Per Student Per Year Cost[5]		
		High	Median	Low	High	Median	Low
Assistant to:[3]							
Administrator	3	$ 24,000	$ 21,000	$ 18,000	$ 15	$ 13	$ 11
Teacher-Senior	2	16,000	14,000	12,000	10	9	8
Technical Supervisor	2	16,000	14,000	12,000	10	9	8
Special Service	3	24,000	21,000	18,000	15	13	11
Business/Personnel Manager	1	22,000	18,500	15,000	14	12	9
Monitors[4]	8	51,200	44,800	38,400	32	28	24
Health Officer	1	14,000	12,000	10,000	9	7	6
Social Service—Case Worker	3	42,000	36,000	30,000	26	22	19
Technical Supervisor	1	22,000	18,500	15,000	14	12	9
TOTALS	24	$231,200	$199,800	$168,400	$145	$125	$105

[1]Each student has four half-days of instruction plus an all-school six-hour Activity Day for Co-curricular and Extra-curricular scheduling.
[2]Fringe benefits included under District costs.
[3]Based on a range of $4.00 to $3.00 per hour for 50 (40-hour) weeks.
[4]Based on a range of $4.00 to $3.00 per hour for 40 (40-hour) weeks.
[5]Figures are rounded and may not total.

APPENDIX T–2
Three-Day Design (Future)
COST ESTIMATES OF SALARIES OF PARAPROFESSIONAL STAFF FOR A 1000-STUDENT LEARNING
CENTER ACCOMMODATING 2000 STUDENTS DURING A FIVE-DAY WEEK[1] (not including Fringe Benefits)[2]
1974-75 Dollars

From Table 9.2

Position	Number	Total Annual Remuneration			÷ 2000 Students = Per Student Per Year Cost[5]		
		High	Median	Low	High	Median	Low
Assistant to:[3]							
Administrator	3	$ 24,000	$ 21,000	$ 18,000	$ 12	$ 11	$ 9
Teacher-Senior	2	16,000	14,000	12,000	8	7	6
Technical Supervisor	2	16,000	14,000	12,000	8	7	6
Special Service	3	24,000	21,000	18,000	12	10	9
Business/Personnel Manager	1	22,000	18,500	15,000	11	9	8
Monitors[4]	11	70,400	61,600	52,800	35	31	26
Health Officer	1	14,000	12,000	10,000	7	6	5
Social Service—Case Worker[6]	3	42,000	36,000	30,000	21	18	15
Technical Supervisor	1	22,000	18,500	15,000	11	9	8
TOTALS	27	$250,400	$216,600	$182,800	$125	$108	$92

[1] Each student has four half-days of instruction plus an all-school six-hour Activity Day for Co-curricular and Extra-curricular scheduling.
[2] Fringe benefits included under District cost.
[3] Based on a range of $3.50 to $2.50 per hour for 50 (40-hour) weeks.
[4] Based on a range of $3.50 to $2.50 per hour for 40 (40-hour) weeks.
[5] Figures are rounded, and may not total.
[6] The addition of a fourth case worker would only increase per student per year cost by $7 (High), $6 (Median), and $5 (Low).

259

Three-Day Design (Future)
COST ESTIMATES OF SALARIES OF PARAPROFESSIONAL STAFF FOR A 1200-STUDENT LEARNING
CENTER ACCOMMODATING 2400 STUDENTS DURING A FIVE-DAY WEEK[1] (not including Fringe Benefits)[2]
1974-75 Dollars

From Table 9.2

Position	Number	Total Annual Remuneration			÷ 2400 Students = Per Student Per Year Cost[5]		
		High	Median	Low	High	Median	Low
Assistant to:[3]							
Administrator	3	$ 24,000	$ 21,000	$ 18,000	$ 10	$ 9	$ 7
Teacher-Senior	2	16,000	14,000	12,000	7	6	5
Technical Supervisor	2	16,000	14,000	12,000	7	6	5
Special Service	3	24,000	21,000	18,000	10	9	8
Business/Personnel Manager	1	22,000	18,500	15,000	9	7	6
Monitors[4]	14	89,600	78,400	67,200	37	32	28
Health Officer	1	14,000	12,000	10,000	6	5	4
Social Service Case Worker[6]	3	42,000	36,000	30,000	18	15	13
Technical Supervisor	1	22,000	18,500	15,000	9	8	6
TOTALS	30	$269,600	$233,400	$197,200	$113	$97	$82

[1] Each student has four half-days of instruction plus an all-school six-hour Activity Day for Co-curricular and Extra-curricular scheduling.
[2] Fringe benefits included under District cost.
[3] Based on a range of $4.00 to $3.00 per hour for 50 (40-hour) weeks.
[4] Based on a range of $4.00 to $3.00 per hour for 40 (40-hour) weeks.
[5] Figures are rounded, and may not total.
[6] The addition of two more case workers would only increase per student per year cost by $12 (High), $10 (Median), and $8 (Low).

Three-Day Design (Future)
COST ESTIMATES OF WAGES FOR STUDENT ASSISTANT—1974-75 Dollars

From Table 9.2

Position	Number	Total Annual[2] Remuneration ÷ 800 =	Annual Per Student Cost
Assistant to:[1]			
Administrator	2	$ 3,400	$ 4
Teacher-Senior	2	3,400	4
Teacher-Specialist	22	37,400	46
Technical Supervisor	6	10,200	13
Special Service	4	6,800	8
Business/Personnel	1	1,700	2
Health	1	1,700	2
Social Work Services	2	3,400	4
Totals	40	$68,000	$85

NOTE 1: If student population
rose from 800 to 1000, and 10
extra student assistants
were added =   10 @ $1,700 = $17,000 $17
LESS: Saving (68,000 ÷ 1000 = $68 subtracted from $85) =   - 17
                                                                      $ 0 additional

NOTE 2: If 1200 students,
and 20 extra assistants @ 1,700 = $34,000 $28
LESS: Saving (68,000 ÷ 1200 = $57 subtracted from $85)=   - 28
                                                                      $ 0 additional

[1]Based on a minimum wage of $2.50 per hour for a maximum of 16 hours per week
for 40 weeks.
[2]For example of calculation, see Footnote 2, Appendix N.

Three-Day Design (Future)
COST ESTIMATES OF FRINGE BENEFITS FOR PROFESSIONAL
INSTRUCTIONAL STAFF (Except District Staff)[1]
1974-75 Dollars

	Total Annual Remuneration	Total Annual Fringe Benefits	Fringe Benefits Per Student Per Year		
			For 1600	For 2000	For 2400
From Appendix S−1 *Professional Staff*					
High	$358,000	$107,400 (30%)	$67		
Median	310,500	93,150 (30%)	58		
Low	263,000	78,900 (30%)	49		
From Appendix S−2 *Professional Staff*					
High	398,000	119,400 (30%)		$60	
Median	345,500	103,650 (30%)		52	
Low	293,000	87,900 (30%)		44	
From Appendix S−3 *Professional Staff*					
High	438,000	131,400 (30%)			$55
Median	380,500	114,150 (30%)			48
Low	323,000	96,900 (30%)			40

[1]This is Instructional Staff only; thus, District Administrative Staff is omitted; however, fringe benefits for District Media Specialist Staff are included in calculations in Appendix J since this personnel is supplemental to the Instructional Staff.

Three-Day Design (Future)
COST ESTIMATES OF FRINGE BENEFITS FOR PARAPROFESSIONAL
INSTRUCTIONAL STAFF (Except District Staff)[1]
1974-75 Dollars

	Total Annual Remuneration	Total Annual Fringe Benefits	Fringe Benefits Per Student Per Year		
			For 1600	For 2000	For 2400
From Appendix T–1					
Paraprofessional Staff					
High	$231,200	$69,360 (30%)	$43		
Median	199,800	59,940 (30%)	38		
Low	168,400	50,520 (30%)	32		
From Appendix T–2					
Paraprofessional Staff					
High	250,400	75,120 (30%)		$38	
Median	216,600	64,980 (30%)		33	
Low	182,800	54,840 (30%)		27	
From Appendix T–3					
Paraprofessional Staff					
High	269,600	80,880 (30%)			$34
Median	233,400	70,020 (30%)			29
Low	197,200	59,160 (30%)			25

[1]This is Instructional Staff only; thus, District Administrative Staff is omitted; however, fringe benefits for District Media Specialist Staff are included in calculations in Appendix J since this personnel is supplemental to the Instructional Staff.

APPENDIX W
Three-Day Design (Future)

ESTIMATES OF COSTS FOR NONHUMAN MEDIA AND MEDIA SERVICES (EXCLUDING DISTRICT SERVICES) FOR 800-1200 STUDENT LEARNING CENTER DESIGNED TO ACCOMMODATE 1600 TO 2400 STUDENTS IN TWO ALTERNATING SHIFTS (PLUS ALL-SCHOOL ACTIVITY DAY) DURING FIVE-DAY WEEK[1]

From Appendix I

Category	Percent of Extra Use Factor[2]	Stated in 1977 Dollars — Capital Outlay					Dollars Per Student Per Year — Annual Outlay				
		For 800 +	Extra Use $	For 1600[3]	For 2000[4]	For 2400[5]	For 800 +	Extra Use $	For 1600	For 2000	For 2400
Equipment and Facilities	30%	$567 +	$170	$369	$307	$246	$ 8 +	$ 3	$ 6	$ 5	$ 4
Media Preparation Equipment	30%	30 +	9	20	17	13					
Media Preparation Supplies	30%										
Media Materials	30%	58 +	17	38	32	25					
Replacement of Equipment & Materials	30%						74 +	22	48	40	32
Miscellaneous (parts, etc.)	50%						10 +	5	8	6½	5
Additional Equipment for:											
Art, Music, etc.	30%	90 +	27	59	49	39	10 +	4	7	6	5
Replacement of above	30%										
TOTALS (does not include interest)		$745 +	$223	$486	$405	$323	$102 +	$34	$69	$58	$46

[1] Experience might indicate a six-day week as preferable in some communities where the three-day or four-day work-week was being used.

[2] Erickson's life estimate for nonhuman media was eight years. In reducing this to five years, Willett/Swanson provide a built-in reserve for increased use in both the Five-Day and Three-Day designs. Thus, the 30 percent extra-use factor is deemed adequate, except for parts.

[3] Fifty percent of 800-student figure, plus 50 percent of increased-use factor.

[4] Median between 1600 and 2400. Total is rounded.

[5] 33 1/3 percent of 800-student figure, plus 33 1/3 percent of increased-use factor.

Three-Day Design (Future)
COST ESTIMATES OF *ANNUAL* OUTLAY FOR EQUIPMENT AND SUPPLIES FOR
THE DESIGN AND PREPARATION OF AUDIOVISUAL MEDIA BY DISTRICT STAFF
(12,000 to 24,000 Students)

Total Annual Replacement Cost	Extra Use Factor[1]	New Total	Per Student Per Year		
			12,000	18,000	24,000
From Appendix F— $3,093	EQUIPMENT[2] 200%	$ 9,279			
From Appendix G— $6,143	SUPPLIES 200%	$18,429			
TOTALS		$27,708	$2.31	$1.54	$1.15

[1]Learning Center figure has been tripled as an arbitrary assumption.

[2]Total cost of *initial* outlay for equipment (from Appendix B) is $23,790. If amortized over five years (no interest included) this would only increase the per student per year cost by $.40 for five years based on a minimum of 12,000 students. The addition of interest at 12 percent per year would add another $.11 per student per year.

(Figures are from the Five-Day and Three-Day Designs)
ESTIMATED PERCENTAGE SAVINGS IN PER STUDENT PER YEAR COSTS OVER
WESTERN NEW YORK STATE TRADITIONAL EDUCATION FORMAT[1]

From Table Number:	Willett/Swanson		Western New York			Willett/Swanson Saving—Stated as a Percent over W.N.Y.
	High	Median	Low	High	Median	
8.6	$900		$1055			15%
8.6		$785			$1,137	31%
8.7	745			$1214		39%
8.7		649			1,137	43%
8.8	635		1055			40%
8.8		555			1,137	51%
8.9	955		1055			9.5%
8.9		803			1,137	29%
8.10		685			1,137	40%
8.11	720		1055			32%
8.11		603			1,137	47%
9.3	648		1055			39%
9.3		581			1,137	49%
9.4	580		1055			45%
9.4		521			1,137	54%
9.5	531			1214		56%
9.5		476			1,137	58%
9.6	735			1214		40%
9.6		668			1,137	41%
9.7	678		1055			36%
9.7		619			1,137	46%
9.8		586			1,137	49%

[1]A representative selection of the *more conservative* comparisons has been made from the Tables indicated. The median is shown for each Table. For less conservative comparisons, take for example the Willett/Swanson "Low" of 422 from Table 9.5 and compare it with the Western New York "High" of $1,214, which would yield a saving of 65%.

GLOSSARY

Aggregate demand—the total demand for *all* goods and services in a society.

Alternative cost (Opportunity cost)—the true (or real) cost of doing anything is what could have been done with the same time and/or resources.

Average cost (Average total cost)—total cost divided by total output.

Capital—(see Real capital)

Capital intensive—a condition where the relatively largest percent of the inputs of a production process is in the form of real capital.

Capital outlay—the amount of monetary resources committed to real capital.

Capital stock—the total quantity of real capital (private and public) in a society.

Collaboration (as related to education)—diverse groups of people (e.g., educators, parents, students, and public officials) *working together* to develop solutions to problems.

Common school (American)—"the school which covered the rudiments thought to be essential to the needs of all citizens" (Morrison, 1940:5).

Constant-product curve (or isoquant)—a concave curve which shows all technologically efficient input combinations for producing a specified level of output.

Continuous learning—(see Discontinuous learning)

Cost-benefit (or *benefit-cost*) *analysis*—a type of marginal analysis, which maximizes the use of relatively scarce resources by pushing expenditure on a desired public good (e.g., education) to the point where the extra benefit(s) from the last dollar expended is still greater than (or at least equal to), but never less than, the extra cost(s) associated with that expenditure.

Cost-effectiveness analysis—the use of systematic and quantitative techniques to compare the effects of alternate methods of applying input(s) in order to accomplish desired objective(s), i.e., output.

Decision model—an orderly arrangement of the components of a system into their perceived interrelationships as a basis for making decisions regarding performance and/or policy.

Depreciation—an allowance for the "wearing out" over time of real capital. Also called capital consumption.

Deschooling—complete elimination of present education production functions (or arrangements) with a view to starting over from basic principles of instruction/learning.

Developmental theory—the study of the growth and development of organisms, including human organisms.

Discontinuous learning—"the established practice of reckoning educational progress in terms of time spent rather than in terms of learnings acquired" (Morrison, 1940:666).

Economies (diseconomies) of scale—increasing (decreasing) returns to the scale of production, i.e., proportionately more (or less) output for a given amount of input(s).

Educational output—(see Output, Education)

Educational technology—". . . the application of scientific knowledge, including learning theory, to the solution of problems in education." See note 13, page 22.

Fringe benefit(s)—benefits received by employees in a form other than direct income payments, e.g., medical insurance, pension plan contributions, etc.

Gross national product (GNP)—the sum of all values added in an economy, expressed as a rate of flow, projected for some time period, e.g., one year.

Hardware—the nonhuman, generally mechanical, devices used to receive, store, and transmit information, as well as acting as pre-programmed concept generators, drill and tutorial agents, and as records processors.

Hawthorne effect (or novelty effect)—a sudden but often temporary increase in attention, interest, productivity, etc., due to some previously unused innovation or technique.

Individualization (or instruction/learning)—the capacity of an education system to identify differences and complexity in students and develop the flexibility needed to respond to them.

Innovation—the application of a new idea to a production process. (In Economics, "innovation" is always distinguished from "invention," which is only the new idea.)

Instructional management—the planning, application, and control of management techniques to the individualization of instruction, including needs assessment, proper resource(s) use, evaluation of results, and "feedback" to the planning stage.

Instructional management system—a logical and orderly set of interacting procedures for the utilization of human and nonhuman resources in organizing and making available to educational personnel the information needed to perform the management of individualized instruction of students.

Instructional resource accounting system—a subsystem of an instruction management system which stores and retrieves on the demand of instruction managers (teachers) the alternative learning experiences available which correlate with the learning objectives listed in the student's needs assessment file and the student's progress file.

Investment—any net addition of new real capital to the total capital stock, or to a production process, either private or public.

Isoquant—(see Constant-product curve)

Knowledge-base—the total amount of available knowledge in a society as of some moment of time.

Labor-intensive—a condition where the relatively largest percent of the inputs of a production process is in the form of human resources.

Learning area—a specified space in a learning center for instruction concerning some content area or skill (e.g., arithmetic, reading, etc.).

Learning center—the physical space where instructional activities take place. (In urban and suburban areas, it could be leased space.)

Learning theory (broadly defined)—all research attempting to explain the affective, cognitive, and psychomotor behaviors of people.

Learning theory (narrowly defined)—behaviorism.

Luddite mentality—an attitude which views all technological change as detrimental to society without concern for the goal of the change.

Lump-of-labor—an assumption that, in any society at a given moment in time, there is only so much total work to be done.

Man-machine system—"a set of planned procedures in which man and machine capabilities are used in an integrated manner to achieve results man could not achieve without the machine" (Loughary *et al.*, 1966:5).

Marginal analysis—isolation of the point of decision at the "margin," where the question is: should I, or should I not?

Marginal productivity—the *extra* productivity (i.e., increase in total productivity, either positive or negative) resulting from the addition of one last (or marginal) unit of an input to a production process.

Marginal utility (disutility)—the *extra* satisfaction (dissatisfaction) which a person obtains by the consumption (acquisition) of one *extra* (or additional) unit of a good or service.

Multimedia instruction/learning—the use of all human and/or nonhuman resources in the proportions determined by a needs assessment to deal with the known learning variables: content, age, sex, and socioeconomic background.

Needs assessment—a diagnosis of the cognitive strengths and weaknesses of a student at a given point in time to enable prescription(s) for individualization of instruction to take place.

Opportunity cost—(see Alternative cost)

Optimum population theory—in a given level of technology, there is some point beyond which population cannot increase without resulting in a decrease in the standard of living.

Optimum size (of a production function)—in a given technological horizon, the lowest point on an average total cost curve, which implies that the most efficient combination of inputs has been attained.

Output, Education (Educational output)—(1) in conventional terms, some level of cognitive achievement; (2) in a capital-intensive, individualized system, the attainment of the educational goals of the individual student beyond some given level of competency for citizenship.

Production function—within a given level of technology, the relationship between a desired level of output and the alternative *sets of inputs* which can produce that output.

Production possibility (frontier, or horizon)—a method of determining the alternative *outputs* possible, given the amount of *inputs* available, expressed as a schedule, or a graph. In general, an increase (decrease) in one output will necessitate a decrease (increase) in another output, *unless* there is a change in technology which increases productivity, thereby increasing the amounts possible of all outputs.

Productivity—the ratio of the output divided by the input(s) in a production process. See also Marginal productivity.

Profit (in a not-for-profit production function)—any residual, after provision for all *present* costs. In the words of Peter Drucker, profit is the necessary provision for *future* costs.

Real capital (as contrasted with *money capital*)—produced means-of-production, i.e., buildings, equipment, machinery, tools, etc., which are themselves a product but which also help to produce other goods or services. A synonym is: *physical capital.*

Schooling—the process to which a student is exposed during the specified time spent in an educational institution called a school. It has also sometimes been used, improperly, as a synonym for "education."

Social change—any perceived alteration in the beliefs, customs, practices, or values of a society, or a portion of a society.

Socioeconomic environment—the economic and/or social level(s) observable in the class structure of a society.

Social technology—"the controllable factors that contribute to the existence of a social problem, and thereby to its potential solution" (Katzman, 1971:4).

Software—the programs (curricular and non-curricular) to be used with "hardware."

Systems approach (or systems analysis)—a research strategy which recognizes the interaction and interdependence of functionally-related components. (Since "schooling" involves both human and nonhuman components, its complex of relationships has been referred to throughout this book as a "man-machine system"). See also Man-machine system.

Teaching machine—"any device which arranges contingencies of reinforcement" (Skinner, 1968:65). Can be thought of as synonymous with "programmed instruction."

Technological change—"an advance in knowledge" (Mansfield, 1971:10).

Technology—literally, the study of technique(s)—generally, the application of new knowledge to a productive process: commercial, industrial, social (e.g., education).

Utility—as used in Economics: the capacity of a good or service to satisfy a human need or want.

Weighted average daily attendance (WADA)—the sum of average daily attendance with each category weighted as: $\frac{1}{2}$K = .50; K - 6 = 1.00; 7 - 12 = 1.25.

AUTHOR INDEX

Alexander, Lawrence T., 208
American Institutes for Research, 87
American Library Association, 205
Anastasiou, Nicholas J., 87
Antionetti, J.A., 62, 223
Archer, L. Bruce, 7, 205
Arrow, Kenneth, 205
Ashby, Eric, 52-53, 205
Atkinson, A.B., 205
Averch, Harvey, 5, 28-29, 64, 205

Barnet, Homer G., 37, 205
Barrett, R.S., 62, 211
Baumol, William J., 8-9, 31, 32, 36, 205
Beck, Carlton E., 206
Becker, Gary S., 12, 13, 206
Bell, T.H., 72, 206
Bennett, William S., Jr., 87
Bentham, Jeremy, 206
Bernier, Normand R., 206
Biddle, Bruce J., 216, 218, 219
Blaug, Mark, 22
Block, J.H., 103, 206
Bloom, Benjamin S., 60, 102, 103, 206, 214

Bohm-Bawerk, Eugene von, 22, 222
Bolvin, John O., 72, 206
Bourne, Randolph S., 85, 206
Bowles, Samuel, 27, 206
Buhler, Charlotte, 99, 207
Burkhead, Jesse, 22, 25, 26, 27, 35, 207

Callahan, Raymond E., 44-45, 207
Carnegie Commission on Higher Education, 48, 52, 207
Carroll, Stephen J., 5, 28-29, 64, 205
Carter, Launor, F., 76, 207
Center for Educational Research and Innovation, 186, 207
Central Advisory Council for Education (England), 88, 207
Chamberlain, Neil W., 207
Chase, Clinton I., 111, 112, 114, 207
Christenson, P.E., 76, 208
Cogan, Morris L., 191, 203, 208
Cohn, Elchanan, 208
Coleman, James S., 27, 32, 88, 208
Combs, Arthur W., 97, 111, 208
Committee for Economic Development, 139, 141, 147, 208

273

Conant, Eaton H., 208
Conant, James B., 32, 208
Coombs, Philip H., 60, 119, 208

Dady, Milan B., 87
Dahl, R.A., 208
Davis, Donald A., 88
Davis, Robert H., 208
Dawson, R.L., 5, 28-29, 62, 64, 211
Denemark, George W., 72, 208
Denison, Edward F., 13, 17, 38-39, 209
Dewey, John, 101, 209
Digest of Educational Statistics, 4, 21, 33-34, 36, 209, 211
Donaldson, Theodore S., 5, 28-29, 64, 205
Dunn, Kenneth, 63, 209
Dunn, Rita Stafford, 62-63, 209

Ebel, Robert L., 112, 113, 209
Eckstein, Otto, 30, 209
Economic Report of the President, 1972, 209
Edding, Friederick, 32, 36, 165, 209
Education USA, 150-151, 209
Erickson, Carlton W.H., 138-143, 146, 151, 162, 169, 173, 210
Erickson, Erik H., 99, 102, 106, 210

Falk, R. Frank, 87
Finley, Robert M., 87, 210
Foley, Cornelius J., 210
Frazier, Thomas W., 103-104, 210
Freeman, R.B., 16, 22
Friedman, Milton, 202, 210

Gagne, Robert, 66, 106, 210
Garner, William T., 31, 210
Gartner, Alan, 80-81, 82, 83, 88, 129, 210

Gelula, Mark, 210
Gentile, J. Ronald, 103-104, 210
Gibbons, Maurice, 94, 210
Gibson, R. Oliver, 211
Ginsburg, Herbert, 11-12, 211
Gintis, Herbert J., 31, 211
Glaser, Robert, 62, 211, 215
Goldberg, M.H., 62, 211
Goldman, Thomas A., 30, 33, 211
Goode, William, 190-191, 203, 211
Gordon, George N., 56, 211
Gove, James R., 212
Grant, W. Vance, 4, 21, 33-34, 36, 211
Gray, William S., 86
Gross, Ronald, 216
Guthrie, James W., 45, 46, 211

Hallak, Jacques, 212
Hammond Indiana Public Schools, 88
Hansen, W. Lee, 212
Hanushek, Eric, 31, 212
Harrington, Michael, 212
Harrison, Charles H., 215
Hastings, J.T., 206
Havighurst, Robert J., 100, 106, 212
Hempel, Marvin W., 22, 212
Hermansen, Kenneth L., 212
Hicks, J.R., 212
Hinrichs, Harley H., 31, 212
Hughes, John L., 55, 62, 212
Hughes, Marie, 75, 213
Hurwitz, Emanuel, Jr., 222
Husen, Torsten, 88, 213
Huxley, Aldous, 48, 213

Igoe, Joseph, 213
International Association for the Evaluation of Education Achievement Report, 88
Ireland, V.M., 87

James, H. Thomas, 124, 213
Jamison, Dean, 5-6, 213
Jencks, Christopher, 27, 29, 32, 213
Jevons, William S., 213

Katzman, Martin T., 27-28, 31, 36, 213
Kiesling, Herbert J., 5, 28-29, 31, 52, 63, 64, 138-142, 146-151, 155, 164, 169-173, 205, 213-214
Kindleberger, Charles P., 13, 214
Kliebard, Herbert M., 19, 214
Koerner, James D., 32, 214
Kohler, Mary Conway, 83, 210
Kozol, Jonathan, 32, 214
Krathwohl, David R., 102, 214
Kuznets, Simon, 13-14, 214

Lafornara, Paul, 211
Leggatt, Timothy, 192, 214
Leonard, George B., 3, 214
Lesser, Gerald, 32, 219
Levin, Henry M., 27, 31, 124, 213
Levine, Donald M., 29, 215
Lind, George, 4, 21, 33-34, 36, 211
Lindblom, C.E., 208
Lineberry, William P., 182-183, 215
Lippitt, Peggy, 84, 215
Little, I.M.D., 215
Loughary, John W., 34, 215
Ludlow, H. Glenn, 111, 112, 114, 207
Lumsdaine, A.A., 62, 215
Luskin, Bernard J., 56, 215

MacDonald, James B., 206
McConnell, Campbell R., 22, 215
McCusker, Henry F., Jr., 71-72, 74, 127, 155, 216
McKenna, Bernard H., 216
McMullen, David W., 58, 59-60, 216

McNamara, W.J., 62, 212
McNeil, J.D., 62, 216

Madaus, G.F., 206
Mansfield, Edwin, 40, 41, 215
Marks, Sema, 57, 217
Martin, John H., 215
Masia, B.B., 214
May, Rollo, 101, 215
Mayer, Martin, 32, 215
Mayeske, George W., 27, 215
Mill, John Stuart, 216
Millman, Stephen D., 208
Mills, Donald L., 190, 191, 222
Minar, David W., 222
Morris, Mary C., 103-104, 210
Morrison, Henry C., 3, 19, 39, 51, 53-54, 55, 216
Moynihan, Daniel S., 27, 216
Murphy, Judith, 216
Murray, H.T., Jr., 163, 217
Myint, Hla, 216

National Audio-Visual Association, Inc., 216, 227
Nephew, Charles T., 216
Newsweek, August 13, 1973, 61, 216
Nikolai, Irvin, 216
Novak, J., 163, 217

O'Donoghue, Martin, 23, 217
Oettinger, Anthony G., 57, 150, 182, 217
Ogburn, William Fielding, 38, 217
Organization for Economic Cooperation and Development, 203

Pearl, Arthur, 80, 217
Perry, Oliver, 61-62, 217
Peterson, Gary T., 217
Piaget, Jean, 99, 106, 217
Pigou, Arthur C., 217
Pincus, John, 5, 28-29, 64, 205

Plowden Report, 88
Pope, Lillian, 88
Postlethwait, S.N., 163, 217
Potter, Robert E., 85, 86, 217
Pugh, James B., Jr., 216

Rawls, James R., 61-62, 217
Reder, Melvin W., 217
Richmond, George, 65, 217
Riessman, Frank, 83, 210
Robbins, Lionel, 15, 37, 217-218
Roe, A., 62, 218
Rossi, Peter H., 216, 218-219
Rott, Marilyn Hopkins, 218, 254
Rubin, Louis, 131, 139, 218
Ryan, Charlotte P., 200, 201, 218

Saettler, Paul, 67, 73, 218
Samuelson, Paul A., 22, 218
Schaefer, William T., 163, 218
Schultz, Theodore W., 12, 22, 218
Shapiro, Eli, 16-17, 43, 218
Sidgwick, Henry, 218
Silberman, Charles E., 32, 193, 219
Silberman, Harry F., 55, 219
Simon, Kenneth A., 219
Skinner, B.F., 14, 66, 131, 136, 219
Smith, Adam, 36, 219
Smith, B. Othanel, 59, 195, 219
Sorensen, Philip H., 71-72, 74, 127, 155, 216
State of New York, Department of Audit and Control, 162, 219
Stoddard, Alexander J., 219
Stodolsky, Susan S., 32, 219
Stolurow, Lawrence M., 59, 61, 219-220
Stone, I.F., 181, 220
Street, David, 220
Sullivan, George, 75, 76, 220
Suppes, Patrick, 5-6, 213

Swanson, Austin D., 5, 30, 31, 89, 123, 124, 220-221

Taylor, G.M., 31, 212
Thayer, P.W., 62, 223
Thomas, J. Alan, 35, 221
Tickton, Sidney G., 53, 63, 221
Timmons, Edwin O., 61-62, 217
Toffler, Alvin, 221
Tyack, David S., 18, 45, 221
Tyler, Ralph W., 111-112, 114, 221

U.S. Department of Health, Education, and Welfare, Office of Education, 162, 221-222
U.S. Department of Labor, 222
University of Indiana Reading Center, 88
Usdan, Michael D., 183, 222
Uttal, William R., 55, 222

Vaizey, John, 7, 14, 222
Vincent, William S., 222
Vollmer, Howard M., 190, 191, 222

Walton, Thomas W., 206
Washburne, Carleton W., 86, 222
Weintraub, Sidney, 128, 222
Welch, Finis, 36, 222
Wells, Stuart, 5-6, 213
Welsh, P., 62, 223
White, Peter T., 66, 223
White, William L., 16-17, 43, 218
Whitehead, Alfred N., 103, 223
Whittaker, Edmund, 223
Willett, Edward J., 5, 35, 89, 163, 223
Willey, Lawrence V., Jr., 58, 223
Woodson, Marshall S., 223

Yelon, Stephen L., 208

SUBJECT INDEX

Achievement, 63-65, 81 (See also Cognitive achievement)

Adult assistants (See Staff, paraprofessional)

Affective development (See Growth and development)

Aggregate demand (See Demand)

Alternative cost (See Opportunity cost)

Anti-technology, 35, 37-49, 183

Art, 120, 143

Automation, 41, 76

Average total cost curves, 126, 159-161, 177, 178

Bay City experiment, 80-81, 84-85

Behavioral objectives, 96, 97, 102

Behaviorists, 95, 98

Capital, 15-17, 35, 52
    human, 11-14, 16, 17, 22, 25, 44
    real, 10, 15-17, 43
    stock of, 15

Capital-intensive (See Production function)

Capital resources (See Resources)

Centralization, 38 (See also Decision-making)

Change, 35, 37-39, 41, 42, 57, 65, 69, 131, 181-203

Child care, 76, 189

Class size, 8 (See also Pupil/teacher ratio)

Co-curricular activities, 122, 134, 169

Cognitive achievement, 20, 27, 34, 35, 47, 64, 67, 84

Cognitive development (See Growth and development)

Collective bargaining, 141

Common school, 9, 19, 54, 65, 83, 125, 126, 129, 187, 199

Community-based learning, 108, 116-117, 186

Competency-based education, 97

Computer, 53, 54, 56, 57, 59, 123, 151, 187

Computer-assisted instruction, 56-61, 122, 143, 149-151

Constant-product curves, 119

Continuous schooling, 19, 53, 54, 65, 98 (See also Discontinuous schooling; Common school)

Cooperative work-experience, 108
Cost
  developmental, 195-196
  educational, 4, 14, 18, 19, 22,
    69, 80, 182, 184-194, 199
    capital, 141-151, 155, 160,
      169
    instruction, 8, 142-151, 159,
      160
    labor, 5, 70, 140-142, 151,
      155, 159, 160, 169
    technology, 139-140
  output, 24, 47, 132
Cost-benefit analysis, 6, 29, 38, 196
Cost-effectiveness analysis, 30-31,
  38
Criterion-based objectives, 96-97
Curriculum, 18, 78, 79, 97, 185,
  191, 196
  industrial influence on, 19
Cybernetics, 41 (See also Feedback)

Dalton plan, 84, 85
Decentralization (See Decision-
  making)
Decision-making
  education, 18, 131-132, 186,
    201
  individual, 87
Demand, 41-42, 47
Developmental tasks, 100, 102, 106
Developmental theory, 99
Diagnosis (See Needs assessment)
Dial-access information retrieval,
  122
Discontinuous schooling, 3, 19, 53
Division of labor (See Specializa-
  tion)

Economic growth, 11-14, 17
Economics of education, 14
Education
  consumers of (See Parents; Stu-
    dents)

dependent variable, 21, 22, 32
economic value, 13
efficiency (See Efficiency)
independent variable, 21, 22, 32
information systems, 96, 98,
  100-102, 104, 107, 151
post-school, 42
pre-school, 42
production function (See Production function)
revolutions in, 52
Educational objectives, 112 (See
  also Behavioral objectives; Criterion-based objectives)
  taxonomy of, 102
Educational plans (See Individualization, planning)
Educational politics (See Politics)
Effectiveness, 27
Efficiency, 8, 23, 27, 28, 32, 33, 47
Efficiency cult, 44
Employment Act of 1946, 42
Equal educational opportunity, 26,
  27
Evaluation, 13, 59-60, 73, 74, 77,
  79, 96-98, 111-113, 134, 139,
  191, 196
Extra-curricular activities (See Co-
  curricular activities)

Family, 18, 82, 101
Feedback, 55, 58, 196 (See also
  Cybernetics)
Fringe employee benefits, 155

Gary plan, 84, 85
Gross national product, 4, 190
Group instruction, 67-68, 86, 196
Growth and development, 91, 96,
  106, 107, 117
  affective, 76, 101-104, 116, 189
  as design concept, 95, 96
  cognitive, 76, 101-104, 116
  dimensions of, 98-101
  portrayal, 104-107

psychomotor, 76, 101-104, 116

Hardware, 34, 70, 78, 79, 143, 185, 196, 197
Heredity, 86
Holism, 96, 98, 101, 104
Homogeneous grouping, 187
Human capital (See Capital)
Human resources (See Resources, human)

Individual differences, 32, 85, 90-95, 118, 196, 198
Individualization, 48, 51, 53, 57, 63, 85, 94, 95, 117, 126, 127
  constraints, 92
  defined, 91
  instruction (See Instruction)
  planning, 67, 73, 74, 77, 79, 87, 93, 115, 117, 134, 191, 196
Individualized learning (See Instruction, individualized)
Industrial revolution, 18
Industry
  education, 9, 14
  non-service, 8
  service, 8
Ineffectiveness (See Effectiveness)
Inefficiency (See Efficiency)
Inflation, 41
Information systems (See Education)
Information transmission, 20, 21, 77, 78, 80-82, 87, 173, 183
Innovation, 6-8, 14, 18, 37, 38
Inputs (See Cost)
Instruction
  individualized, 9, 18, 20, 21, 33, 61-65, 67, 72-74, 77, 84, 86, 89-118, 124, 125, 132, 134, 143, 159, 165, 169, 173, 177, 182, 187, 195, 196, 198
  (See also Individualization)
  traditional (See Production function, labor-intensive)

Instructional management, 91
Instructional management system, 80, 90, 92, 93, 107-117
  design concept for, 90, 95, 104
Instructional media system, 90, 92, 93, 108
Instructional resource accounting system, 110, 114-117
Instructional television, 8, 122, 123, 147
Integrated learning (See Holism)
Intellectual development (See Growth and development, cognitive)
Investment
  education, 10, 11, 14, 16
  real, 17
  social, 10, 11, 16

Job security, 81, 182, 183, 193, 194

Knowledge
  advances in, 17
  stock of, 16, 188

Labor, 119 (See also Production function, labor-intensive)
Labor-intensive (See Production function)
Lancaster system, 80
Learning area, 125, 169
Learning center, 65, 68, 78, 120, 122-126, 132, 134, 143, 146, 159, 169, 192, 198
Learning environment, 61, 68, 84, 120-123, 136, 177, 179, 188, 192
Learning module, 97, 110, 115
Learning theory, 14, 19, 22, 65, 78, 79, 186, 203
Life-long learning (See Education, post-school)
Lock-step learning, 19, 75, 86, 103
Luddite mentality, 37, 39-40, 44, 48, 183

Lump-of-labor, 40
Lunch, 122

Management, 23, 24
  scientific, 44-45
Man-machine systems, 21, 34, 44, 51-66, 69, 73, 77, 78, 81, 84, 87, 93, 117, 119-129, 140, 142, 159, 165, 177, 182, 183, 202
Marginal analysis, 29, 36
Marginal productivity (See Productivity)
Marginal rate of substitution, 119
Mass education, 9, 18, 19, 38, 39, 53, 118, 126, 187, 188, 198
Mechanization and modernization agreement, 194
Media
  human, 21, 24, 125, 126, 196
  non-human, 24, 125, 126, 142, 146, 149, 173, 185, 187, 196
Monopoly, 24, 28, 35
Music, 120, 143

National Institute of Education, 195
Natural ability (See Heredity)
Natural resources (See Resources)
Needs, 90, 95, 110-111, 123
Needs assessment, 73, 77, 87, 90-93, 97, 117, 134, 191, 196
Needs assessment system, 73, 74, 79, 107, 110-114

Opportunity cost, 6, 7, 8, 12, 14
Optimum population theory, 40
Outcomes (See Output)
Output
  education, 5, 27, 29, 36, 39-40, 46-48, 188, 190

Paraprofessional (See Staff)
Parents, 49, 182, 189, 197-199, 201, 202

Personality development (See Growth and development)
Physical education, 120, 143
Pilot models of capital-intensive education, 179, 195-197
Planning, programming, budgeting, and evaluation systems, 36
Politics, 183
Post-school education (See Education)
Pre-school education (See Education)
Prescription (See Individualization, planning)
Price, 24 (See also Cost)
Print medium, 78, 143, 146, 151
Production function
  capital-intensive, 16, 20, 33, 34, 41, 42, 44, 48, 53, 61, 67-88, 95, 118-120, 123, 124, 126, 127, 131-180, 181-184, 186-187, 193, 195, 198, 199
  defined, 23
  education, 20, 21, 24-36, 42, 44, 48, 53, 61, 67-88, 119, 173
  labor-intensive, 4, 16, 20, 21, 33, 69, 70, 73, 80, 81, 87, 95, 117, 123, 124, 126, 140, 142, 159, 160, 173, 177, 184, 190, 198, 200, 202
  traditional (See Production function, labor-intensive)
Production possibility(ies), 8, 25, 26
Productivity, 8, 16, 17, 24, 31, 32, 34, 41-43, 45-48, 52, 126, 177, 184, 185, 189, 190, 193
  marginal, 13
Professional (See Staff)
Professionalization, 62, 81, 182-184, 190-194 (See also Teacher, professional organizations)
Profit, 24

Programmed learning (See Teaching machine)
Psychomotor development (See Growth and development)
Pupil/adult ratio, 71-74, 155, 203 (See also Pupil/teacher ratio)
Pupil/teacher ratio, 4, 33, 34, 68, 73, 139-141

Quality
  education, 8

Reading, 162
Real capital (See Capital)
Research, 5, 189, 202
Resources
  allocation of, 10, 14, 29, 42, 89, 160
  capital, 16
  economic, 10
  human (See Capital, human)
  natural, 16
Retirement, 185, 194
Retraining, 185, 193-195, 198, 199

Salary (See Wages)
Satisfaction (See Utility)
Savings, 182, 184-186, 189, 194, 197, 198
Scheduling, 110
Schooling, 10, 12, 13, 18, 20, 27, 47, 48, 86, 88
  cognitive emphasis in, 27, 46, 102
  compulsory, 18
  continuous (See Continuous schooling)
  supply (See Supply)
Science, 143
Size
  district, 123-124, 132
  learning center, 123-126, 132, 159
Social change (See Change)

Socialization, 76, 87, 88, 186
Socioeconomic
  effect, 26, 28, 35, 46, 86
  mix, 120
Software, 71, 79, 143, 185, 196, 197
Specialization, 68, 74, 75, 78, 79, 81, 84, 87, 124, 132, 134, 173, 182, 184, 187, 191-194
Staff
  administrative, 134, 136, 162
  health officer, 137, 138, 162
  instructional, 8, 21, 68, 74, 122, 126-127, 173, 177
  multimedia preparation, 123, 143
  paraprofessional, 68, 71, 74-78, 80-82, 84, 87, 123, 126-128, 132, 134, 141, 151, 162, 169, 173, 192, 196, 199
  professional, 4, 21, 68, 71, 74, 77-80, 126-128, 132, 134, 136, 141, 151, 166, 169, 173, 196, 199, 201, 202
  ratio of professional/paraprofessional, 71-73, 136, 165
  social service, 137, 138, 169
  special service, 134, 135, 169
  student assistants, 68, 74, 77, 78, 80, 82-84, 123, 126-127, 132, 134, 136, 151, 162, 169, 196
  technical supervisor, 136, 138
Student(s), 46, 49, 93, 95, 119, 187-189, 197, 199, 201, 202
  as self-directed, 95
Student assistant(s) (See Staff, student assistants)
Student/teacher ratio (See Pupil/teacher ratio)
Supply, 47
Systems approach, 125

Taxes, 184, 185

Taxpayer, 182, 184, 189-190
Teacher
  behavior, 31, 75, 76, 81
  professional organizations, 141,
    182, 190-194, 198
  role as manager of instruction,
    75, 76, 90, 93, 125, 134,
    136, 190, 193
  role as transmitter of informa-
    tion, 75, 76, 78, 80, 81, 87,
    90, 190, 193
  training, 192, 195, 197-199
Teaching, 8, 32
Teaching machine, 8, 54, 55, 61,
  62, 66, 76, 85-86, 141, 147,
  151, 173
Team teaching, 85, 169, 192
Technocracy, 41
Technological change (See Change)
Technological structure, 8, 9
Technological unemployment (See
  Unemployment)
Technology
  educational, 5, 19, 21, 22, 33,
    34, 40, 44, 53, 55, 57, 62,
    64, 69, 72, 74, 84, 87, 89,

    94, 123-125, 138, 139, 141,
    142, 144, 177, 186, 190, 203
  social, 27, 190
Television
  educational, 56, 122 (See also
    Instructional television)
Test (See Evaluation)
Textbook (See Print medium)
Time
  in learning, 120, 121, 173, 187
  in school, 84-86, 132, 187, 189

Unemployment, 40, 41, 43, 44 (See
  also Job security)
Unions (See Teacher, professional
  organizations)
Unit costs, 184-185
Utility, 22, 47

Values (See Growth and development, affective)

Wages, 66, 160, 184, 185, 194
Winnetka plan, 84, 86
Work-study, 189
Work-week, 132